Lecture Notes of the Institute for Computer Sciences, Social Informatics and Telecommunications Engineering   142

More information about this series at http://www.springer.com/series/8197

Victor C.M. Leung · Roy Xiaorong Lai
Min Chen · Jiafu Wan (Eds.)

Cloud Computing

5th International Conference, CloudComp 2014
Guilin, China, October 19–21, 2014
Revised Selected Papers

 Springer

Editors
Victor C.M. Leung
Electrical and Computer Engineering
The University of British Columbia
Vancouver, BC
Canada

Roy Xiaorong Lai
Cofederal Networks Inc.
Renton, WA
USA

Min Chen
School of Computer Science
    and Technology
Huazhong University of Science
    and Technology
Wuhan
China

Jiafu Wan
School of Mechanical and Automotive
    Engineering
South China University of Technology
Guangzhou
China

ISSN 1867-8211   ISSN 1867-822X (electronic)
Lecture Notes of the Institute for Computer Sciences, Social Informatics
and Telecommunications Engineering
ISBN 978-3-319-16049-8   ISBN 978-3-319-16050-4 (eBook)
DOI 10.1007/978-3-319-16050-4

Library of Congress Control Number: 2015932982

Springer Cham Heidelberg New York Dordrecht London

Printed on acid-free paper

Springer International Publishing AG Switzerland is part of Springer Science+Business Media
(www.springer.com)

Preface

It is a great pleasure to present the Proceedings of the 5th International Conference on Cloud Computing (CloudComp 2014). This year's conference continued its tradition of bringing together researchers, developers, and industry professionals to discuss recent advances and experiences in clouds, cloud computing, and related ecosystems and business support. The conference also provided a forum for presenting the recent advances and results obtained in the wider area of cloud computing, giving users and researchers equally a chance to gain better insight into the capabilities and limitations of current cloud systems.

CloudComp 2014 received 72 paper submissions, from which the Technical Program Committee (TPC) selected 25 regular papers for presentation and publication in these proceedings after rigorous reviews by expert TPC members. The acceptance rate was 34.72 %. The conference consisted of six symposia that covered a broad range of research aspects. In addition to these paper presentations, CloudComp 2014 also featured some inspiring invited talks, tutorials on advanced storage architectures for cloud and cloud-assisted big data application, and a Workshop on Cloud Computing in Industrial Systems and Applications was also given on the last day of the conference. We hope that the conference proceedings served as a valuable reference to researchers and developers in the area.

Located in the charming and cultural city of Guilin at an enchanting time of the year, CloudComp 2014 was an exciting and stimulating event. It surely advanced our understanding of cloud computing and doubtless opened up new directions for research and development.

October 2014

Victor C.M. Leung
Roy Xiaorong Lai
Min Chen
Jiafu Wan

Organization

Conference Committees

General Chair

Victor C.M. Leung — University of British Columbia, Canada
Roy Xiaorong Lai — Confederal Networks Inc., USA

TPC Chairs

Yin Zhang — Huazhong University of Science and Technology, China
Chuanpei Xu — Guilin University of Electronic Technology, China

Workshop Chair

Honggang Wang — University of Massachusetts Dartmouth, USA
Jiafu Wan — South China University of Technology, China

International Advisory Committee Chair

En-Dong Wang — Inspur, China

Publication Chair

Kai Lin — Dalian University of Technology, China

Local Chair

Zhi Li — Guilin University of Aerospace Technology, China

Publicity Chair

Chin-Feng Lai — National Ilan University, Taiwan
Zhuanli Cheng — Huazhong University of Science and Technology, China

Web Chair

Ran Li — Huazhong University of Science and Technology, China

Contents

CLOUDCOMP Workshop

CLOUDCOMP Technical Sessions

A Hybrid Remote Rendering Approach
for Graphic Applications
on Cloud Computing

Chin-Feng Lai[1]([⊠]), Han-Chieh Chao[2], Zong-Ruei Tsai[1], Ying-Hsun Lai[3],
and Mohammad Mehedi Hassan[4]

[1] Department of Computer Science and Information Engineering,
National Chung Cheng University, Chiayi, Taiwan
`cinfon@ieee.org, tzongruey@gmail.com`
[2] Department of Computer Science and Information Engineering,
National ILan University, Yilan, Taiwan
`hcc@niu.edu.tw`
[3] Smart Network System Institute,
Institute for Information Industry, Taipei, Taiwan
`teddylai@iii.org.tw`
[4] College of Computer and Information Sciences,
King Saud University, Riyadh, Saudi Arabia
`mmhassan@ksu.edu.sa`

Abstract. Due to the fast development of mobile devices, the requirement of graphics processing has grown rapidly in recent years. Graphic processing unit provides the computing of 3D effect in mobile devices, such as user interface and 3D application. Comparing with personal computer, the computing power of mobile devices is much lower. The concept of remote rendering is connecting the graphic processing unit in the server to improve the local rendering ability. However, when network bandwidth is unstable or even unreachable, the user experience would extremely drop. In the recent research, there are a couples mount of topics in association with decreasing network packet transmission. In the unstable network environment, the correlation research is still lacking. This paper proposes a hybrid remote rendering approach for craphic applications on cloud computing. It takes local rendering ability and network bandwidth as input arguments and dynamically sets the frames drawing sequence on client and rendering server. In this study, the experiment chooses 3 applications and runs in 2 different network environments. In the 10 % higher than the lowest requirement bandwidth, this framework could improve 44.99 % frames in each second. In lowest bandwidth requirement, it could improve 44.57 % frames and 30.86 % in 10 % lower than lowest requirement. In the unstable bandwidth, there are around 33.74 % increasing in frame rate.

Keywords: Hybrid remote rendering · Graphic applications · Cloud computing

© Institute for Computer Sciences, Social Informatics and Telecommunications Engineering 2015
V.C.M. Leung et al. (Eds.): CloudComp 2014, LNICST 142, pp. 3–17, 2015.
DOI: 10.1007/978-3-319-16050-4_1

1   Introduction

With continuous development of science and technology, cloud computing technology has been used to extensively improve the quality of network services. However, there remain applications of complex operations in the graphic applications. When the user runs this drawing program, the image processor cannot instantly complete calculation, resulting in picture delay, thus, user experience is reduced. In the application of cloud service, data transfer often occupies the network bandwidth. If part of the client-side mathematical capability is combined with the server calculation, the complex parts are calculated by the server, meaning the use of network bandwidth can be reduced, allowing the user to use network transmission smoothly when using cloud services. Common cloud services mostly accelerate CPU operations, and with the performance improvement of the Graphic Processing Unit in recent years, cloud services for GPU acceleration have appeared, and the research subjects regarding remote rendering have gradually received greater attention. It was originally implemented by open source [1]; while the hybrid rendering architecture, etc., were proposed in recent years [2–5]. However, there is no study regarding a remote rendering system on network speed and quality. In view of this, this study intends to use the graphics computing capacity of the current PC to enhance the graphic capability of mobile devices. As more network bandwidth will be consumed during remote rendering, this study considers the image processing capacity of mobile devices, current graphic capability of devices, and current network transmission rates and quality as the decision parameters of the hybrid rendering system of this study. Finally, the image processors of the client-side and server simultaneously execute calculation. Based on this parameter calculation, the user can use a remote server for drawing even when the network transmission is unstable.

2   Related Works

2.1   General Remote Rendering

The remote rendering system, as proposed by Simon Stegmaier [6], is constructed mainly on an X Server, with GLX protocols, and through dynamic linking, and developers can use this system in application without modifying the application source code. In most common remote rendering architectures, in order to reduce packet transmission quantity, the computing time of the rendering server must be prolonged. For better user experience, the interactive feedback of the user application is increased, and packet transmission quantity shall be upgraded. Marc Levoy proposed a solution [7] by dividing the complex rendering operation into two parts. One is a simple geometrically physical architecture, and the other is the final texture mapping, light effect, and fog effect. Figure 1 shows the remote rendering system, as proposed by Marc Levoy.

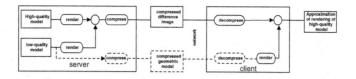

Fig. 1. General remote rendering system.

2.2   Hybrid Remote Rendering

Audrius Jurgelionis proposed the mode-optional remote rendering system based
on the Game_Large architecture [8]. When the user-side hardware or network
connection quality is low, graphics rendering is handed over to the server by
video streaming, and the result is compressed into video streaming for the user.
When the mathematical capability of user's hardware is high and the network
connection is stable, 3D Streaming is used to hand the 3D information to the
user for drawing calculation. The client-side shall have better processing core and
faster network connection. Figure 2 shows the hybrid remote rendering system
proposed by Audrius Jurgelionis.

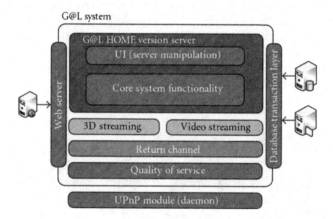

Fig. 2. Hybrid remote rendering system.

The red part in Fig. 2 is the home edition of the Game_Large system, and
for data transmission with the client-side, the indigenous Game_Large system
nucleus and display interface are used. The left part of Fig. 2 shows the web
server, which is an Apache server combined with PHP and sqLITE modules,
and the application menu is displayed on the webpage. The right part of Fig. 2
shows the Database Transaction Layer, which is used for data transmission with
the database system and accessing the application files. The lower part shows
server rendering, when the user is connected to the server, this subsystem selects
3D Streaming or video streaming according to the Quality of Service (QoS).
This system uses the aforesaid three major subsystems as program operating
cores, the user is connected to the web server, and the database installation
program data are accessed, via this interface, in order to run applications.

3   Approach Architecture

This paper proposes a hybrid remote rendering approach for graphic applications on cloud computing. When the local side rendering capability is insufficient, the 3D application menu fluency can be enhanced by cloud computing power in order to enhance the user's experience. The Cloud rendering server is connected via the network, and whether or not to use the server for rendering is judged according to current network connection speed and quality. When the network connection speed and quality are good, the rendering server is used for rendering operations. When the network connection speed and quality are poor, the GPU of the current mobile device is used for drawing calculations. The hybrid remote rendering platform is implemented in the aforesaid manner. Figure 3 shows the proposed approach architecture. The local side receives the function call from the upper application. First, the Bandwidth Measurement Module collects current network connection speed and quality, and submits the result to the Rendering Selection Module for rendering decision. If the decision result is a local drawing, the drawing instruction is directly processed systematically by GPU calculation. If the decision result is submitted to the Rendering Server for drawing calculation, the teledrawing function transfers the instruction, via the network, to the server. When the rendering server completes the drawing, the image is coded and fed back to the local side. The local side can obtain the drawing result from the Frame Decoder. Finally, the drawing Buffer Manager decides when the picture should be displayed on the Display, and the local side hybrid rendering process is completed.

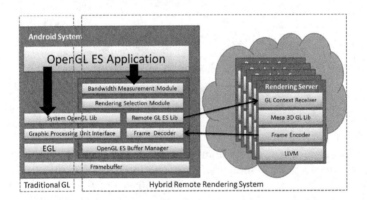

Fig. 3. Proposed approach architecture.

At the rendering server side, when the mobile device transfers the drawing instruction to the server, the Rendering Context Receiver receives the drawing program environment settings and drawing instructions. Afterwards, the drawing instruction is drawn by the 3D graphics library, and calculated by the hardware. Finally, the drawing result is coded and transferred to the local side. In many common server architectures, the Virtual Machine only virtualizes the CPU; therefore, the 3D drawing is less supported in the virtual machine environment, and at the rendering server side, the Low Level Virtual Machine (LLVM) is used to translate the drawing instruction into the CPU machine code, and 3D rendering is implemented by CPU. If the current picture is rendered by the server, in order to reduce the consumption of network bandwidth, the picture is coded before it is transferred via the network. The client-side must decode the picture before it is used. The server rendering sequence diagram is shown, as follows:

3.1 Bandwidth Measurement Module

The bandwidth measurement module measures the current network bandwidth, network stability, and current application drawing complexity. In terms of network bandwidth, the upload and download bandwidths of client-side and server-side, as well as the current maximum bandwidth consumption, are measured. In terms of network stability, the rate of change in the previous network bandwidth is observed, current network stability is obtained from the rate of change, and the bandwidth for the next time interval is determined. Application drawing complexity is related to current application drawing instructions. The more complicated the application, the more drawing instructions shall be transferred, the more drawing instructions there are, and the larger the consumption of network bandwidth. The detailed theories and implementation modes of the aforesaid three items are described, as follows:

Measurement of Network Bandwidth: As mentioned above, regarding the measurement of network bandwidth, the client-side measures the upload and download bandwidths. The measured maximum upload bandwidth is expressed as Eq. 1, and the download bandwidth is expressed as Eq. 2.

$$B_{up} = Bandwidth(upload) \tag{1}$$

$$B_{down} = Bandwidth(download) \tag{2}$$

Network Stability Measurement: The measurement of network stability, in addition to current bandwidth measured by the aforesaid two equations, is expressed as Eq. 3.

$$UploadChangingRate = (CR_{up}) \frac{\sum_2^N \left| \frac{B_{up(n-1)} - B_{up(n)}}{B_{up(n-1)}} \right|}{N-1} \tag{3}$$

The download bandwidth stability is expressed as Eq. 4.

$$DownloadChangingRate =$$
$$(CR_{down}) \frac{\sum_2^N \left| \frac{B_{down(n-1)} - B_{down(n)}}{B_{down(n-1)}} \right|}{N-1} \tag{4}$$

Current Application Drawing Complexity: In this study, the application drawing instruction complexity is defined as the number of packets of an instruction to be transferred for the application to draw one single picture. Generally speaking, when the drawing instruction is complex, as there are more required scenes or objects, higher mathematical capability is required. If it is implemented by remote rendering, more upload network bandwidth shall be occupied. The application drawing instruction complexity is defined as Eq. 5.

$$K_{up} = \frac{UploadBytes}{FrameCount} \tag{5}$$

The upload bandwidth is used mainly for transferring drawing instruction, while the download bandwidth is used for transferring coded pictures. The coded picture is related to current picture compression ratio, defined as Eq. 6.

$$K_{down} = \frac{DownloadBytes}{FrameCount} \tag{6}$$

The drawing complexity is usually related to the picture of a current scene, and when the picture contains a large number of objects, the complexity is high. It is unnecessary to measure the complexity when the complexities are similar to each other. This study proposes using drawing instruction triggering to measure drawing complexity. When the calculation and measurement of the aforesaid three items are complete, the network packet transfer time for remote rendering can be calculated. The required time for packet transfer is in the unit of one single picture, the upload time can be defined as Eq. 7, and the download time can be defined as Eq. 8.

$$T_{upload} = \frac{K_{up}}{((1 - CR) \times 50\% + 50\%) \times B_{up}} \tag{7}$$

$$T_{download} = \frac{K_{down}}{((1 - CR) \times 50\% + 50\%) \times B_{down}} \tag{8}$$

3.2   Rendering Decision Module

The rendering decision module decides the rendering position of each picture during the next period of time, and the bandwidth measurement module obtains the current network transmission rate and quality as the basis of deciding one item. When the rendering position in the next time interval is decided, the drawing instruction is transferred to the corresponding library by dynamic library linking. The hybrid rendering system, as designed in this study, uses a remote server to accelerate local rendering, and considers the local drawing computing power and current network connection speed and quality. In terms of the network connection information, the required information is obtained by the bandwidth measurement module. An equation is defined for local graphic capability in this study, Rendering Factor, expressed as Eq. 9.

$$RenderingFactor(RF) = \frac{CT_{client}}{CT_{server}} \tag{9}$$

The CT_{client} represents the computing time of the client, which represents the client hardware computing power. The larger the value, the longer the computing time, and the mathematical capability is lower. The smaller the value, the shorter the computing time, and the mathematical capability is higher. It is generally known as local side computing performance, and is related to applications and hardware computing power. When the application complexity is low, the hardware computing power is relatively high; and when the application is complex, the hardware computing power is relatively weak. The CT_{server} represents the computing time of the server, which represents the time for server rendering, and this rendering process is as shown in Fig. 4. Therefore, it is related to the client hardware computing power, server computing power, and network speed and quality.

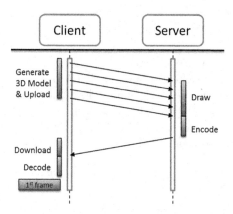

Fig. 4. Rendering process.

The client hardware performance is different from the aforesaid CT_{client}. The CT_{client} is mainly related to CPU and GPU operations. In comparison to CT_{client}, the CT_{server} is only related to CPU computing power. The server computing power is related to the rendering operation of the server, i.e. the speed of processing OpenGL ES instruction. The network connection speeds are the upload and download times, which are obtained by the bandwidth measurement module. The network connection quality is also obtained by the bandwidth measurement module. As stated above, the CT_{server} can be expressed as Eq. 10.

$$CT_{server} = f(P_c, P_s, B, K, T_{enc}, T_{dec}) \tag{10}$$

In Eq. 2, CT_{server} represents the time for server rendering, as related to six factors. Table 1 lists the meanings of the six factors.

The six factor times in Eq. 2 are summed up, and defined as Eq. 11.

$$CT_{server} = P_c + P_s + T_{enc} + T_{down} + T_{dec} \tag{11}$$

The above two items of CT_{client} and CT_{server} are calculated as Eq. 1, in order to obtain the local side and Server computing performance proportion.

Table 1. Six factors of the CT_{server}

Factor name	Meanings
P_c	The required 3D model computing time when the graphics application is executed at the Client, e.g. vector vertex, rotation angle, matrix operation, etc
P_s	The server responds to the drawing function call, and the time is spent on rendering. This item is mainly related to the server GPU
B	Measured by the bandwidth measurement module, current network bandwidth, and stability
K	Measured by bandwidth measurement module and complexity proportion of current application
T_{enc}	Picture coding time at Server
T_{dec}	Picture decoding time at Client

When the server performance is higher, most rendering can be completed by server rendering; however, a few pictures are still drawn by the local side. On the contrary, if the local side performance is higher, most picture rendering is implemented by the local side. The Rendering Factor (RF) is calculated by Eq. 9, and this factor is calculated by Eq. 12 to obtain the local side and Server rendering picture configurations in the next time interval.

$$\left(\frac{1}{CT_{client}} - F_{sub} \right) + (F_{sub} \times RF) = 30 \tag{12}$$

In Eq. 12, F_{sub} represents how many frames shall be subtracted from the frames per second of the local drawing at the client. This study intends to use the hybrid operation model in order to increase the picture refresh rate per second to 30 frames. The value of F_{sub} is the time of rendering the pictures that shall be reduced by the local side, and this time is rendered by remote server to increase the picture refresh rate. Equations 9 and 12 are changed into simultaneous equations, expressed as Eq. 13.

$$\begin{cases} Rendering\ Factor(RF) = \frac{CT_{client}}{CT_{server}} \\ \left(\frac{1}{CT_{client}} - F_{sub} \right) + (F_{sub} \times RF) = 30 \end{cases} \tag{13}$$

The F_{sub} is obtained from simultaneous equations, expressed as Eq. 14.

$$F_{sub} = \frac{30 - 1/CT_{client}}{RF - 1} \tag{14}$$

Table 2 shows the meanings of F_{sub} in this work.

FPS_{client} is the number of pictures to be rendered by the local side in the next time interval, expressed as Eq. 15.

$$FPS_{client} = \frac{1}{CT_{client}} - F_{sub} \tag{15}$$

Table 2. Meanings of F_{sub} in various conditions

Condition	Meanings
$F_{sub} < 0$	When F_{sub} is smaller than 0, it means RF is smaller than 1, and local side rendering performance is greater than remote performance
$0 < F_{sub} \leq 1/CT_{client}$	When Fsub meets this condition, it means the hybrid rendering system of this study can be used for picture rendering configuration
$F_{sub} > 1/CT_{client}$	When Fsub meets this condition, it means that only remote rendering is allowed, and the current network environment is inapplicable to hybrid rendering

FPSserver is the number of pictures to be rendered by the server in the next time interval, expressed as Eq. 16.

$$FPS_{server} = F_{sub} \times RF \tag{16}$$

After Eq. 9 calculation, the number of pictures rendered by the client is calculated by Eq. 15, and the number of pictures rendered by the server is calculated by Eq. 16. When the rendering picture configuration in next time interval is completed, the rendering sequence shall be completed.

According to the aforesaid assumptions, the server drawing rate must be higher than the client drawing rate. Therefore, in the picture rendering time sequence, the client pictures are equally allocated in the server rendered picture, as shown in Fig. 5, thus, the time delay is distributed evenly in the rendering time sequence. If the rendering time sequence is allocated nonuniformly, there will be unsteadiness when the user views pictures. In a uniformly distributed rendering time sequence, there is still unsteadiness; however, this phenomenon can be eliminated by the buffer management mechanism in the next section.

3.3   Rendering Decision Module

Figure 6 shows the flow of this system. The operation flow of this system is described below, as per initialization, bandwidth measurement, calculating RF, rendering process, and picture display.

This study uses three application working programs as the test programs. The three application working programs are tested, where each application is tested in both stable and unstable network environments of variable bandwidths. In the experimental network environment, adjustment is based on the upload bandwidth, and the upload and download speeds are limited by speed limiting software. The network transmission rates are different when the applications

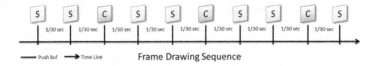

Fig. 5. Picture rendering time sequence.

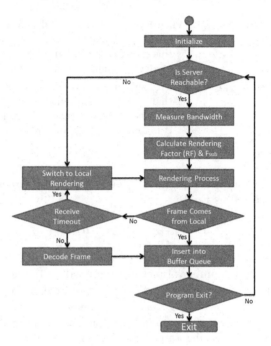

Fig. 6. System flow.

are tested in the same manner, as drawing instructions are often related to applications. When the drawing program is complex, the number of drawing instructions to be transmitted increases. In terms of download bandwidth, as the rendered picture is transferred, it is related to the image compression ratio and resolution.

4   Analysis of Approach Implementation Results

In this section, the results of three application programs on stable/unstable network condition are analyzed.

4.1   Stable Bandwidth

In terms of application I, the following figure shows the tested network bandwidth and picture refresh rate of application I. In the case of stable bandwidth, and in terms of picture configuration, the server renders 20 frames, the local side renders 10 frames, and the overall picture refresh rate is 30 frames. For current bandwidth, the download bandwidth consumption is smaller than the upload bandwidth consumption. As the system calculates download and upload times, the upload bandwidth greatly influences the picture refresh in decision making (Fig. 7).

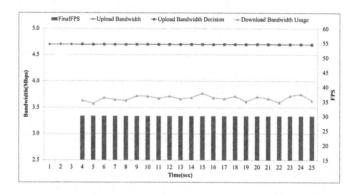

Fig. 7. Application I on stable bandwidth.

Application working program II is also tested in highly stable bandwidth, and this working program is correlated with texture mapping. The client computing power is lower in rendering, thus, at the same network speed, as Client rendering time is very different from the server rendering time, the RF is large. In terms of the allocation proportion of pictures, more pictures will be rendered by the server. The following figure shows the tested network bandwidth and picture refresh rate of application II. In the case of stable bandwidth, in terms of picture configuration, the server renders 27 frames, the local side renders 3 frames, and the overall picture refresh rate is 30 frames. For current bandwidth, the download bandwidth consumption is smaller than the upload bandwidth consumption. As the system calculates the download and upload times, the upload bandwidths greatly influence the picture refresh in decision making (Fig. 8).

Application working program III is tested in highly stable bandwidth, and this program is the 3D graphics application for 3D blocks flying to the user. The application calculates the rotation angle and color setting of each block, and transfers the information to the GPU or rendering server for drawing. The following figure shows the tested network bandwidth and picture refresh rate of application III. In the case of stable bandwidth, and in terms of picture configuration, the server renders 26 frames, the local side renders 4 frames, and the overall picture refresh rate is 30 frames. For current bandwidth, the download bandwidth consumption is smaller than the upload bandwidth consumption. As the system calculates the download and upload times, the upload bandwidths greatly influence the picture refresh in decision making (Fig. 9).

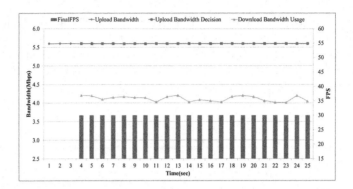

Fig. 8. Application II on stable bandwidth.

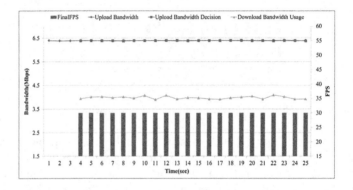

Fig. 9. Application III on stable bandwidth.

4.2   Unstable Bandwidth

This experiment analyzes the scenario of unstable bandwidth, the network change script of a wireless network connection, and speed limiting software changes the network transmission rate every second. The three application working programs are tested in this network environment and the results are analyzed. Application I is an OpenGL ES example program, and the following text analyzes the drawing performance of application I using the hybrid rendering architecture, as designed in this study, in unstable bandwidth. The following figure shows the tested network bandwidth and picture refresh rate of application I. The above figure shows application I tested in unstable network bandwidth. The picture refresh rate at the fourth and the fifth time point is 30, which is hybrid rendering, where the server renders 20 frames, while the local side renders 10 frames. The remote rendering mode is at the 6th to the 19th time point, and all pictures are rendered by the server. The hybrid rendering mode is at the 21st and 23rd time point, where there is an error between the decided bandwidth and actual bandwidth, thus, the current rendering configuration is wrong, and server rendering fails to be completed on time. However, in the hybrid rendering architecture, the basic picture refresh rate is maintained by the local side, thus, reducing the changes in the picture refresh rate (Fig. 10).

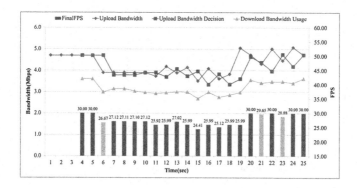

Fig. 10. Application I on unstable bandwidth.

Application II is an OpenGL ES program related to texture mapping. The following text analyzes the drawing performance of application II using the hybrid rendering architecture, as designed in this study, in unstable bandwidth. The following figure shows the tested network bandwidth and picture refresh rate of application II. The above figure shows that application II is tested in unstable network bandwidth. The picture refresh rate at the fourth and the fifth time point is 30, which is hybrid rendering, the server renders 27 frames, and the local side renders 3 frames. The remote rendering mode is at the 6th to the 19th time point, and pictures are rendered by the server. The hybrid rendering mode is at the 21st and the 23rd time point, where there is an error between the decided bandwidth and actual bandwidth, thus, the current rendering configuration is wrong, and server rendering fails to be completed on time. However, in the hybrid rendering architecture, the basic picture refresh rate is maintained by the local side, thus, reducing the changes in the picture refresh rate (Fig. 11).

Application III is the application of squares flying to the user. In an unstable network environment, the picture rendering decision varies with the network environment. The following figure shows the tested network bandwidth and picture refresh rate of application III. The above figure shows application III tested in an unstable network bandwidth. The picture refresh rate at the fourth and the fifth time point is 30, which is hybrid rendering, and the server renders 25 frames, while the local side renders 5 frames. The remote rendering mode is at the 6th to the 19th time point, and the pictures are rendered by the server. The hybrid rendering mode is at the 20th and the 24th time point, where there is an error between the decided bandwidth and actual bandwidth, thus, the current rendering configuration is wrong, and server rendering fails to be completed on time. However, in the hybrid rendering architecture, the basic picture refresh rate is maintained by the local side, thus, reducing the changes in the picture refresh rate (Fig. 12).

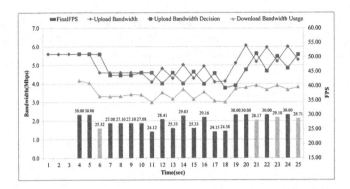

Fig. 11. Application II on unstable bandwidth.

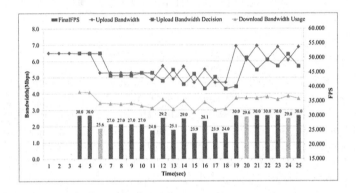

Fig. 12. Application III on unstable bandwidth.

5   Conclusion

Most previous studies selected only one rendering mode. This paper designs a hybrid rendering system, which is combined with the rendering server and local side computing power, and reduces the dependence of the remote rendering system on network speed. In good bandwidth, each application can increase the picture refresh rate to 30 frames through the server computing power. In poor bandwidth, working program I can increase the picture refresh rate by 30.86 % in the architecture designed in this study. In unstable bandwidth, as the bandwidth is variable, the bandwidth estimation is wrong, and the overall picture refresh is increased by 33.74. In future research, if the packet size and quantity of drawing instructions transferred by applications can be reduced, the rendering efficiency of the rendering system can be increased. As this study uses real-time drawing instruction processing, the user control response delay can be reduced; however, the load of the upload bandwidth is increased.

Acknowledgment. The authors would like to thank the National Science Council of the Republic of China, Taiwan for supporting this research under Contract NSC 101-2628-E-194-003-MY3, 101-2221-E-197-008-MY3 and 102-2219-E-194-002.

References

1. Mark, W., McMillan, L., Bishop, G.: Post-rendering 3D warping. In: Proceedings of the 1997 Symposium on Interactive 3D Graphics, pp. 7–16, April 1997
2. Engel, K., Ertl, T., Hastreiter, P., Tomandl, B., Eberhardt, K.: Combining local and remote visualization techniques for interactive volume rendering in medical applications. In: Proceedings of the Conference on Visualization, pp. 449–452, October 2000
3. Jurgelionis, A., Fechteler, P., Eisert, P., Bellotti, F., David, H., Laulajainen, J.P., Carmichael, R., Poulopoulos, V., Laikari, A., Per, P., De Gloria, A., Bouras, C.: Platform for distributed 3D gaming. Int. J. Comput. Games Technol. **2009**, 1–15 (2009)
4. Zhu, M., Mondet, S., Morin, G., Ooi, W.T., Cheng, W.: Towards peer-assisted rendering in networked virtual environments. In: Proceedings of the 19th ACM International Conference on Multimedia, pp. 183–192, November 2011
5. De Winter, D., Simoens, P., Deboosere, L., De Turck, F., Moreau, J., Dhoedt, B., Demeester, P.: A hybrid thin-client protocol for multimedia streaming and interactive gaming applications. In: Proceedings of the 2006 International Workshop on Network and Operating Systems Support for Digital Audio and Video, pp. 86–92, May 2006
6. Stegmaier, S., Magallon, M., Ertl, T.: A generic solution for hardware-accelerated remote visualization. In: Proceedings of the Symposium on Data Visualisation, pp. 87–94, May 2002
7. Levoy, M.: Polygon-assisted JPEG and MPEG compression of synthetic images. In: Proceedings of the 22nd Annual Conference on Computer Graphics and Interactive Techniques, pp. 21–28, September 1995
8. Nave, I., David, H., Shani, A., La ikari, A., Eisert, P., Fechteler, P.: Games@ large graphics streaming architecture. In: IEEE International Symposium on Consumer Electronics, pp. 1–4, April 2008

A Policy-Based Application Service Management in Mobile Cloud Broker

Woojoong Kim[(✉)] and Chan-Hyun Youn

Department of Electrical Engineering, KAIST, Daejeon, Korea
{w.j.kim, chyoun}@kaist.ac.kr

Abstract. In this paper, to deploy scientific application service among advanced computing applications to the mobile cloud environment, we integrate mobile cloud system with policy-based resource management providing SLA adaptive resource management called as mobile cloud broker. However, we do not use the conventional policy-based resource management because of some problems which cannot guarantee the performance of cloud resource required by user. To resolve this problem, we propose the policy based resource management for the mobile cloud system providing scientific application service to provide the cost efficient SLA adaptive resource management to guarantee SLA required by cloud service user while minimizing cost. We describe the function and architecture of mobile cloud broker and the proposed policy-based resource management scheme in the mobile cloud broker. In addition, we show that the proposed policy-based resource management guarantee the QoS of scientific application and reduces the cost compared to the conventional cloud broker system through the evaluation.

Keywords: Mobile cloud computing · Mobile cloud broker · Policy-based resource management

1 Introduction

As the demand for high computing-intensive mobile application have been increased, there have been the attempts to apply cloud computing service to mobile environment for various mobile services [1]. Through mobile cloud computing, it is expected that the limited resources of mobile device can be overcome and mobile device accommodates the high performance computing application. To realize mobile cloud computing, a main way is to build the mobile cloud system to provide the specific mobile services to mobile users. There are many previous works in this way providing the various services such as mobile business, mobile commerce, mobile learning and mobile healthcare [4–7]. In the case of advanced computing application service (e.g. scientific application service focused on this paper) which is computing-intensive and requires many computing and storage resource [2], it is important to guarantee service level agreement (SLA) such as deadline, budget required by user [3]. However the conventional mobile cloud systems have difficulty to guarantee the SLA required by user because they do not have some functions to realize SLA adaptive resource management which enables dynamic virtual machine (VM) scaling to control QoS

© Institute for Computer Sciences, Social Informatics and Telecommunications Engineering 2015
V.C.M. Leung et al. (Eds.): CloudComp 2014, LNICST 142, pp. 18–28, 2015.
DOI: 10.1007/978-3-319-16050-4_2

based on SLA for high performance computing. Y. Jinhui et al. [8] proposed the mobile-cloud framework to constitute and execute scientific workflow on bioinformatics using mobile device. This framework supports the collaboration of researchers on an experiment of genome bioinformatics in mobile device. However, only the basic functions such as service repository, service composition, service execution and the user interface are considered to execute scientific workflow on mobile device. In addition, the SLA required by user is not considered and the resource scheduling and provisioning on each sub-task within workflow also is not considered for executing scientific workflow. To resolve this problem of the conventional mobile cloud system, we apply the policy-based resource management. There is the previous work on policy-based resource management proposed by Ren et al. [9]. However it is difficult for Ren's work to guarantee the performance of cloud resource required by user. Even in the same VM specification (the number of CPU cores, memory size and storage size), there are different performance between cloud resources provided by CSPs because of the heterogeneity [10] of cloud resource. However, Ren's work considers the VMs which have the same VM specification as the same performance so, cannot provide the optimal resource on performance and cost. In this paper, to resolve this problem of Ren's work, we propose the policy based resource management scheme for the mobile cloud system providing scientific application service to provide the cost efficient SLA adaptive resource management to guarantee SLA required by cloud service user while minimizing cost.

2 Mobile Cloud Broker for Scientific Application

To provide a brokering service for scientific application in mobile cloud, we integrate the mobile cloud system with the proposed policy-based resource management which provides cost effective and SLA adaptive resource management. This system is called as mobile cloud broker in this paper. The mobile broker system for scientific application in mobile cloud is described with its functionality in Fig. 1. There is connector which is the mobile application installed in mobile device to access to the mobile cloud broker. Connector is mobile application and provides easy interface for user to sign up and login. After login, connector accesses user's own virtual device provided by mobile cloud broker and show remote control screen of the virtual device through VNC client. In the mobile cloud broker system, the virtual device service which provides the augmented resource virtualized to mobile environment (called as Virtual Device in this paper) with various contents providing some services (e.g. scientific application service, business application service) is provided. Mobile cloud broker admits user to virtual device service and provides the connection between mobile device and virtual device. Mobile cloud broker basically store and maintain the executable file and metadata of content for the specific service through virtual device. Especially for typical scientific application services represented by workflow, mobile cloud broker provides workflow designer through virtual device to receive the requirement (i.e. SLA) from user and submit it to the policy-based resource management function (Figs. 2 and 3).

The proposed policy-based resource management is the key function which makes it possible for the mobile cloud system to provide scientific application while satisfying

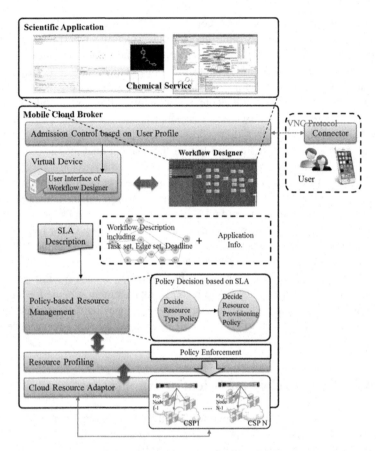

Fig. 1. The model of the integrated broker for scientific application in mobile cloud

user's SLA by providing cost effective SLA adaptive resource management. Policy means the strategy to satisfy SLA required by user for providing service. Policy-based resource management provides the convenient and transparent resource management interface for system to be adaptive about user SLA [16, 17]. In our case, we define two phases of policy – resource type policy, resource provisioning policy. Resource type policy is the strategy to decide the resource type (i.e. VM flavor type) for each sub-task within requested workflow based on given SLA (e.g. deadline, budget). Resource provisioning policy is the strategy to decide the certain physical node of the certain cloud among multi-cloud for creating VM based on given SLA (e.g. computing-intensive application, network-intensive application). The proposed policy-based resource management in the mobile cloud broker provides several policies for each phase and the adaptiveness on various user's SLA. The detail of these policies will be explained in Sect. 3. Scientific application services considered in this paper are represented as Directed Acyclic Graph (DAG) as [3] and are submitted by user with SLA description to the policy-based resource management function through workflow designer of virtual device in the mobile cloud broker. The SLA description which user should specify in the workflow designer is composed of user id *uid*, application information *A* and workflow description *G*. Application information *A* represents the characteristics of an application such as computing-intensive and network-intensive. To represent the workflow *G* of DAG, n_i denotes the *i* th node of workflow *G* (node is identical to sub-task) in our notation. The connection or dependency from node *i* to *j* in the workflow is represented as edge $e_{i,j}$ and the set of edge is represented as *E*. In addition, the deadline D, i.e. the execution time constraints required by user for requested workflow, is also included in the workflow. The workflow description is represented as $\{N = \{n_1, n_2, \ldots, n_k\}, E, D\}$.

Firstly, the workflow in the submitted SLA description is parsed and divided into sub-tasks. Then, the two phases of policy are decided based on the submitted SLA. Secondly, the flavor type of VM is allocated for each sub-task based on the decided resource type policy and the scheduled workflow description *g* including task-VM flavor type mapping information is returned. Finally, each sub-task within workflow is executed based on the scheduled workflow description by provisioning VM with the decided resource provisioning policy. This provisioning process is support by resource profiling function that predicts and evaluates the computing performance of each physical node (i.e. Server Rack) provided by cloud service providers in multi-cloud environment and maintains the network performance between VMs provisioned by each user. After completing the workflow, the result of requested service is returned through the virtual device.

3   Policy-Based Resource Management

As mentioned in Sect. 2, the proposed policy-based resource management provides two phases of policy for cost effective SLA adaptive resource management.

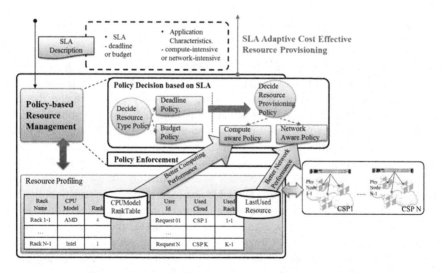

Fig. 2. The procedure of policy-based resource management in C-ARCF

When a request is submitted, the policy-based resource management makes a decision on two phases of policy sequentially for that request. In resource type policy, there are two policies – deadline policy, budget policy according to given SLA from the request. If user requests a service with deadline in SLA, the policy-based resource management decides the deadline policy to satisfy the requested deadline for scheduling workflow while minimizing the cost for leasing VM. If user requests a service with budget in SLA, the budget policy is decided to satisfy the requested budget for scheduling workflow while minimizing the total execution time. These policies use heuristic based traditional workflow scheduling with VM Packing [13] for deadline policy and Loss/Gain [15] for budget policy.

In resource provisioning policy, there are also two policies – compute-aware and network-aware resource provisioning policy according to given SLA. If the application information in submitted SLA has compute-intensive, the compute-aware resource provisioning policy is decided to provide the cloud resource having better computing capability in fixed cost, considering the heterogeneity [10] of cloud resource. To achieve this object, we use CPU model rank table based on benchmark program provided from [14]. The available racks in multi-cloud environment are sorted based on rank in CPU model rank table and the high-ranked rack is provisioned with high priority. Algorithm 1 shows the compute-aware resource provisioning policy.

Algorithm 1. Compute-aware resource provisioning policy
Input : uid^k, f (uid^k : request id, f : flavor type)
Output : created VM

01: **if** P^k is compute-aware provisioning policy
02:     sort availableRacks using CPU Model Rank Table based on benchmark program
03:     **for** $r^i \in$ availableRacks
04:         **if** r^i is available for flavor type f
05:             createdVM = createNewVM(r^i, f)
06:             **return** createdVM
07:         **end if**
08:     **end for**
09: **end if**

If the application information in submitted SLA has network-intensive, network-aware resource provisioning is decided to provide the cloud resource having better network performance on the past created VM for each user. For the application which need lots of data transmission between tasks, this policy can guarantee the data transmission time between VMs. To achieve this object, last used resource table is maintained for each user. When user request first, in order words, there is no available last used resource information, load-balancing based provisioning is done so VM is provisioned to the rack having maximum remaining resource capacity. After creating the VM, the cloud and rack of the created VM is recorded to last used resource table. When user requests later and there is available last used resource information, the VM in the same rack with the last used resource is provisioned if possible. If there is not available resource capacity in last used resource for requested flavor type, new rack as close as possible to the rack of last used resource is decided. After finding the new rack and creating VM, the new rack is updated to last used resource table for the corresponding user. After policy decision process, workflow scheduling and executing process with resource provisioning are continued based on two decided policies and the result of the request is returned to user. Algorithm 2 show the network-aware resource provisioning policy.

Algorithm 2. Network-aware resource provisioning policy

Input : uid^k, f (uid^k : request id, f : flavor type)

Output : created VM

01: **if** $LastUsedResource$ of uid^k is available

02:      cloud c^k, rack r^k ← get $LastUsedResource$ of uid^k

03:      **if** rack r^k in cloud c^k is available for flavor type f

04:          createdVM = createNewVM(r^k, f)

05:          **return** createdVM

06:      **else**

07:          sort availableRacks in closest order from r^k

08:          **for** r^i ∈ availableRacks

09:              **if** r^i is available for flavor type f

10:                  createdVM = createNewVM(r^i, f)

11:                  record {uid^k, c^k, r^k} into LastUsedResource

12:                  **return** createdVM

13:              **end if**

14:          **end for**

15:          **return** null

16:      **end if**

17: **else**

18:      maxCapacityRack ← max(remainCapacity(r^j))   ⋯   (r^j ∈ rackSet of c^i, c^i ∈ cloudSet)

19:      **if** maxCapacityRack is available for flavor type f

20:          createdVM = createNewVM(maxCapacityRack, f)

21:          record {uid^k, c^k, r^k} into LastUsedResource

22:          **return** createdVM

23:      **else**

24:          **return** null

25:      **end if**

26: **end if**

In conclusion, C-ARCF can guarantee the several user's SLA adaptively for scientific application in the policy-based resource with two phases of policy management.

4   Experiments

We evaluate the proposed policy-based resource management in this paper compared to the policy-based resource management of Ren's work. Especially, we evaluate the performance of the proposed policy, i.e. compute-aware resource provisioning policies (Algorithm 1), of the resource provisioning policy phase in this paper except the network-aware resource provisioning policy and the policies in the resource type policy phase which uses traditional workflow scheduling. For the experiment of compute-aware resource provisioning policy, we use QSAR service of MapChem service [9] as compute-intensive application which is an integrated chemical application for collaborative pharmaceutical research and the available input data types are sdf30, sdf100, sdf200(sdf100 means the input data which includes a hundred of chemical compounds info expressed by structure data format [12]). We use openstack cloud environment and the available resource policies in openstack cloud environment are small type(1 CPU, 2 GB MEM, 10 GB Disk), medium type(2 CPU, 4 GB MEM, 10 GB Disk) and large type(4 CPU, 8 GB MEM, 10 GB Disk). The SLA of QSAR service is defined as deadline and it is set in random on each request. We build the cloud testbed using 6 nodes with the deployment of openstack cloud environment [11]. Node 1, 5 is nova controller and node 2, 3, 4, 6 are nova compute nodes. Nova controller manages the operation between the nova compute nodes such as create or delete instance or snapshot and received the result from the nova compute nodes. Each node has the hardware specification described in Table 1.

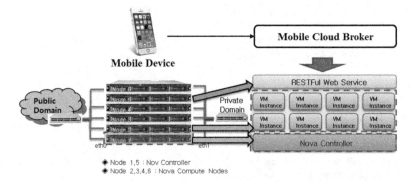

Fig. 3. The experiment environment of integrated broker with openstack

Table 1. The specification of computing node in openstack environment

	Node1	Node2	Node3	Node4	Node5	Node6
Function	Nova Controller Node	Nova Compute Node	Nova Compute Node	Nova Compute Node	Nova Controller Node	Nova Compute Node
Specification	**H/W**: Intel, Xeon E5620 2.4G, Core 16, MEM 16G, HDD 1T **OS**: Ubuntu 12.04				**H/W**: Intel, Xeon W3520 2.67G, Core 8, MEM 16G **OS**: Ubuntu 12.04	
IP address	Eth0 (143.248. 152.64)	Eth0 (143.248. 152.61)	Eth0 (143.248. 152.62)	Eth0 (143.248. 152.63)	Eth0 (143.248. 152.16)	Eth0 (143.248. 152.17)

In this experiment environment, to evaluate the adaptiveness on SLA required by user, we measure the SLA violation when the requests are occurred in the fixed interval over a period of time first. Second to evaluate the ability which guarantees SLA required by user while minimizing cost, we measure the total cost when the requests are occurred in the fixed interval over a period of time. We repeat the experiment with different request interval over a period of time. In addition, we refer the metrics which Ren et al. use for evaluation so, we use *relative cost* [9] which does not have monetary meaning in reality but, the cost has theoretical meaning for comparison between algorithms or models. A lower relative cost means the lower monetary cost in reality. Therefore, we can save the monetary cost in reality by reducing the relative cost.

- **The result of policy-based resource management.**

We make the request in the different interval time (4 s, 3.6 s, 3.2 s, 2.8 s, 2.4 s, 2 s, 1.6 s, 1.2 s, 0.8 s) within 3 min. The input data type of the request is randomly chosen from available input data such as sdf30, sdf100, sdf200. QSAR service of MapChem service is used and the deadline is chosen randomly as mentioned above. Since QSAR service of MapChem service is compute-intensive application, compute-aware resource provisioning policy (Algorithm 1) is decided in this experiment.

Table 2. Cost performance comparison of proposed system and conventional system

Request Interval Time(sec)	The Total Cost of Integrated broker(RC)	The Total Cost of MapChem Broker(RC)
4	2107242	9239967
3.6	2355759	7844055
3.2	2812881	7227801
2.8	3120249	5403198
2.4	3850263	11913414
2	4251492	8037645
1.6	5781423	12119163
1.2	7465920	17783175
0.8	10515201	20728950

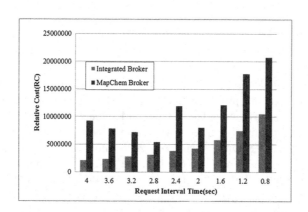

Fig. 4. Cost performance comparison of proposed system and conventional system defined in Table 2

In Fig. 4, we see that the total cost of Ren's work is higher than that of the proposed policy-based resource management over all interval times of the request. Ren's work prepares the extra VM in advance with auto-scaling to reduce the delay from VM initiation time. According the proposed auto-scaling in Ren's work, at least one empty

Table 3. SLA violation comparison of proposed system and conventional system

Request Interval Time(sec)	Total SLA Violation of Integrated broker(#)	Total SLA Violation of MapChem Broker(#)
4	5	7
3.6	6	5
3.2	2	4
2.8	6	9
2.4	10	13
2	6	16
1.6	16	23
1.2	15	38
0.8	21	61

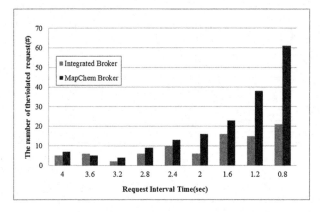

Fig. 5. SLA violation performance comparison of proposed system and conventional system defined in Table 3

VM is always kept. This mechanism makes the waste of resource and occurs the high cost. On the other hand, the proposed policy-based resource management do not makes the extra resource because we judge that the VM initiation time is not critical compared to the execution time of a request. Since the proposed policy-based resource management launches VM only when a request is submitted and release VM immediately after the requests in VM are finished, the cost of the proposed policy-based resource management is lower than that of Ren's work. In addition, the proposed policy-based resource management can allocate the proper amount of cloud resource for the request to guarantee the SLA while minimizing the cost with predicted performance. However, Ren's work cannot allocate the proper amount of cloud resource based on the SLA of the request because Ren's work allocated VM statically based on the size of the input data type. For example, sdf30 is only mapped to small type and sdf100 is only mapped to medium type and sdf200 is only mapped to large type.

For measuring SLA violation, we also makes the request in the different interval time (4 s, 3.6 s, 3.2 s, 2.8 s, 2.4 s, 2 s, 1.6 s, 1.2 s, 0.8 s) within 3 min with the same environment as above experiment. The metric of SLA violation is defined as the number of request which violate the deadline required by user.

Figure 5 shows that Ren's work has the higher SLA violation over the entire request interval time compared to the proposed policy-based resource management. In addition, as the interval time of request decrease, the gap of SLA violation between Ren's work and the proposed policy-based resource management is increased. Therefore, in the high rate of request, the proposed policy-based resource management will show better performance on SLA violation. In the same reasons on the result of cost experiment, Ren's work cannot allocate the proper amount of cloud resource based on the SLA of the request because Ren's work allocated VM statically based on the size of the input data type and does not consider the SLA required by user. However, the proposed policy-based resource management can achieve cost effective SLA adaptive resource management which guarantee the SLA while minimizing the cost.

5 Conclusion

In this paper, we integrate the mobile cloud system with the policy-based resource management for scientific application to provide the scientific application service such as chemical and bio applications with satisfying the SLA required by user in mobile cloud environment. However for this, we do not use the conventional policy-based resource management because of some problems mentioned in Sect. 1. Therefore, to resolve the problem, we propose the policy based resource management for the mobile cloud system providing scientific application service to provide the cost efficient SLA adaptive resource management to guarantee SLA required by cloud service user while minimizing cost. Finally, we evaluate that the proposed policy-based resource management guarantee the SLA required by user and reduces the cost compared to the conventional policy-based resource management. Therefore, we prove that the proposed policy-based resource management can achieve cost effective SLA adaptive resource management which guarantee the SLA while minimizing the cost for providing scientific application service in mobile cloud broker.

Acknowledgments. This research was supported by Next-Generation Information Computing Development Program through the NRF funded by the Ministry of Education, Science and Technology (2010-0020732) and the MSIP (Ministry of Science, ICT & Future Planning), Korea in the ICT R&D Program 2014.

References

1. Srirama, S.N., Paniagua, C., Flores, H.: CroudSTag: social group formation with facial recognition and mobile cloud services. Procedia Comput. Sci. **5**, 633–640 (2011)
2. Ostermann, S., Iosup, A., Yigitbasi, N.M., Prodan, R., Fahringer, T., Epema, D.: An early performance analysis of cloud computing services for scientific computing. Technical report PDS-2008-006, TU Delft, 3 December 2008. http://www.eecs.berkeley.edu/Pubs/TechRpts/2009/EECS-2009-28.html

3. Yu, J., Buyya, R.: Scheduling Scientific Workflow Applications with Deadline and Budget Constraints Using Genetic Algorithms Scientific Programming, pp. 217–230. IOS Press, Amsterdam (2006)
4. Huang, D., Zhang, X., Kang, M., Luo, J.: Mobicloud: a secure mobile cloud framework for pervasive mobile computing and communication. In: Proceedings of 5th IEEE International Symposium on Service-Oriented System Engineering (2010)
5. Yang, X., Pan, T., Shen, J.: On 3G mobile e-commerce platform based on cloud computing, pp. 198–201, August 2010
6. Gao, H., Zhai, Y.: System design of cloud computing based on mobile learning. In: Proceedings of the 3rd International Symposium on Knowledge Acquisition and Modeling (KAM), pp. 293–242, November 2010
7. Doukas, C., Pliakas, T., Maglogiannis, I.: Mobile healthcare information management unitizing cloud computing and android OS. In: Annual International Conference of the IEEE on Engineering in Medicine and Biology Society (EMBC), pp. 1037–1040, October 2010
8. Yao, J., et al.: Facilitating bioinformatic research with mobile cloud. In: The Second International Conference on Cloud Computing, GRIDs, and Virtualization, CLOUD COMPUTING 2011 (2011)
9. Ren, Y.: A cloud collaboration system with active application control scheme and its experimental performance analysis, Master thesis, Korea Advanced Institute of Science and Technology (2012)
10. Farley, B., et al.: More for your money: exploiting performance heterogeneity in public clouds. In: Proceedings of the Third ACM Symposium on Cloud Computing. ACM (2012)
11. Openstack foundation (2012). http://www.openstack.org/
12. Dalby, A., Nourse, J.G., Hounshell, W.D., Gushurst, A.K.I., Grier, D.L., Leland, B.A., Laufer, J.: Description of several chemical structure file formats used by computer programs developed at molecular design limited. J. Chem. Inf. Model. **32**(3), 244 (1992)
13. Kang, D.-K., et al.: Cost adaptive workflow scheduling in cloud computing. In: Proceedings of the 8th International Conference on Ubiquitous Information Management and Communication. ACM (2014)
14. CPU model rank table. http://www.cpubenchmark.net/
15. Sakellariou, R., Zhao, H.: Scheduling workflows with budget constraints. In: Gorlatch, S., Danelutto, M. (eds.) Integrated Research in GRID Computing. CoreGRID Series, pp. 189–202. Springer, New York (2007)
16. Changkun, W.: Policy-based network management. In: Proceedings of IEEE WCC 2000-ICCT (2000). inf.ufrgs.br
17. Simplifying network administration using policy-based management - DC Verma, IBMTJWR Center, Y Heights - Network, IEEE (2002). ieeexplore.ieee.org

Personalized Video Recommendations with Both Historical and New Items

Zhen Zhang, Zhongnan Huang, Guangyu Gao,
and Chi Harold Liu[✉]

School of Software, Beijing Institute of Technology, Beijing, China
zhenzhenclaire7@gmail.com, zhongnanh@hotmail.com,
{guangyugao,chiliu}@bit.edu.cn

Abstract. Recommender systems have been proven as an essential tool to solve the information overload problem due to the burst of Internet traffic, however traditional approaches only consider to recommend items that users have not seen before, and thus ignore the significance of those items in a user's historical records. This is motivated by the fact that users often revisit those items they have watched before, especially for TV series. Based on this, in this paper, we introduce a new concept called "revisiting ratio", to uniquely represent the ratio between the new and old items. We also propose a "preference model" to aid selecting the most related historical records. Finally, theoretical analysis and extensive results are supplemented to show the advantages of the proposed system.

Keywords: Recommender system · Revisiting ratio · Reference model

1 Introduction

When the original conceptual foundation of the Internet was laid back in the 50s, no one had the slightest idea of how easy it will be for us to receive information. With the easy access to the Internet, users can acquire the most recent knowledge and information, including daily news, friend's moments, new movies, almost everywhere with their laptop, iPad, smartphones, and other forms of smart devices. Meanwhile, users gradually feel stressful to make wise decisions on what piece of information to choose, since there exists far more amount of available information than a user can consume, and thus, information overload on the Internet has become a series problem. In order to address this issue, recommender systems have been widely investigated and proposed as an essential tool for users to navigate the plethora of contents according to their personal interests [1]. For example, most e-Commerce websites (e.g., Amazon.com, Netflix, Last.fm, etc.) have already embedded this feature into their products, both static and mobile, to provide convenient and personalized services for users.

This work is financially sponsored by National Natural Science Foundation of China (Grant No. 61300179).

© Institute for Computer Sciences, Social Informatics and Telecommunications Engineering 2015
V.C.M. Leung et al. (Eds.): CloudComp 2014, LNICST 142, pp. 29–42, 2015.
DOI: 10.1007/978-3-319-16050-4_3

The use of recommender systems not only brings high monetary benefits to the service operators (e.g., through precise ads), but also significantly aids the use of their services. As a result, a number of recommendation engines (i.e. item-based recommendation [2], user-based recommendation [3], Collaborative Filtering (CF) algorithm [4], and SVD algorithm [5]) have blossomed.

Nevertheless, there are still many fundamental issues to be considered from theoretical analysis perspectives [6]. One is the ignorance of recommending historical items as the part of final recommendation list to users. Most recommender systems only recommend new items since they claim that users will not revisit those items they have seen before [7]. It might be the case in some scenarios, e.g., for on-line bookstore since customers barely read the same book they have selected before. However, in most of other practical scenarios like online video sharing the viewing website, users may prefer to repeatedly watch the same video (or more likely the same channel) they viewed before. This always happens when a famous TV series are lively broadcasting online. Therefore, an ideal recommender system (and its embedded algorithm/strategy) should fully consider everything a user prefers and those items they are in need of [8], and then use these pieces of information to optimally recommend corresponding items to individual users in a timely manner [9]. Unfortunately, most existing recommender systems did not consider this, and as a result users are forced to browse their viewing history. Towards this end, in this paper, we aim to design a novel online video recommender system, whose final recommendation list to individual users contains both the historical and new recommended items. Our main contribution of this paper is three-fold:

- We propose a new concept of "revisiting ratio", to represent the percentage of new recommended items and old ones. It will be dynamically calculated every time when new usage data feed into the system to follow the migration of user's interest.
- We propose a preference model to represent a user's preference to an item, where three parameter metrics are considered: a newly defined loyalty value, an item's watching times and the last watching time by a user.
- We build a large-scale, distributed computing environment to evaluate our proposed recommender system on a real on-line video website data set.

The rest of the paper is organized as follows. In Sect. 2, we depict the related work. In Sect. 3, we introduce a formal model of our system. Section 4 describes the design of two selection models and the architecture of the whole proposed recommender system. A complete case study is presented in Sect. 5, and finally conclusions and future work is presented in Sect. 6.

2   Related Work

Plenty of research activities on recommender systems across different aspects have been recently proposed [10–15]. Collaborative Filtering (CF, [4]) is one of the earliest and most successful recommendation algorithm, that assumes users will not change their preference over time [16,17]. Specifically, the process of making recommendations can be summarized as three steps. First, it measures a user's distance by calculating the similarity between their preferences. Second, it selects the K nearest users as neighbors of the target user [18]. Finally, the system predicts how much the targeted user may be interested in a particular item according to his/her neighbors' attitudes [19]. Since pure CF strategy does not require any information about items, it can handle every recommended objects including unstructured complex objects such as music and movies. However, this approach also has some shortcomings. As it is based on the historical data, it has the cold start problem to new users and items [20]. In addition, it also requires much computation resource since user preferences are often stored in a sparse matrix [21].

Furthermore, content-based recommendations [22] have been widely used in the field of information retrieval and information filtering, that emphasizes the content of an item. Different from CF, it does not require a user's evaluation of that item, but uses his/her interests and preferences extracted from the description about the content, and uses machine learning techniques to make recommendations [23]. Focusing on an item's feature, this approach can achieve high accuracy without the help of large amount of users, and thus it has the capability to work in situations where no-one in a community has ever rated those items. However, it requires good structural characteristics during the extraction, which are often difficult to obtain [24].

All these recommender systems so far focus on exploiting new items that a user may prefer, and ignore the significance of historical records. In practice, users often revisit those items they are interested in, especially for TV series. Therefore, it's important and necessary to make recommendations including both new and historical items.

3   System Model

In this section, we first present a formal model to describe the system architecture, and then introduce the system flow.

We assume that there is a dynamic recommender system embedded in an on-line video website/smart device application, where users regularly browse our recommended items, and click the ones they are interested in to browse. The website/application will store all usage files $l(t)$ as a log into a back-end persistent database at the end of day. We define $T(t)$ as the training data set, consisted of N daily logs in the reverse order starting from day t, as: $T(t) = \{l(t), l(t-1), ..., l(t-N)\}$. The proposed recommender system will use $T(t)$ as the input after the daily backup is completed, and re-train the system model background using the new training set $T(t+1)$. During this process, we find out a user's current viewing behavior by analyzing his/her historical records, and determining how many new and old recommended items should be added into the final recommendations. Meantime, we propose a novel concept of "preference model" to select old items from current user profile. Since the training set of

Table 1. List of notations and descriptions

Notation	Explanation
$l(t)$	Log file at day t
$T(t)$	The set of all $\ell(t)$ at day t
$R_n(t)$	The set of items produced by original recommender system
$R_o(t)$	The set of items produced by historical model
$u(t)$	User profile at day t
λ_r	Revisiting ratio of recommendation list
λ_u	Revisiting ratio of user profile
Ψ	Loyalty value
ℓ	Viewing times of the item
$\jmath$	Distance from the last view

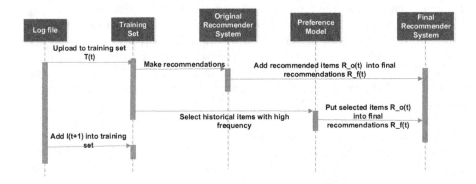

Fig. 1. Sequence diagram of the proposed recommender system operations.

this model changes on the daily basis, recommendations will be different. Thus, users will receive daily personalized recommendations every time they log in the website/application. Table 1 shows the list of notations used in this paper.

Figure 1 illustrates the procedure of the proposed recommender system with historical items and new recommendations, and this can be summarized as follows:

First, the system takes $l(t)$ as the input and performs pre-processing, including data cleaning and reduction. For the former, we directly delete records that are lack of attribute values or contain errors because their amount is relatively very small. Meantime, we remove less important attributes to obtain a reduced representation of $l(t)$. Then, preprocessed data is added into $T(t-1)$ to compose the new training set $T(t)$. After, our recommender system (see Sect. 4.4) generates new recommended items, donated as $R_n(t)$. Meanwhile, the proposed preference model (see Sect. 4.3) selects old ones from a user profile, denoted as $R_o(t)$. Finally, we combine $R_n(t)$ and $R_o(t)$ to make the final recommendations $R_f(t)$, and push it to the targeted user's front-end website/application.

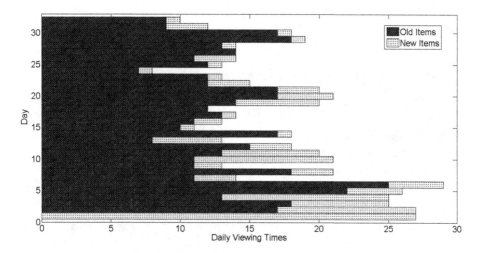

Fig. 2. User1's profile for 30 days. This user watches videos every day and most of them are the old ones he/she has watched before.

4   Proposed Personalized Video Recommender System

In this section, we first describe our observations of user behaviors from a real data set, and then explain the proposed new concepts of revisiting ratio and preference model. Finally, we show how we make final recommendations with an open source recommender system and our proposed preference model. Here, we donate an item as a video in our dataset. Meanwhile, we adopt channels to be the content of our recommendations, which contains videos with similar tags.

4.1   Observations of User Behavior from a Real Data Set

Our data set is made up of forty-one watching logs from a famous on-line video website that contains 1,000,000 users and 2,000 videos in total. An average of 1,500,000 records per file is observed, and its size is around 8 GB each. Each record has 48 attributes, including user ID, item ID, watching time, IP address, user location, etc., describing different aspects of the user's watching behavior. Since user behaviors are a crucial, but dynamic parameter to make personalized recommendations, we specifically select two representative users to analyze and visualize the content of their profiles within 30 days.

Figures 2 and 3 show the profiles of these two representative users, respectively. We first analyze their watching frequencies. It is obvious that user 1 visits the website almost everyday, while user 2 is absent for 18 days. That is, the watching frequency of user 1 is higher than user 2. Then, we compare the number of items they have watched in total. The average daily viewing times of user 1 is 15, while 24 times from user 2. It is worth noting that although user 2's watching frequency is lower than user 1's, the amount of items he/she watched

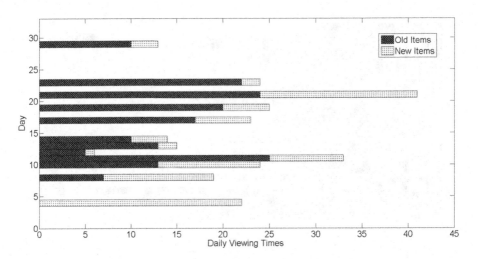

Fig. 3. User2's profile in the same time. This user only watches videos on some days, but the amount he/she watches is a lot each time. Different from user 1, he/she watches roughly the same amount of new items as the old ones.

are eventually more than user 1. Therefore, when the system makes personalized recommendations, it should clearly consider both the frequency and amount of the watching to decide how many recommendations it should make every day to different users.

Finally, we examine at the composition of the daily user profiles. We separate all items into two categories: new items and old ones. Among all of them, new items indicate those items that have never occurred in a user profile before, while old ones represent those items a user has viewed. It is clear that both of users not only watch new items but also review old ones most of the time. But the ratio of new and old items is different for each user, and also tends to change every day. Take user 1 for example, the average of this ratio is 0.63 for the first three days (except day 1 since we believe that all appeared items are new to the user at the beginning). This indicates that he/she has the similar preference to new items and old ones. However, only using this parameter to decide whether a user likes new items or not is unreasonable, since he/she may change his/her preference after that. We observe that the average value of the ratio from day 4 to day 15 is 0.30, and it falls down to 0.15 from day 15 to day 32. These information indicates that this user prefers old items than new ones. From Fig. 2, it is clear to see that old items occupy a large portion of all viewing times, and thus, only the overall trend of the ratio between the number of new and old items can best reflect a user's preference.

Different from user 1, user 2 tends to watch more new items than old ones. During the 12 days when he/she watches videos, the maximum value of the ratio is 0.7, and the average is 0.49. Thus, we believe that this user does not have special preferences to new or old items, and it is understandable that the system should recommend roughly the same amount of old items as new ones.

4.2 Revisiting Ratio

As mentioned earlier, the ratio of new and old items is different for each user and can largely reflect a user's viewing preferences/behavior. Thus, it is important to observe the trend of this parameter in a user profile, and adjust the composition of the final recommendation list each day according to this time-varying ratio. Here, we call it as the "revisiting ratio". The value between 0 to 0.5 indicates that a particular user prefers old items while the ratio between 0.5 to 1 indicates he/she prefers new ones more. Since there are two item lists (i.e., user profile and recommendation list) to be used in our recommending process, we use λ_u and λ_r to denote them, respectively. We claim that revisiting ratios of a user profile from $u(0)$ to $u(t-1)$ can best reflect a user's preference at a particular day t, so that the ratio of recommendation list λ_r can be also predicted by using the Moving Average (MA) approach. MA is a calculation to analyze data points by creating a series of averages of different subsets of the full data set and is used to predict the future trend of this time series [25]. Here, we adopt an unweighted form of its variation, named Simple moving average(SMA), that simply calculates the average of the full data set and use it as the prediction of the next day [26]. If the value is high, it means that this user prefers new items than the old ones; otherwise, old recommended items should be more emphasized in the final recommendation list. Since users' interests may be changed and/or affected by seasonal trends, λ_r is time-varying and should be recalculated every day using the most recent user profile, as:

$$\lambda_r(t) = \frac{\lambda_u(t-1) + \lambda_u(t-2) + \cdots + \lambda_u(0)}{t-1}. \tag{1}$$

4.3 Preference Model

Without loss of generality, three parameters are key to affect a user's preference to an item. The more frequent the user views an item, the more he/she may like it. Thus, historical viewing times, denoted as ℓ, is the first parameter of our concern to the system design. Furthermore, we consider a user's last viewing of an item, denoted as $\jmath$. If an item has not been watched for a relatively long period of time, one may conclude that this user highly likely has already lost interests of it. Finally, we introduce a new metric called "loyalty value", to uniquely represent the *cyclical* viewing behavior of a user. That is, if an item has been viewed on every Saturday, it is more likely to be viewed again next Saturday. This always happens for TV series that has predefined showing time. Loyalty value can be computed by two variables, the number of intervals ϵ and loyalty times ϖ as:

$$\Psi = \frac{\epsilon}{\varpi}. \tag{2}$$

An example to calculate the loyalty value is shown in Fig. 4. First, we pick the days when the item has been watched by a user. Second, we number the intervals of neighboring two days and mark the ones lower than the loyalty cycle (i.e., 7 days) as ϖ. Third, we sum up the overall number of intervals as ϵ.

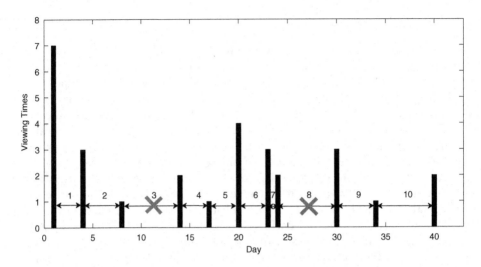

Fig. 4. The way to calculate loyalty value by using the video watching. In this scenario, 10 intervals are observed in total, and the user is not "loyal" in the third and eighth day, marked by a red cross. Thus, $\varpi = 0.8$ (Color figure online).

Finally, we calculate the loyalty value as shown in (2). As shown in the figure, we randomly select a video watching log of a user, and arbitrarily set the loyalty cycle to five days. It is clear that there are ten ϵ and eight ϖ in this example. Therefore, the loyalty value of this user to this particular video is 0.8, that shows a high degree of user loyalty to this item.

Then, we compute a user's preference Θ to an item as:

$$\Theta = a \times \Psi^2 + b \times \ell + c \times \jmath + d, \tag{3}$$

where a, b, c, d are four parameters estimated by logistic regression.

4.4   Open Source Recommender System - Myrrix

In our design, we leverage an open source recommender system, called "Myrrix" [27] to make new recommendations. Myrrix is an open source project powered by Apache Mahout, and it is proposed to build a temporal, high-scalability recommendation engine in big data environment. As shown in Fig. 5, by using machine learning model updated by the computation layer, serving layer can answer requests, records input and provides recommendations in real-time. Considering that user ratings are not usually available, it employs a generalized model that can ingest any event (e.g. clicks, views) besides ratings. Therefore, we believe that the fundamentals of Myrrix serve as the ideal recommender system due to its simplicity, scalability and universality.

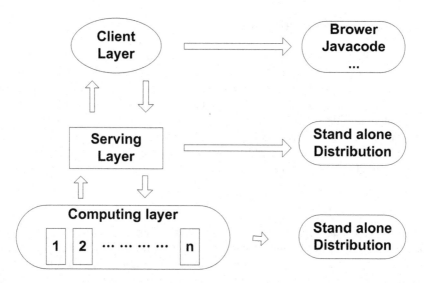

Fig. 5. Open source recommender system Myrrix's architecture [27].

4.5   Making Final Recommendations

As mentioned above, the final recommendation list $R_f(t)$ consists of two parts: $R_n(t)$ and $R_o(t)$. Therefore, after integrating $l(t)$ into $T(t)$, we follow the following steps to produce $R_f(t)$:

Step-1: We first make a prediction on the size of $R_f(t)$ by using SMA approach [25], as:

$$|R_f(t)| = \frac{\sum_{i=0}^{t-1}|R_f(i)|}{t-1}. \tag{4}$$

Step-2: The size of $R_o(t)$ and $R_n(t)$ can be computed:

$$|R_o(t)| = \begin{cases} \dfrac{1}{1+\lambda_r(t-1)} \times |R_f(t)|\, , t \geq 1 \\[2mm] 0.5 \times |R_f(t)|\, , t \doteq 0 \end{cases} \tag{5}$$

$$|R_n(t)| = \begin{cases} \dfrac{\lambda_r(t-1)}{1+\lambda(t-1)} \times |R_f(t)|\, , t \geq 1, \\[2mm] 0.5 \times |R_f(t)|\, , t \doteq 0, \end{cases} \tag{6}$$

where $\lambda_r(t)$ donates the revisiting ratio of recommendation list on this day, $|R_f(t)|$ denotes the number of final recommended items, $|R_o(t)|$ denotes the number of old items, and $|R_n(t)|$ is the number of new items.

Step-3: The system first makes $|R_f(t)|$ recommendations using Myrixx, and pick top $|R_n(t)|$ items as the list $R_n(t)$. Then, we calculate the preference value of each item in the user profile $U(t)$, and select the highest $|R_o(t)|$ items as $R_o(t)$. After, final recommendations provided to the user can be donated as:

$$R_f(t) = R_o(t) \cup R_n(t). \tag{7}$$

5   Performance Evaluation

Having described the design of our proposed recommender system, in this section we evaluate its correctness and effectiveness on a real data set. We first explain our experiment environment, and then show the results. Since there is no direct information showing a user's interests to items (i.e. through user ratings), without loss of generality, here we assume that a user's number of viewing times can directly indicate his/her preference, i.e., higher frequency users click an item, the more he/her likes it. Based on this, open source project Myrrix [27] is selected to build explicit ratings of user and item.

5.1   Environment

We use Apache Hadoop [28], as an open-source platform to develop reliable, scalable, and distributed computing, allowing for the distributed processing of large data sets across clusters of computers using simple programming models. Considering the scale of our used data set, we implement a Hadoop cluster with 11 nodes, one as the Master Node and the others as Data Nodes. These nodes are all virtual machines supported by VMware with Intel Core i-5 CPU, 20G disk and all running Ubuntu 12.04. All virtual machines are connected with a 10 Mbps switch as a local network. In our experiment, we use log data from $l(0)$ to $l(10)$ as original training set, denoted as $T(0)$. Since there are an average of 1,500,000 records per file, $T(0)$ contains 15,000,000 records on average. Meanwhile, it is worth noting that in order to avoid the problem of data sparsity, *channels* are considered as our final recommended items, which is a combination of a set of online videos with same tags/features. However, our proposed model is still applicable to recommend single items.

5.2   Results

First, we compare the performance of two historical records selection strategies. One is our proposed preference model, and the other one is called "frequency model", i.e., to simply select the most highest frequently viewed items in the current training set as the final recommendations. Clearly, frequency model neither considers the impact of the last viewing of an item nor a user's periodical viewing behavior, compared with our proposed model.

Figure 6 shows the performance of these two strategies from day 11 to day 40. This is done by setting the loyalty cycle to five days, and evaluating system performance as the training set accumulates. We first pick data from day 1 to day 10 as the initial training set. Then, we recommend ten items based on these two models every day, and calculate the accuracy of our recommendations. After the evaluation, the newest record is added into the new training set.

From the figure, it is clear that the preference model performs better than frequency model most of the time. The precision of the preference model reaches 80 % three times, while the highest accuracy achieved by the frequency model is only 70 %. Furthermore, there are four times when the attained precision is lower

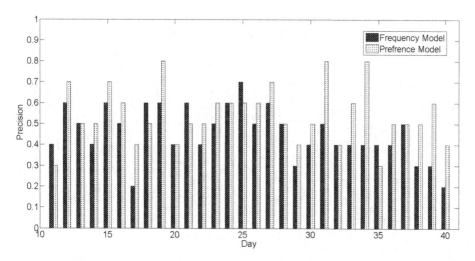

Fig. 6. Comparison of two historical records selection strategies, preference model and frequency model.

than 40 % by frequency model, while only two times by the preference model. On day 17 and day 40, the precision of frequency model even falls to 20 %, indicating that only 2 out of 10 recommendations has eventually been watched by the user on the next day. Then, we compare the change of the accuracy as more training data accumulates from time being. We observe that these two models has a huge contrast from day 31 to day 34, that the average accuracy of preference model is 65 % while only 42.5 % achieved by the frequency model. When we examine the corresponding user profile of this period of time, we find that most of the items the user have watches are on day 30. Since their appearances are not frequent, frequency model does not recommend them to the user. Instead, these items are selected by our proposed preference model, since the user watched them recently and in turn their revisiting ratios j are high. It is also worth to explain the reason why the accuracy of preference model reaches 60 %, while frequency model has achieved only 30 %. From the profile, we find that most of them are TV series. Take one item for example, the user has watched it on day 17, 23, and 30, respectively. Since its appearance frequency is far lower than others', the frequency model will not recommend it. However, our proposed preference model detects this regular cyclic behavior and recommends it for its high loyalty value. Thus, our preference model can successfully adapts its decision based on a user's dynamic behavior and make accurate recommendations on time.

In order to explain the impact of the three proposed considerations (i.e., historical viewing times, the user's last viewing, and loyalty value) in our proposed preference model, we evaluate its performance in Fig. 7. On day 19 and 20, most of the items a user watched are those he/she watched regularly (i.e., heavy hitters). Thus, the preference model fully considering a user's viewing times achieves the best performance. However, on day 12, 16, 21, and 26, the

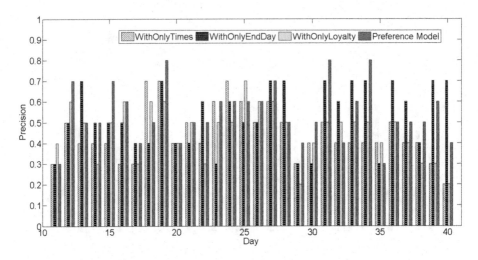

Fig. 7. System performance with three parameters considered in our proposed preference model.

best model should be the one using the loyalty value, because most of items the user watched these days are the ones he/she watched periodically. Thus, the model integrated with loyalty value have the capability to detect a user's periodical viewing behavior. However, when the user changes his/her interests, above two models cannot make accurate recommendations anymore since both of them rely on the precise analysis of a user's historical records. For example, the user watches many new items on day 27. Since they are new to training set, only this model can quickly find out these items and recommend them on the next day. Therefore, when we consider the capability to respond to the user dynamic, the model with a user's last viewing of an item get the best performance.

6   Conclusion and Future Work

In this paper, we have shown how to use the revisiting ratio and preference model to design and implement a novel recommender system that recommends both new and historical items. Our solution fully considers the probability of an item's appearance and uniquely incorporates new concepts of revisiting ratio and loyalty value. Extensive experimental results on a real data set have fully explained the advantages of our proposed preference model and indicates the necessity of factors we concerned in this model. As for the future, a meaningful study will be considering how to control the dynamics of users. Since users may change their preferences, it can be useful to find a solution for maintain the stability of a recommender system.

References

1. Chen, M., Mao, S., Liu, Y.: Big data: a survey. ACM/Springer Mob. Netw. Appl. (ACM MONET) **19**, 171–209 (2014)
2. Sarwar, B., Karypis, G., Konstan, J., Riedl, J.: Item-based collaborative filtering recommendation algorithms. In: ACM WWW 2001, pp. 285–295 (2001)
3. Song, S., Wu, K.: A creative personalized recommendation algorithm; user-based slope one algorithm. In: IEEE Systems and Informatics (ICSAI 2012), pp. 2203–2207 (2012)
4. Shi, Y., Larson, M., Hanjalic, A.: Collaborative filtering beyond the user-item matrix: a survey of the state of the art and future challenges. ACM Comput. Surv. (CSUR) **47**, 3:1–3:45 (2014)
5. Ba, Q., Li, X., Bai, Z.: Clustering collaborative filtering recommendation system based on svd algorithm. In: IEEE Software Engineering and Service Sciences (ICSESS 2013), pp. 963–967 (2013)
6. Zhang, D., Hsu, C.H., Chen, M., Chen, Q., Xiong, N., Lloret, J.: Cold-start recommendation using bi-clustering and fusion for large-scale social recommender systems. IEEE Trans. Emerg. Top. Comput. **2**, 239–250 (2014)
7. Song, J., He, L., Lin, X.: Improving the accuracy of tagging recommender system by using classification. In: IEEE Advanced Communication Technology (ICACT 2010), vol. 1, pp. 387–391 (2010)
8. Bedi, P., Agarwal, S.K.: Preference learning in aspect-oriented recommender system. In: IEEE Computing Intelligence and Communication Networks (CICN 2011), pp. 611–615 (2011)
9. Ghazanfar, M.A., Prugel-Bennett, A.: A scalable, accurate hybrid recommender system. In: IEEE Knowledge Discovery and Data Mining (WKDD 2010), pp. 94–98 (2010)
10. Ricci, F., Rokach, L., Shapira, B.: Introduction to Recommender Systems Handbook. Springer, Boston (2011)
11. Jafarkarimi, H., Sim, A.T.H., Saadatdoost, R.: A naive recommendation model for large databases. Int. J. Inf. Educ. Technol. **2**, 216–219 (2012)
12. Talabeigi, M., Forsati, R., Meybodi, M.R.: A hybrid web recommender system based on cellular learning automata. In: IEEE Granular Computing (GrC 2010), pp. 453–458 (2010)
13. Diaby, M., Viennet, E., Launay, T.: Toward the next generation of recruitment tools: an online social network-based job recommender system. In: ACM ASONAM 2013, pp. 821–828 (2013)
14. Xia, P., Xiao, J., Shu, C.: An application of recommender system with mingle-topn algorithm on b2b platform. In: IEEE Advanced Cloud and Big Data (CBD 2013), pp. 170–176 (2013)
15. Zhang, Y., Wang, L., Hu, L., Wang, X., Chen, M.: Comer: cloud-based medicine recommendation. In: QShine 2014, pp. 18–19 (2014)
16. Bouneffouf, D., Bouzeghoub, A., Gançarski, A.L.: Following the user's interests in mobile context-aware recommender systems: the hybrid-e-greedy algorithm. In: IEEE Advanced Information Networking and Applications Workshops (WAINA 2012), pp. 657–662 (2012)
17. Verma, S.K., Mittal, N., Agarwal, B.: Hybrid recommender system based on fuzzy clustering and collaborative filtering. In: International Conference Computing and Communication Technology (ICCCT 2013), pp. 116–120 (2013)

18. Jin, J., Chen, Q.: A trust-based top-k recommender system using social tagging network. In: Fuzzy Systems and Knowledge Discovery (FSKD 2012). pp. 1270–1274 (2012)
19. Sarwar, B.M., Karypis, G., Konstan, J.A., Riedl, J.T.: Application of dimensionality reduction in recommender system-a case study. Technical report, DTIC Document (2000)
20. Herlocker, J.L., Konstan, J.A., Terveen, L.G., Riedl, J.T.: Evaluating collaborative filtering recommender systems. ACM Trans. Inf. Syst. (TOIS) **22**, 5–53 (2004)
21. Beel, J., Langer, S., Gipp, B.: A comparative analysis of offline and online evaluations and discussion of research paper recommender system evaluation. In: ACM RepSys 2013, pp. 7–14 (2013)
22. Mooney, R.J., Roy, L.: Content-based book recommending using learning for text categorization. In: ACM Conference on Digital Libraries, pp. 195–204 (2000)
23. Gupta, R., Jain, A., Rana, S., Singh, S.: Contextual information based recommender system using singular value decomposition. In: Advances in Computing, Communications and Informatics (ICACCI 2013), pp. 2084–2089 (2013)
24. CSDN: Item-Based Collaborative Filtering Recommendation Algorithms. http:// blog.csdn.net/huagong_adu/article/details/7362908
25. Hamilton, J.D.: Time Series Analysis, vol. 2. Princeton University Press, Princeton (1994)
26. Alsultanny, Y.: Successful forecasting for knowledge discovery by statistical methods. In: IEEE Information Technology: New Generations (ITNG 2012), pp. 584–588 (2012)
27. Apache: Myrrix. http://myrrix.com/
28. Apache: Hadoop. http://hadoop.apache.org/

A VM Reservation-Based Cloud Service Broker and Its Performance Evaluation

Heejae Kim, Yoonki Ha, Yusik Kim,
Kyung-no Joo, and Chan-Hyun Youn$^{(\boxtimes)}$

Department of Electrical Engineering, Korea Advanced Institute
of Science and Technology (KAIST), Daejeon, Korea
{kim881019,milmgas,yusiky,eu2198,chyoun}@kaist.ac.kr

Abstract. We deal with a reservation-based cloud service broker (R-CSB). The main role of the R-CSB is to provide application execution services or Software-as-a-Service. The R-CSB makes a profit by an arbitrage between cloud service consumers and providers, and service fees from the consumers. In this paper, we first present detail concepts and architecture of the R-CSB. Also, to reduce the VM leasing cost, we discuss two schemes. The VM reservation scheme (C-VMR) makes the R-CSB reduce the VM leasing cost via leasing an appropriate number of reserved VMs. In addition to the C-VMR, we also present the VM allocation scheme (C-VMA) to allocate applications to VMs cost-effectively. Performance evaluation results show that the C-VMR has lower cost than other approaches and the C-VMA shows has higher average VM utilization than the conventional methods in most cases.

Keywords: Cloud service brokers · VM reservation · VM allocation

1 Introduction

According to Gartner, cloud service brokers (CSBs) are one of the top 10 strategic technology trends for 2014 [1]. There are many related companies to provide services for selecting best services of multiple clouds, adding monitoring services, metadata managing services, and providing Software-as-a-Service (SaaS). Liu et al. [2] classified these services as three forms: service intermediation to improve services by adding new value-added features, service aggregation to combine and integrate services into new services, and service arbitrage to arbitrage and aggregate service with not fixed services.

We suppose that a CSB operates independently to cloud service providers (CSPs) and cloud service consumers (CSCs). It means that the CSB is a business entity which creates values between CSPs and CSCs, and we call it as a VM reservation-based CSB (R-CSB). The main role of the R-CSB is to provide application execution services or SaaS using virtual machines (VMs) leased from CSPs. Because it is difficult for most CSCs to perform effective VM allocation and application execution management, the R-CSB has advantages of choosing the optimal resources to execute the applications with characteristics of CSCs (e.g. geographical location, network topology, various types of resource requests, etc.), and reallocating VMs in dynamic situations via

© Institute for Computer Sciences, Social Informatics and Telecommunications Engineering 2015
V.C.M. Leung et al. (Eds.): CloudComp 2014, LNICST 142, pp. 43–52, 2015.
DOI: 10.1007/978-3-319-16050-4_4

monitoring performance. Also, because we consider the actual and general pricing policies of CSPs, the R-CSB is easily applicable in today's industry.

In this paper, we present detail concepts and architecture of the R-CSB, and its VM reservation and allocation schemes. The VM reservation scheme (C-VMR) and the VM allocation scheme (C-VMA) especially focus on reducing the VM leasing cost. The C-VMR is designed to lease an appropriate number of reserved VMs (RVMs) by demand with time. Also, as an extension of BestFit, the C-VMA is operated with both on-demand VMs (OVMs) and RVMs by considering residual times of VMs.

The remainder of this paper is organized as follows. Section 2 describes related work. Section 3 presents detail concepts and architecture of the R-CSB. Sections 4 and 5 present the C-VMR and C-VMA respectively. In Sect. 6, we evaluate the C-VMR and C-VMA. Finally, Sect. 7 concludes this paper.

2 Related Work

For VM reservation in clouds, Chaisiri et al. [3] proposed the OVMP algorithm to optimize resource provisioning and VM placement. The authors formulated the optimization problem to minimize the total cost of resource provisioning using stochastic integer programming and presented a method to solve it using Benders decomposition and sample-average approximation algorithms. Wang et al. [4] presented VM reservation strategies to minimize the VM leasing cost using dynamic programming and the corresponding approximation algorithms for CSBs.

For VM allocation in clouds, Genaud et al. [5] divided strategies for it into four categories: 1VM4ALL, 1VMPerJob, Bin-Packing, and Relax. 1VM4ALL allocates every job to a single VM, 1VMPerJob allocates each job to a VM, Bin-Packing allocates jobs to VMs using heuristics such as FirstFit, BestFit, and WorstFit, and Relax considers SLAs by including a bound on the waiting time. Leitner et al. [6] presented a scheme to minimize the sum of changes of the VM leasing cost and the SLA penalty cost. They described the change of the VM leasing cost after the VM κ is selected to allocate the application as depicted in Eq. (1) where T^{req} is the execution time of the application requested to execute, T_{κ}^{res} is the residual time of the VM κ, BTU_{κ} is billing time unit (BTU) of the VM κ, and p_{κ}^{BTU} is the price of the VM κ in the BTU.

$$\Delta lc_{\kappa} = \begin{cases} \left| \frac{T^{req} - T_{\kappa}^{res}}{BTU_{\kappa}} \cdot p_{\kappa}^{BTU} \right|, & \text{if } T^{req} > T_{\kappa}^{res} \\ 0, & \text{if } T^{req} \leq T_{\kappa}^{res} \end{cases} . \tag{1}$$

We note that selecting a VM to minimize the change of the VM leasing cost is the extension of BestFit which selects a VM whose residual time is longer than the execution time and the nearest to it. We call it as modified BestFit (MBF) in the remainder of this paper. In addition, WorstFit is identical to the BestFit except that it selects a VM whose residual time is the farthest to the execution time. We call the corresponding extension of the WorstFit as modified WorstFit (MWF). Shen et al. [7] presented a scheme using a portfolio of integer programming problems (IPP) and heuristics-based approaches. In the scheme, VM allocation strategies are produced by the IPP and the various heuristics in limited time, and the best strategy is selected as its VM allocation decision. They also extended the scheme to consider both OVMs and RVMs by determining the number and types of RVMs. A scheme presented by Deng et al. [8] used a trace-based simulator to select a suitable strategy for each VM provisioning, job selecting, and VM selecting in a portfolio. In addition, they propose an algorithm to enlarge the chance of selecting the best policy in limited time.

3 Reservation-Based Cloud Service Broker

The R-CSB executes applications on behalf of CSCs or provides SaaS using VMs leased from CSPs. A profit of the R-CSB is made by an arbitrage between CSCs and CSPs, and service fees from CSCs. To increase the profit, the VM leasing cost of the R-CSB should decrease, and we solve it via cost-effective VM reservation and allocation. The VM reservation is based on the following fact. The resources provided by CSPs is generally divided by OVMs and RVMs. The OVMs and the RVMs refers to VMs leased in comparatively short BTUs (e.g. an hour) and long BTUs (e.g. a month, a year) respectively. Prices of RVMs during unit time is set to be cheaper than those of OVMs, and the VM reservation can reduce the VM leasing cost. However, because BTUs of RVMs are much longer than those of OVMs, the cost-effectiveness of the VM reservation can rather decrease if utilizations of the RVMs are low. Therefore, the R-CSB should lease an appropriate number of RVMs.

In addition to the VM reservation, the VM leasing cost can be reduced by the effective VM allocation via increasing average VM utilization. If the number of leased RVMs is greater or equal to the current demand to the R-CSB, it is enough to allocate applications to the RVMs, and the OVM leasing cost is not imposed. Otherwise, an additional OVM should be leased to allocate the application. Therefore, increasing average VM utilization decrease the number of OVMs leased additionally, and it results in the reduction of the VM leasing cost.

Figure 1 depicts architecture of the R-CSB. A VM reservation module is to determine the number of RVMs to be leased by time. The VM reservation strategizing in the VM reservation module is performed based on demand monitoring and prediction. RVMs leased by the VM reservation module and OVMs additionally leased are managed in a VM pool management module. We divide the VM pool into two kinds: VM pools which contains VMs whose status is idle (an idle VM pool) and VMs on which the applications is executed (an active VM pool). For application execution requests of CSCs via a user interface, the R-CSB parses the requests and profiles the applications if the profiling isn't done before. The applications are scheduled and allocated to appropriate VMs in the idle VM pool, and VM scaling is performed if it is empty. Then, the application execution module starts to execute the applications via a cloud interface. To guarantee performances of applications in the dynamic nature of public clouds, the R-CSB is designed to reallocate VMs if performance degradations are monitored or current VM allocation cannot satisfy SLAs of CSCs. In addition, we need a security and authentication management module for a secure service of R-CSB.

CSCs
application execution requests

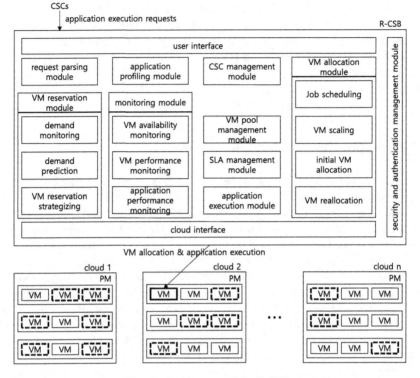

Fig. 1. Architecture of the R-CSB.

4 C-VMR

The C-VMR is presented to determine the appropriate number of RVMs to be leased in the VM reservation module. In this section, we suppose that BTUs of OVMs and RVMs are fixed as BTU_{OVM} and BTU_{RVM} respectively. The basic idea of the C-VMR is adaptively determining the number of RVMs to be leased based on predicted demand. The demand refers to the number of VMs needed to service application execution requests of CSCs.

The C-VMR uses the auto regressive integrated moving average (ARIMA) model to predict demand based on Brockwell et al. [9], Fang et al. [10], and Ha et al. [11]. The demand prediction is performed with the following three steps. First, time series of the demand are preprocessed to apply the ARIMA model. Because the ARIMA model is only applicable with stationary time series, the non-stationary time series of the demand should be processed to be stationary. It can be achieved by obtaining derivations of the time series. Second, the order of the ARIMA model is determined based on the auto correlation function (ACF) and the partial auto correlation function (PACF) of the preprocessed time series. Validity of the ARIMA model is also checked in this step. Third, the ARIMA model is applied to predict the demand.

A mechanism of the C-VMR is as follows. The C-VMR is operated every period T_r. At each time t at which the C-VMR is operated, the demand from the time t for T_p is predicted. Then, $n^l_{RVM}(t)$ which denotes the number of RVMs to be leased at the time t is determined as Eq. (1) where $D_p(t)$ is the predicted demand during $[t, t+1]$, and $n^e_{RVM}(t)$ is the number of RVMs in the VM pool at time t.

$$n^l_{RVM}(t) = \left\lfloor \frac{1}{T_p} \sum_{k=t}^{t+T_p} D_p(k) - n^e_{RVM}(k) \right\rfloor. \tag{2}$$

Algorithm 1. C-VMR

Input: historical demand information during $[t - T_h, t - 1]$ where T_h is a period to be used as the historical demand in the demand prediction

1: predict the demand during $[t, t + T_p]$

2: Obtain $n^l_{RVM}(t)$

3: Lease additional RVMs as much as $n^l_{RVM}(t)$

---

5 C-VMA

The C-VMA is operated as online VM allocation. We assume that the applications are indivisible. To reduce the VM leasing cost, the C-VMA focuses on increasing VM utilization. Whenever each application execution request is arrived, the C-VMA is operated as follows. If there exist OVMs which satisfy $\alpha <$ the residual time – the predicted application execution time $< \beta$ in the idle VM pool, the MBF is applied for the OVMs. Otherwise, if there exist RVMs in the idle VM pool, one of the RVMs is selected. Finally, if there does not exist the corresponding OVM or RVM, the MBF is applied for all the VMs in the idle VM pool. Obviously, an additional OVM is leased and added to the idle VM pool if it is empty.

Algorithm 2. C-VMA

Input: an application execution request

1: **if** there exists OVMs which satisfy $\alpha <$ the residual time – the predicted application execution time $< \beta$ **then**

2: apply the MBF for the OVMs

3: **else if** there exists RVMs in the idle VM pool **then**

4: allocate the application to one of the RVMs

5: **else**

6: apply the MBF for all the OVMs in the idle VM pool

7: **end if**

---

6 Performance Evaluation

6.1 C-VMR

In this section, we evaluate the C-VMR. For the evaluation, the actual demand is generated for 4 years as depicted in Fig. 2(a) as a solid line. The actual demand is unit of the average number of VMs needed to service application execution requests of CSCs per hour. We use ASTSA package in R [12] for the demand prediction using the ARIMA model, and the prediction result is also depicted in Fig. 2(a) as a dotted line. In the evaluation, we suppose that there are 5 RVMs in the VM pool initially, BTUs of OVMs and RVMs are 1 h and 1 month, and the leasing costs are \$0.24 per an hour and \$131.4 per a month respectively. We note that the VM leasing costs are from the pricing policy for large standard cloud servers in GoGrid [13]. Also, we set T_r, T_p, and T_h as 1 week, 1 month, and 30 weeks respectively.

We compare the C-VMR with three other approaches: No VM reservation, Fixed VM reservation, and BTU-fixed VM reservation). The No VM reservation is the approach which uses no RVM. Therefore, application execution requests are serviced using only OVMs. The Fixed VM reservation is the approach which reserves an optimal fixed number of RVMs for every time. The optimal fixed number is determined to minimize the VM leasing cost. The BTU-fixed VM reservation is the approach which reserves an optimal fixed number of RVMs for each period as much as BTU. Therefore, the optimal fixed number is recomputed at each period. Figure 2(b) shows the result. The result shows that the VM leasing cost of C-VMR is less than other three approaches.

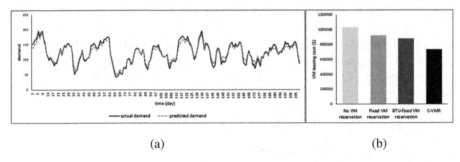

(a)   (b)

Fig. 2. An example of VM allocation in the R-CSB: (a) VM allocation when it is not necessary to lease OVMs, (b) VM allocation when it is necessary to lease OVMs additionally.

6.2 C-VMA

In this section, we evaluate the C-VMA. The evaluation is performed in our cloud testbed based on OpenStack Essex [14] as depicted in Fig. 3. Each physical machine (PM) in the testbed uses two quad-core processors with Hyper-Threading [15] (Intel® Xeon® Processor E5620). It also has 14 GB for the main memory and 1000 GB for the hard disk. For the evaluation, we developed the several modules highlighted in Fig. 3, and the modules are operated on Apache Tomcat 7.0 [16]. The experimental procedure is as follows. We start the experiment after building VMs which have 1 VCPU, 1 GB of memory, and 10 GB. Five VMs of them are set for the initial RVMs in an idle VM pool, and we suppose that BTU of the RVMs are longer than the experiment period. Application execution requests are arrived to the R-SPCSB via RESTful web services via Jersey [17] during an hour by inter-arrival times which follows a Poisson distribution whose mean is 5 s. For the applications, we use three applications whose expected execution times are 15.99, 38.23, and 60.08 s and they are based on Map-Chem [18] which performs a high performance bio and chemical analysis. We note that the inter-arrival time and the application for each request is predetermined randomly before the experiment. Application execution requests are written in JavaScript Object Notation (JSON) [19] via Gson [20] and transmitted to the R-CSB via a POST method. After receiving each request, the R-CSB parses the request using Gson, and a VM to execute the application is selected by a VM allocation strategy. Then, the application is executed on it. We suppose that BTU of OVMs is 100 s, and extra delay to lease new VMs including transaction time is 5 s. These are considered as scaled down values of BTU and extra delay in real world respectively.

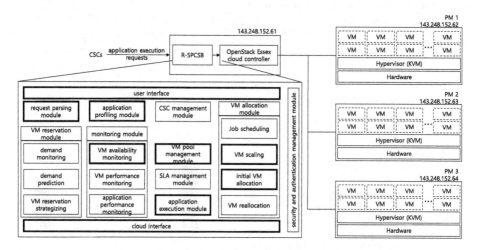

Fig. 3. The experimental environment for evaluating the C-VMA.

We evaluate the C-VMA for six cases by difference between predicted and expected application execution times.

Case 1 (predicted application execution times ≪ expected application execution times). Predicted application execution times of the three applications are 10.99, 26.23, and 40.08 s respectively. $\alpha = 7$ and $\beta = 27$.

Case 2 (predicted application execution times < expected application execution times). Predicted application execution times of the three applications are 10.99, 30.23, and 50.08 s respectively. $\alpha = 5$ and $\beta = 25$.

Case 3 (predicted application execution times = expected application execution times = actual application execution times). Predicted application execution times of the three applications are 15.99, 38.23, and 60.08 s respectively. $\alpha = 0$ and $\beta = 20$.

Case 4 (predicted application execution times = expected application execution times). Predicted application execution times of the three applications are 15.99, 38.23, and 60.08 s respectively. $\alpha = 0$ and $\beta = 20$.

Case 5 (predicted application execution times > expected application execution times). Predicted application execution times of the three applications are 20.99, 46.23, and 70.08 s respectively. $\alpha = -5$ and $\beta = 25$.

Case 6 (predicted application execution times ≫ expected application execution times). Predicted application execution times of the three applications are 20.99, 52.23, and 80.08 s respectively. $\alpha = -7$ and $\beta = 27$.

We note that the experiment for the case 3 was performed with just waiting (i.e., executing sleep()) during the corresponding expected application execution times instead of executing application actually.

Figure 4 depicts the results. We compare the C-VMA with the MBF, the MWF, and reservation-based MBF (R-MBF). We note that the R-MBF is identical to the MBF except that it tries to allocate applications to RVMs first. The results of the MBF shows that the average VM utilization gets lower as the predicted application execution times are farther from the expected application execution times. Because the MBF is based on the prediction of application execution times, the MBF can fail to select VMs whose residual time is the closest to the actual application execution times. In addition, the unnecessary VM leasing cost can occur if the predicted application execution times are shorter than the actual application execution times in the selected VMs. Therefore, the C-VMA is designed to overcome these problems via using the specific bound of the residual time – the predicted application execution time. On the other hand, the results

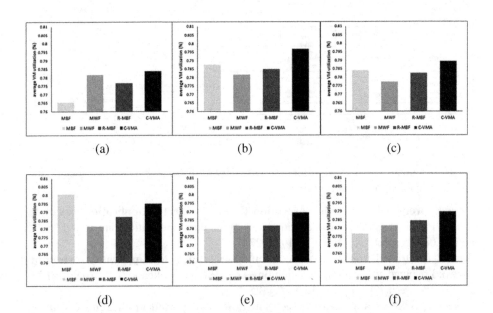

Fig. 4. The average VM utilization of the MBF, the MWF, the R-MBF, and the C-VMA: (a) case 1, (b) case 2, (c) case 3, (d) case 4, (e) case 5, and (f) case 6.

of the MWF are the same for all the cases except for the case 3 because it selects a VM whose residual time is the longest regardless of the predicted application execution times. In the results of the R-MBF, the average VM utilizations of the R-MBF are higher than those of the MWF if the predicted application execution times are close to the expected application execution times. Otherwise, the average VM utilizations are higher than that of the MBF because the R-MBF checks RVMs whether there exist RVMs available to allocate first. Finally, the average VM utilization of the C-VMA is the highest for all the cases except for the case 4.

7 Conclusion

In this paper, we presented a VM reservation-based cloud service broker and its performance evaluation. Among many issues enabling to be addressed in the R-CSB, we focused on reducing the VM leasing cost. To achieve it, the C-VMR and the C-VMA were presented for cost-effective VM reservation and allocation respectively. The evaluation for the C-VMR showed that the VM leasing cost of the C-VMR is the lowest compared with the other methods. To evaluate the C-VMA, we implemented a prototype of the R-CSB. The results showed that the average VM utilization of the C-VMA is the highest compared with the conventional methods in most cases. As on-going and future work, we are extending the C-VMR and the C-VMA to consider various types of OVMs and RVMs of multiple CSPs, and constraints such as budget, performance, etc.

Acknowledgments. This research was supported by the MSIP (Ministry of Science, ICT & Future Planning), Korea in the ICT R&D Program 2014, and the MSIP under the ITRC (Information Technology Research Center) support program (NIPA-2014(H0301-14-1020)) supervised by the NIPA (National IT Industry Promotion Agency).

References

1. Top 10 Strategic Technology Trends for 2014. http://www.gartner.com
2. Liu, F., Tong, J., Mao, J., Bohn, R., Messina, J., Badger, L., Leaf, D.: NIST cloud computing reference architecture. NIST Special Publication 500-292 (2011)
3. Chaisiri, S., Lee, B.S., Niyato, D.: Optimization of resource provisioning cost in cloud computing. IEEE Trans. Serv. Comput. **5**(2), 164–177 (2012)
4. Wang, W., Niu, D., Li, B., Liang, B.: Dynamic cloud resource reservation via cloud brokerage. In: 33rd IEEE International Conference on Distributed Computing Systems, pp. 400–409 (2013)
5. Genaud, S., Gossa, J.: Cost-wait trade-offs in client-side resource provisioning with elastic clouds. In: 4th IEEE International Conference on Cloud Computing, pp. 1–8 (2011)
6. Leitner, P., Hummer, W., Satzger, B., Inzinger, C., Dustdar, S.: Cost-efficient and application SLA-aware client side request scheduling in an infrastructure-as-a-service cloud. In: 5th IEEE International Conference on Cloud Computing, pp. 213–220 (2012)
7. Shen, S., Deng, K., Iosup, A., Epema, D.: Scheduling jobs in the cloud using on-demand and reserved instances. In: Wolf, F., Mohr, B., an Mey, D. (eds.) Euro-Par 2013. LNCS, vol. 8097, pp. 242–254. Springer, Heidelberg (2013)

8. Deng, K., Song, J., Ren, K., Iosup, A.: Exploring portfolio scheduling for long-term execution of scientific workloads in IaaS clouds. In: 25th International Conference on High Performance Computing, Networking, Storage and Analysis (2013)
9. Brockwell, P.J., Davis, R.A.: Introduction to Time Series and Forecasting. Springer, New York (2002)
10. Fang, W., Lu, Z., Wu, J., Cao, Z.Y.: RPPS: a novel resource prediction and provisioning scheme in cloud data center. In: 9th IEEE International Conference on Services Computing, pp. 609–616 (2012)
11. Ha, Y., Youn, C.H.: A study on efficient VM reservation method for cloud broker. In: 41st Conference of the KIPS (2014)
12. R. http://www.r-project.org
13. GoGrid. http://www.gogrid.com
14. OpenStack Essex. http://www.openstack.com
15. Intel Hyper-Threading Technology. http://www.intel.com
16. Apache Tomcat 7.0. http://tomcat.apache.org
17. Jersey. http://jersey.java.net/
18. Ren, Y.: A Cloud Collaboration System with Active Application Control Scheme and Its Experimental Performance Analysis, Master's thesis, KAIST (2012)
19. JavaScript Object Notation. http://www.json.org
20. Gson. https://code.google.com/p/google-gson

Virtualizing IMS Core
and Its Performance Analysis

Lingxia Liao[1](✉), Victor C.M. Leung[1], and Min Chen[2]

[1] Department of Electrical and Computer Engineering,
University of British Columbia, Vancouver, Canada
{liaolx,vleung}@ece.ubc.ca
[2] School of Computer Science and Technology,
Huazhong University of Science and Technology, Wuhan, China
minchen@ieee.org

Abstract. Current IP Multimedia System (IMS) industry faces the issue that the complicated architecture of IMS and the huge early investment in its network construction has slowed down its deployment and service innovation. Furthermore, IMS network also causes more computing and network resource waste than current telecom network becuase no existed method can be used to predict the capacity of data service with guaranteed Quality of Service (QoS) in IMS network. Present research and practice consider that virtualizing IMS core and running it on cloud can be a way to solve these problems. However, current research shows the virtualization brings at least five times longer response delays to IMS and makes it unfeasible to be used. We argue that hardware-assisted virtualization technology can improve the virtual machine performance, and through carefully tuning the virtual machine parameters, the overhead caused by virtual machines can be minimized. We choose OpenIMSCore as an IMS core network, IMS Benchmark SIPp as a traffic generator, design and conduct a performance test. The results show that running IMS core network on virtual machines has comparable response delays with it running on bare boxes. It is feasible to virtualize the IMS core network and run it on private clouds.

Keywords: Cloud computing · Virtualization · IMS architecture · Performance testing

1 Introduction

IP Multimedia Subsystem (IMS) is an all-IP core network architecture designed by 3GPP to replace the current mobile circuit switch communication system and support wide range of multimedia applications [1]. It has been deployed in current Long-Term Evolution (LTE) systems to provide core network control for both voice and data services with Quality of Service (QoS) guaranteed. However, IMS network architecture is fully new and very complicated, which creates a big difficulty in network understanding and deployment, and causes huge early

© Institute for Computer Sciences, Social Informatics and Telecommunications Engineering 2015
V.C.M. Leung et al. (Eds.): CloudComp 2014, LNICST 142, pp. 53–65, 2015.
DOI: 10.1007/978-3-319-16050-4_5

investment and resource waste. These issues have slowed down the IMS network deployment and service innovation in the reality. Finding a way to reduce the deployment difficulty and the resource waste is significant for IMS industry.

Cloud Computing is a model for enabling convenient, on-demand network access to a shared pool of configurable computing resource that can be rapidly provisioned and released with minimal management effort or service provider interaction [2,3]. The Platform-as-a-Service (PaaS) provided by a cloud can dynamically scale up and down the resource without interrupting the applications running on top of it. Virtualizing IMS core network and running it on cloud PaaS environment can be a way to reduce IMS network deployment difficulty, early investment, and resource waste. Because IMS core is an application with rigid network requirement especially for response delay and applications running on public clouds may have undecidable network overhead caused by the uncontrollable network infrastructures for application service providers, virtualizing IMS core on a private cloud environment with fully controlled network infrastructure can greatly reduce the possible negative network performance influencing factors, which can be a way to solve the problems in current IMS industry without sacrificing the performance.

Currently, there are a couple of research work on IMS core virtualization. Reference [4] is focused on the scalability. It avoids the response delay comparability between running IMS core network on virtual machines and physical machines. Reference [5] targets to building a virtual IMS test bed with acceptable performance, but it doesn't provide the definition of an acceptable performance, and its way to measure delays lacks accuracy. Reference [6] presents a feasibility research on IMS core virtualization and gives five times longer response delay when running it on a virtual machine comparing to run it on a physical machine. However, to the best of our knowledge, all of them are based on software virtualization technology, and no effort has been made to investigate the feasibility to virtualize IMS core on hardware-assisted [7,8] virtual machines, which has shown the great performance improvement on I/O and network benchmark testing. This paper argues that virtualizing IMS core network on hardware-assisted virtual machines and running it on private clouds can be feasible. A performance test is designed and conducted to show the comparable network latencies when running IMS core network on a bare box and virtual machines.

The main contributions of this paper are three folds: (1) the mainstream virtual machines and the virtualization technologies used are summarized, and the parameters affecting the performance of virtual machines are highlighted; (2) a performance testing is designed and conducted to quantitatively compare the performance that running IMS core on bare boxes and different virtual machines; and (3) running IMS core on hardware-assisted supported virtual machines have comparable network latency as running it on bare boxes.

The rest of this paper is organized as follows. The background of IMS and cloud computing is introduced in Sect. 2; the mainstream virtual machines and the virtualization technologies they used are summarized in Sect. 3. The performance testing is provided in Sect. 4 and the conclusions are drawn in Sect. 5.

2   Background

IMS and Cloud Computing are concepts belonging to the telecom and the Internet domains. In this section, the basic concepts in IMS and Cloud Computing domains are introduced.

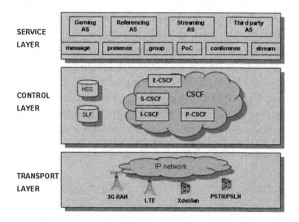

Fig. 1. IMS layered architecture.

2.1   IMS

IMS is a layered reference architecture. A simplified IMS architecture consists of three layers from the bottom up: the transport layer, the control layer, and the service layer as shown in Fig. 1 [9]. The transport layer enables the access from the different access networks and ensures the network inter-connectivity and bearer controlling with the collaboration of the IP core domains. The transport layer supports multiple access mechanisms and provides inter-connectivity to multiple networks [10]. The control layer is the IMS core network. It provides the call session controls, user managements, multimedia service resource controls and multimedia applications supporting, network inter-working. The service layer consists of various media capabilities servers and application servers, and has the ability to provide multiple multimedia services.

The main features of IMS can be summarized as the follows: (1) decoupling the access from applications to be the transport layer and the control from applications to be the control layer, such that the multimedia application services can be an independent layer on top of both; (2) the control is IP based through Session Initiation Protocol (SIP) to control call sessions, such as session creating, modifying and terminating. By working with Session Description Protocol (SDP), the media identification and negotiation is achieved; the QoS can be guaranteed for both voice and other multimedia services over IP. The major concerns of IMS include the complication of its system architecture and the possible performance bottleneck in its core and access components.

2.2   Cloud Computing

Cloud computing is defined by National Institute of Standards and Technology (NIST) as a model for service sharing. It is a layered architecture with three service delivery models and three service deployment models [11]. Hoff presents this layered architecture in [12] as shown in Fig. 2, in which the three service delivery models from the bottom up are Infrastructure-as-a-Service (IaaS), Platform-as-a-Service (PaaS), and Software-as-a-Service (SaaS). In such architecture, the lower level services form the base of the upper level services. IaaS provides the infrastructure, including network resources, servers, and storage space, in a way of on-demand usage and pay as you go hardware provisioning. PaaS facilitates the environment for developing, testing and implementing applications without having any control over the underlying operating system and hardware infrastructure. It is often termed as the development platform for SaaS. SaaS is the most commonly used service delivery model that provides software or application, on-demand, to the customer, using the Internet.

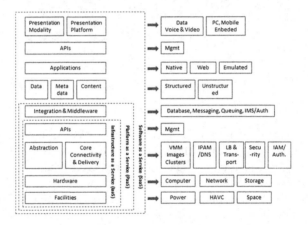

Fig. 2. Cloud layered architecture.

Based on the network infrastructure, physical location of the computing resources, the cloud deployment model can be classified to private cloud, public cloud, hybrid cloud. Private cloud is the infrastructure fully operated and used by a single enterprise with full control over the underlying hardware and software environment. Public cloud is owned by the cloud service provider, and the services are offered to and shared by public users based on the resource's usage through the Internet. Hybrid cloud is a mix of private and public cloud model. In this model, companies connect their private cloud to public clouds. It is used in the scenario where companies want to store and process the critical data in their private cloud and take the advantage of highly available and scalable resource in the public cloud as well.

Cloud computing has known the features as (1) On-demand self-service; (2) Broad network access; (3) Resource pooling; (4) Rapid elasticity; (5) Measured service. The major concerns in cloud computing consist of accurately billing and auditing, QoS monitoring, network troubleshooting and inter- operating, performance isolation, and security.

2.3   Virtualizing IMS Core

As we have mentioned in last subsection, IMS is a layered architecture, which decouples the access and control from applications and provides independent interface for the service on top of them. It is designed and supposed to greatly reduce the difficulty in new service innovation and integration. However, this layered structure itself is complicated, which causes the difficulty in system understanding and implementation and further slows down the third party multimedia service innovations and deployments in the reality. And furthermore, such layered structure in theory avoids the central bottleneck but splits the bottleneck into many points, especially for the control functions and database in its core network. In order to have guaranteed QoS for each service, the core has to have the capability to handle a big number of requests in a short time from both voice and other multimedia users. However, as a fully new IP core to support both voice and data services with guaranteed QoS, there is no existing ways to predict the usage of IP users, which can cause huge resource waste or service degrading. Even the IMS network provider can bear this huge resource waste, no matter how much resource has been reserved, there is always a day when the resource is used up with the users growing, and a system capacity expansion is unavoidable, which means the serve interruption and all the invest in the old system is wasted.

Since cloud can provide elastic environment to support resource scaling up and down without service interruption, virtualizing IMS core and running it on cloud can be a way to achieve the goal of reducing deployment difficulty and resource waste, and provide system capacity expansion without service interruption. As public cloud is traditionally considered as a platform for CPU consumed applications rather than network consumed applications, an application such as IMS core with rigid network requirement may not be fitted into its environment. However, private cloud model gives the applications on top of it the fully computing and network resource controlling, which can greatly reduce the possible factors to influence the application performance. On the other hand, telecom service providers have the experiences and requirements to fully control the network and services, and constructing a private cloud in their data center is workable for telecom service providers.

The big difference on running IMS core on bare boxes and private cloud is the computing resources on private cloud are virtualized; and virtual machines contributes most part of the performance difference. Virtual machines with different virtualization technology employed perform varied. Choosing the right virtual machines can reduce the performance influence to minimum and it is the key for virtualizing IMS core.

3   Virtualization technologies

Virtualization for x86 architecture (such as IA32 and IA64) was happening in recent a couple of years [13]. The main obstacles to virtualize x86 systems are the visibility of privileged state and lack of traps when privileged instructions run at user-level. The main approaches are used to conquer these two obstacles are Binary Translation (BT) and special privileged partition. Regarding to the various approach, current virtualization technology, which creates a virtual machine working like a real computer with an operating system to provide an isolated running environment to the applications on top of it, can be categorized into the following three types:

- Full virtualization: It almost completely simulate of the actual hardware to allow an unmodified guest OS and other applications to be run in isolation. The key technology used in full virtualization is BT, which translate the guest binary code (including all privileged instructions) to mostly user-mode instructions, such that they can be safely used on host OS with high performance. VirtualBox fills in this category.
- Para virtualization: It has not to totally simulate a hardware environment, but it offers a special API to modify the guest OS such that it can be run in this environment. Instead of using BT to handle the privileged instructions, para virtualization addresses it by creating a special privileged partition, whose privilege is lower than host OS privilege instructions but higher than the host OS user-mode instructions. The guest OSes run in this special partition and all the privilege system calls made by guest applications are also directed to run in this partition, for example, the Dom0 of Xen.
- Hardware assisted virtualization technology is a way of improving the efficiency of hardware virtualization. It involves employing specially designed CPUs and hardware components that help improve the performance of a guest environment, for example the Intel VT and AMD-V.

Table 1 lists some popular open source or free virtual machines. Kernel-based Virtual Machine (KVM) is a full virtualization solution for Linux on x86 hardware [14]. It consists of a loadable kernel module to provide the core virtualization infrastructure and a processor specific module. It has shown great I/O and network performance improving in many performance testings. VirtualBox is a virtualization product of Oracle using full virtualization technology [15]. It supports x86 and AMD64/Intel64, and easy to use with rich features. It is freely available for enterprise as well as home users. Xen is a virtualization solution using a Para virtualization technology [13]. It is first developed by the University of Cambridge Computer Laboratory and now it is open-source and maintained by Xen community.

There is no simple way to compare the performance of different virtual machines. Different test scenario and configuration makes big difference in performance testings. However, Hardware-assisted method shows a big performance improving [16–20], some best practice in tuning the virtual machine performance are widely used [21, 22]:

Table 1. Virtual machine and the virtualization technoligies used

Virtual machines	Virtualization type	Hardware-assisted supported
KVM	Full	Yes
Virtualbox	Full	Yes
Xen	Para and Full	Yes

- Image type: each type of virtual machine defines its own image format to support some advanced functionality, but raw images always get the better performance and compatibility.
- Cache mode: the write cache mode affects the performance of disk I/O. Virtual machines normally support three write cache modes: none, write through, and write back. None is the mode without cache; write through is the mode that the host page cache is enabled while the virtual machine disk cache is disabled; write back is the mode that both the host page cache and virtual machine disk cache are enabled. Cache back mode has the best disk performance because the virtual machine disk cache improves the disk performance greatly.
- Device driver type: Virtual machines normally support para virtualized device drivers, these device drivers have been performance optimized. Using virtio to enable para-virtualized device drivers gets better performance.
- Network type: virtual machines normally supported two networking types: Network Address Translator (NAT) and Bridged. Bridged mode has the better performance.

4 Performance Benchmark

In order to demonstrate that hardware-assisted virtual machine can reduce the performance overhead, we design and conduct a performance test. We introduce the test bed and test scenarios used and discuss the test result in the rest of this section.

4.1 OpenIMSCore and IMS Benchmark SIPp

OpenIMSCore [23] is an open-source implementation of IMS core network. It realizes the fundamental functions of IMS core network, which includes the Call-Session Control Functions (P-CSCF, I-CSCF, S-CSCF), and a lightweight Home Subscriber Server (HSS) developed in compliance to the IMS architecture standards given by the 3GPP. P-CSCF is the first point connecting to users. It receives the service requests and transfers them to the next point. I-CSCF is the gateway point of IMS, it allocates the service requests to a particula S-CSCF, answers the routing requests, and hides the topology of the IMS domain. S-CSCF is the key control element in IMS. It controls the call sessions, user data, and user registration authentication. HSS stores all the information about the subscribers. It is a database including all the data about the basic identifications, routing information, and the QoS levels. OpenIMSCore implements

CSCFs in C and HSS on MySQL database. The IMS Bench SIPp [24] is a free open source traffic generator for the SIP protocol. It is a test tool that meets the criterion of IMS Performance Benchmark specification, ETSI TS 186.008 [25]. The whole test system consists of three modules:

- one manager instance that controls the whole benchmark running,
- a fixed number of SIPp load generators,
- a monitoring tool for the System Under Tests (SUT) to collect information about CPU load and memory consumption.

The manager instance uses a xml file to predefine the test configuration, which consists of the IP of each load generator, the IP and Port number of the SUT, the distribution of scenarios, and the number of Inadequately handled Scenario(HIS). The test system also provides some Perl scripts to add new user to HSS, to report the test data, and to analysis the test data.

4.2 Test Bed

We choose OpenIMSCore as IMS core network to test the performance, especially the delay when it runs on bare mental and multiple virtual machines. IMS benchmark SIPp is used to generate the test traffic. Our test bed consists of two PCs, one is the SUT, which runs the OpenIMSCore and the SIPp monitoring module; the other is the test system, which runs the SIPp with one manager instance and one load generator. The SUT and the test system is connected through a Syslink compact wireless broadband router with 4 Ethernet ports. Table 2 lists the test bed hardware configurations.

We run P-CSCF, I-CSCF, S-CSCF, and HSS modules of OpenIMSCore in a bare mental as the base line. Two test cases are considered: running P-CSCF, I-CSCF, S-CSCF, and HSS modules of OpenIMSCore in one virtual machine instance and in 4 virtual machines. Each virtual machine in our test has 1 CPU, 1 G memory, 10 G raw image file, the write back cache, the bridged network, the virtio device driver, and hardware-assisted enabled. We use this configuration for each virtual machine instance under test.

4.3 Test Result and Discussion

In this sub section, we analyze three typical scenarios: calling, messaging, and registering. We present the test results and discuss the possible reasons to cause them.

Calling Scenario: A full IMS calling scenario consists of three sub-scenarios: session setup, invite arrive, and session release. The session setup is the period from a caller sending a SIP INVITE request to a callee receiving the corresponding ACK message; the invite arrive is the period from a caller sending a SIP INVITE request to a callee receiving a SIP INVITE request, and the session release is the period from the first BYE to the corresponding 200 OK. We test the delays under different test load for each sub-scenario on each type of the virtual machines. The test

Table 2. Performance benchmark test bed

Machine	CPU	Memory	Hard disk	Network	OS
SUT	Intel Core i7-2600, 3.4 GHz*8	8 G	400 G	1000 Mb/s	Ubunbu 12.04 LTS
Test machine	Intel Core i3-M370, 2.4 GHz	4 G	200G	1000 Mb/s	CentOS 6

load is expressed in Scenarios Attempts Per Second (SAPS), which are 10, 15, 20 in our testing. SIPp calculates the number of delay in mean, minimum, maximum, percentile 50, percentile 90, percentile 95, and percentile 99. We choose the data in percentile 90 and draw them in Figs. 3, 4, and 5 for the delays in each sub-scenario. It can be observed that the 90 percentile of delay is in the range of 4 to 9 ms during the session setup sub scenario, 1 to 3.5 ms during the invite arrive sub scenario, and 2 to 5 ms during the session release sub scenario, and they does not increase with the increase of the number of SAPS during the testing. The delay in 4 VMs is longer than the one in 1 VM, because the Round Traffic Time(RTT) between virtual machines is longer than the communication time between the applications inside a virtual machine instance. Among the three types of virtual machines, Xen with hardware-assisted supported has the shortest delay, which is even shorter than the delay on physical machines. The most possible reason for it is the Xen virtual machine creates a performance isolation environment for the OpenIMSCore running on top it, whereas the performance of OpenIMSCore running on the physical machine can be affected by the other applications sharing the same running environment (Fig. 7).

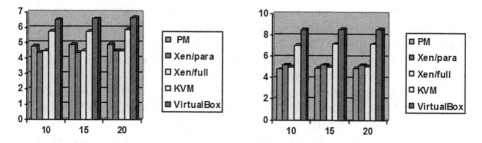

Fig. 3. Delay in call session setup (left: running on 1 VM, right: running on 4 VMs).

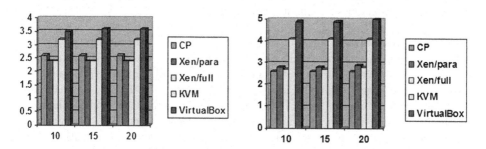

Fig. 4. Delay in call invite arrival (left: running on 1 VM, right: running on 4 VMs)

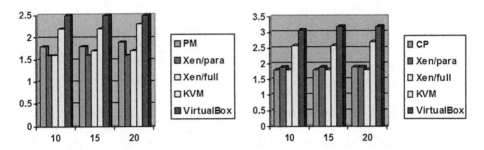

Fig. 5. Delay in call session release (left: running on 1 VM, right: running on 4 VMs)

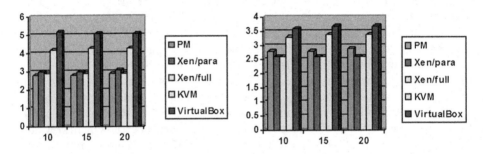

Fig. 6. Delay in message scenario (left: running on 1 VM, right: running on 4 VMs)

Messaging Scenario: IMS benchmark specification includes a message scenario. The delay is the time in milliseconds between the sending of a message and the corresponding 200 OK. We test this scenario under different load of 10, 15, 20 SAPS for each type of virtual machines. Figure 6 shows the test results in 90 percentile. It can be observed that the 90 percentile of delay is in the range of 2 to 6 ms in this scenario, and it does not increase with the increase of the number of SAPS. The delay in 4 VMs is longer than the one in 1 VM in terms of longer RTT between virtual machines than application in the same virtual machine. Xen has the shortest delay among the three types of virtual machines. The delay for all the OpenIMSCore modules running in a Xen virtual machine instance has even shorter delay than the one running in the physical machine in terms of the possible reason mentioned in last subsection.

Registration Scenario: A full IMS registration scenario consists of 2 subscenarios: between the first SIP Register request and the 401 Unauthorized response and between the second Register message and the corresponding 200 OK message. We test the delay under different test load of 10, 15, 20 SAPs for each sub-scenario on each type of virtual machine. Figures 5 and 6 show the test results in 90 percentile. It can be observed that the 90 percentile of delay does not increase with the increase of the number of SAPS during the testing. For each type of virtual machine, the delay in 4 VMs is longer than in 1 VM in terms of the longer RTT between virtual machines than applications within the same

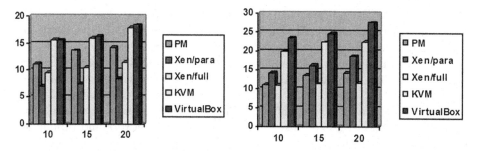

Fig. 7. Delay in first registration (left: running on 1 VM; right: running on 4 VMS)

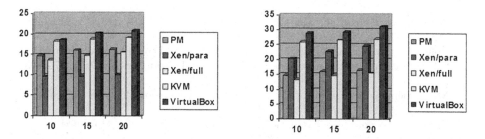

Fig. 8. Delay in second registration (left: running on 1 VM; right: running on 4 VMS).

virtual machine. The delay on Xen is the shortest among the three types of virtual machines. The same, the delay of OpenIMSCore running in one Xen virtual machine instance is shorter than the one running in the physical machine, the possible reason has been mentioned in last subsection.

Discussions: We conduct an IMS core network performance test by virtualizing OpenIMSCore on KVM, Xen, and VirtualBox virtual machines with Hardware-assisted virtualization technology supported. We use IMS Benchmark SIPp as test tool to compare the performance of running OpenIMSCore on a bare box and the virtual machines. The results show that the response delay of running on virtual machines is comparable to that running on bare boxes, which greatly improves the delay (at least 10 times longer) provided by current researches. Hardware-assisted virtualization technology and current best practice in virtual machine performance tuning can really improve the network performance. Under our test scenarios, the Xen presents the shortest delay among all three types of virtual machines tested in either para or full virtualization mode Fig. 8.

5   Conclusions

In order to solve the problem that the complicated architecture, the huge early invest, and the big possible resource waste in IMS network deployment has slowed down the IMS network deployment and its service innovation, this paper firstly introduces the basic concepts in IMS and cloud computing, then designs and conducts a performance testing to test the response delays of OpenIMSCore under different loads and configurations. The test bed, the test tool, and test scenarios are provided in detail, and the results are advanced discussed. The test results show that running OpenIMSCore on virtual machines with Hardware-assisted virtualization technology enabled can greatly reduce the response delays, and all the response delays running on all the virtual machine types used are comparable to those on bare boxes. Virtualize IMS core network and running it on a private cloud is feasible.

References

1. Poikselk, M., Mayer, G.: The IMS: IP Multimedia Concepts and Services. John Wiley and Sons, New York (2009)
2. Rings, T., Caryer, G., Gallop, J., et al.: Grid and cloud computing: opportunities for integration with the next generation network. J. Grid Comput. **7**(3), 375–393 (2009)
3. Nokia Siemens Network. Cloud computing-business boost for communications industry (2011). http://bit.ly/nVlxRI/
4. Umair, M.: Performance Evaluation and Elastic Scaling of an IP Multimedia Subsystem Implemented in a Cloud (2013)
5. Corte, G.D., et al.: An IMS-based virtualized architecture: performance analysis. In: Proceedings of the 11th WSEAS International Conference on Mathematical Methods and Computational Techniques in Electrical Engineering. World Scientific and Engineering Academy and Society (WSEAS) (2009)
6. Chuan, S., Xiaoyong, H., Xiaodong, D.: Feasibility of the virtualization based on OpenIMSCore. In: Yang, G. (ed.) Proceedings of the ICCEAE2012. CCIS, vol. 181, pp. 539–544. Springer, Heidelberg (2013)
7. INTEL CORPORATION. Intel virtualization technology specification for the IA-32 Intel architecture, April 2005
8. AMD. AMD64 Virtualization Codenamed 'Pacifica' Technology: Secure Virtual Machine Architecture Reference Manual, May 2005
9. 3GPP, IP Multimedia Subsystem (IMS), TS 23.228, Release 6 (2004)
10. 3GPP, IP Multimedia Subsystem (IMS), TS 23.228, Release 7 (2007)
11. Mell, P., Grance, T.: The NIST definition of Cloud Computing. Special Publication Draft-800-145 (2011)
12. Hoff: The Frogs Who Desired a King: A Virtualization and Cloud Computing Security Fable Set To Interpretive Dance (2009). http://www.rationalsurvivability.com/presentations/Frogs.pdf
13. Barham, P., et al.: Xen and the art of virtualization. ACM SIGOPS Oper. Syst. Rev. **37**(5), 164–177 (2003)
14. Linux: 2.6.20 Kernel release notes. Virtualization support through KVM (2007). http://kernelnewbies.org
15. Oracle Corporation. Oracle and Virtualization (2010). http://www.oracle.com/us/technologies/virtualization/index.html
16. Deshane, T., et al.: Quantitative comparison of Xen and KVM. Xen Summit, pp. 1–2, Boston, MA, USA (2008)

17. Danti, G.: Vmware vs Virtualbox vs KVM vs XEN: virtual machines performance comparison (2010). http://www.ilsistemista.net/index.php/virtualization/1-virtual-machines-performance-comparison.html

18. Chen, W., et al.: A novel hardware assisted full virtualization technique. In: The 9th International Conference for. IEEE (2008)

19. Adams, K., Agesen, O.: A comparison of software and hardware techniques for x86 virtualization. ACM SIGOPS Operating Systems Review **40**(5), 2–13 (2006). ACM

20. Menon, A., et al.: Diagnosing performance overheads in the xen virtual machine environment. In: Proceedings of the 1st ACM/USENIX International Conference on Virtual Execution Environments. ACM (2005)

21. IBM. Kernel Virtual Machine (KVM): Tuning KVM for performance. http://www-01.ibm.com/support/knowledgecenter/linuxonibm/liaat/liaattuning.pdf

22. VMware. Best Practices for performance Tuning of Latency Sensitive. http://www.vmware.com/files/pdf/techpaper/VMW-Tuning-Latency-Sensitive-Workloads.pdf

23. OpenIMSCore Project official website. http://www.openimscore.org

24. IMS bench SIPp official website. http://sipp.sourceforge.net/imsbench/intro.html

25. Institute, E.T.S.: Telecommunications and Internet converged Services and Protocols for Advanced Networking (TISPAN); IMS/NGN Performance Benchmark. ETSI TS **186**, 1–8 (2007)

VM³: Virtual Machine Multicast Migration Based on Comprehensive Load Forecasting

Feng Guo[✉], Dong Zhang, Zhengwei Liu, and Kaiyuan Qi

State Key Laboratory of High-end Server and Storage Technology,
System Soft Department of Inspur, Jinan 250101, China
{guofengbj,zhangdong,liuzhw,qiky}@inspur.com

Abstract. Although Virtual Machine (VM) is a fundamental technique for Cloud Operation System (Cloud OS), lack of task model and dynamic usability evaluation are great challenges in VM migration. Hence, this paper proposes a VM multicast migration based on comprehensive load forecasting mechanism named VM³. In this paper, we design a VM placement algorithm based on comprehensive load forecasting, which provides an accurate selection of destination host according to the comprehensive network performance including bandwidth, latency, etc., while only the computing node offloading is considered in the tradition algorithms. Furthermore, we propose a multicast migration mechanism to reduce the computation before migration, and support parallel migration. Through implements and experiments it proves that VM³ improves the accuracy and efficiency of VM cluster migration, and it is practical and widely applicable.

Keywords: Cloud operation system · Virtual machine · Multicast · Placement algorithm · Migration mechanism

1 Introduction

Cloud computing is a kind of computing model and service model driven by business. From the prospect of computing resources, it is a computing model that provides users with services accessing to computing resources through the network. Users can conveniently use computing resources (i.e. data, software, hardware, network bandwidth, etc.) according to their own demand, without understanding the details of the process of services.

From the perspective of the specific application, cloud computing offers the resource services at three levels, i.e. software as a service (SaaS), Platform as a Service (PaaS) and Infrastructure as a Service (IaaS) [1]. These three levels focus on different applications, but they meet the same challenges, such as resources and tasks scheduling. For example, Amazon Elastic Cloud ensures utilization of each VM through reasonable scheduling. Enterprise Resources Plan (EPR) of Eight Hundred Passengers improves customer satisfaction and loyalty with more reasonable task scheduling. Scheduling is an important issue of cloud computing, which directly affects the system stability, resource usage efficiency, user

© Institute for Computer Sciences, Social Informatics and Telecommunications Engineering 2015
V.C.M. Leung et al. (Eds.): CloudComp 2014, LNICST 142, pp. 66–75, 2015.
DOI: 10.1007/978-3-319-16050-4_6

satisfaction and operational costs. Therefore, scheduling plays a significant roles in cloud computing.

Virtualization is one of the cornerstones to build a cloud computing system, especially the server virtualization technology, which provides the infrastructure layer for cloud computing [2]. Specifically, High Availability (HA) [3,4] is able to maintain real-time synchronous mirroring for VM, avoiding one single physical machine breakdown impacting on other VMs. Live Migration [3,4] enables rapid online VM migration among different physical machines without interrupting VM operation. These techniques can effectively improve availability of VM, maintenance convenience and energy efficiency of physical machine.

With continued growth in demand demands, the number of VMs in the data center is increasing rapidly, which brings up a new challenge to the resource scheduling. In large-scale VM cluster, the number of VMs and VM loads often change along with demands. Then static resource allocation will cause waste of resources or lack of resources, while artificial dynamic resource adjustment have obvious limitation in efficiency, practicability, etc. Therefore, dynamic resource scheduling is available for VM. When the number of VMs is small and average load is low, we can migrate VMs onto fewer physical machines and shut down part of others to save energy and improve the calculation/energy ratio. When the number of VMs is large and average load is high, we can activate more backup physical machines for load balancing. Moreover, because the application load on VM changes over time, the more resource should be timely allocated for VMs in the high load level.

At present, the server virtualization applications are mostly implemented with static resource allocation, in which VMs do not have good adaptability to load changes. In scheduling the VM cluster, most applications on the physical machines are still based on the traditional task scheduling strategy. Since the task-based application does not cover all types of applications, task-based cluster scheduling has significant limitations. Furthermore, scheduling granularity is large, so it is difficult to adapt to the special advantages of VM cluster.

In terms of VM resource allocation under a single physical node, most researches focused on the Virtual Machine Manager (VMM), such as VM CPU time slice allocation algorithm, paged memory management, and distribution. Only a small amount of literatures proposed dynamic resource allocation based on VM load. In [5], Menasce et al. proposed a dynamic scheduling of CPU resources under a single node. In [6], Zhao et al. proposed an approach for load balancing of memory between VM under a single-node. In [7,8], Song et al. proposed a dynamic resource allocation within a single node, and a multi-layer VM cluster task scheduling. Dynamic resource allocation under single node has the features of high speed and small overhead, but the scheduling range is limited within a single node, and only CPU and memory resources on VM can be dynamic allocated.

In terms of multi-node resource scheduling, VMware's commercial product DRS [9] contains the load balancing of multi-node via virtual machine migration, but there is no analysis of mechanism of scheduling for DRS. In [10],

Hu et al. proposed an approach for scheduling CPU and memory resource under multi-node to save energy. Although various approaches have been proposed for VM scheduling and allocation strategy, there are the following challenges in scheduling [11,12].

- *Lack of task model:* Various resource scheduling policy in cloud computing can be higher practicality only after the verification of properly task model. However, due to the lack of cloud computing task log, most researchers still use only-mathematical models or existing task models to evaluate the performance of resource scheduling policy under parallel system. Because these task models are not built according to task loading under specific cloud environment, the analysis is unconvincing. Hence, it is an urgent issue to build a properly task model under cloud environment.
- *Lack of dynamic availability evaluation:* Currently, there has not been any mature usability evaluation system of resource in cloud computing. Although there are some resources assessment and prediction system in distributed and grid computing, which can be integrated into various scheduling or resource management systems to guide scheduling, these evaluation models are not suitable in cloud computing. Dynamic cloud resource workloads lead to uncertain capacity and availability of resources, which plays an important role in guiding to select the best resources-task scheduling. Therefore, accurate knowledge of the dynamic available resources is a key issues in scheduling decisions.

In this paper, we survey the development status and existing problems of VM scheduling. This paper proposes a VM multicast migration based on comprehensive load forecasting mechanism named VM^3. In this paper, we design a VM placement algorithm based on comprehensive load forecasting, which provides an accurate selection of destination host according to the network performance. Furthermore, we propose a multicast migration mechanism to reduce the computation before migration, and support parallel migration. Through implements and experiments it proves that VM^3 improves the accuracy and efficiency of VM cluster migration, and it is practical and widely applicable.

2   VM Placement Algorithm Based on Comprehensive Load

In the migration of VMs, the host selection is extremely important. Excellent selection algorithms and strategies can greatly improve the efficiency of migration and the stability of VM. This paper presents a novel host evaluation model, considering a combination of factors, such as server comprehensive load, network environment and migration time. According to the proposed algorithm, we can choose the most appropriate host for VM migration.

2.1   Comprehensive Load Evaluation Model

Finding a suitable computing node is to look for one of the most efficient path in the set of computing nodes, which need to consider the following issues:

- *Expected execution time:* refers to the expected time-consuming of completing task of migrate VM to the destination node.
- *Network bandwidth:* refers to the maximum bandwidth provided by the path connecting the VM node to the destination node.
- *Network latency:* refers to the maximum network latency.
- *Comprehensive load of physical machine:* refers to comprehensive load of the destination node. This is an important parameter, which generally has several quantitative indicators, such as, the actual utilization of the CPU, the actual memory usage, the number of tasks, the number of threads, etc.

We assume the constraint function of computing node as presented in Eq. 1. Wherein, $tc(m)$ represents the expected execution time; $bw(m)$ represents the network bandwidth; $dl(m)$ represents the network latency; and $ld(m)$ the comprehensive load of physical machine.

$$res(m) = \frac{A \cdot tc(m) + B \cdot dl(m) + C \cdot ld(m)}{D \cdot bw(m)} \qquad (1)$$

And the constraints is defined in Eq. 2.

$$s.t. \begin{cases} tc(m) < TL \\ dl(m) < DL \\ ld(m) < LD \\ bw(m) < BW \end{cases} \qquad (2)$$

The selection process to find the resource and path meeting the constraints in Eq. 2 while the value of $res(m)$ is as small as possible. Wherein, A, B, C, D are the weights of four constraint conditions, while TL, DL, LD, BW are boundary restrictions, which may be different in various cloud environments.

2.2   Migration Time Prediction Algorithm

Heterogeneous is a very important feature in the entire cloud environment, so the structure of each node, hardware and software environment, and the performance of capacity and throughout will be different. Meanwhile, the situation of network is more complex, so the load of any line at any time will be unpredictable. Because the bandwidth of cloud computing environment is lower than traditional grid environment, so the situation of network will unexpected fluctuation. Therefore, it is a great challenge to calculate the execution speed of the node to complete the migration.

However, in cloud computing, the task is usually assigned to the computing resources with the highest efficient and lowest consumption, which greatly improves the performance. Hence, it's necessary to pre-estimate the execution time of available nodes during the process of allocation.

Considering the heterogeneous and dynamic of cloud computing, we design a prediction algorithm to estimate the execution speed of the next task through accumulating the history value. The algorithm makes separately prediction of efficiency and time spent by each node to complete the next task. This model can be expected to get a relatively accurate prediction no matter what the level of the load of computing resources. Due to the current load degree of each computing node has been known and the load degree of the last completed job can be obtained, so we use the following Eq. 3 algorithm to predict the speed of execution.

$$ET_m^{ld_{k+1}}(k+1) = \frac{ld_{k+1}}{ld_k}((1-\rho)ET_m^{ld_k}(k) + \rho RT_m^{ld_k}(k)) \tag{3}$$

Wherein, $ET_m^{ld_k}(k)$ refers to the k-th predicted execution time of the m-th computing resource; ld_k refers to the k-th prediction of the comprehensive system load, $RT_m^{ld_k}$ refers to the k-th actual execution time of the m-th computing resource; ρ is an adjustable parameters to adjust the specific gravity of the experience value and the predicted value in different cloud environments, in order to achieve the optimum prediction of the model. On each computing node, the node will record the actual loss of time of each migration, which is combined with the previous prediction result to calculate the possible execution time of the next migration. Meanwhile, the comprehensive load ld is recorded.

3   Multicast Migration Mechanism

Multicast Migration mechanism adopts the principle of multicast and calculate the virtual machine migration path in advance, which is stored in the mapping table to be updated regularly. Hence, during the VM migration the path can be directly queried instead of calculation. According to the corresponding path in the mapping table, the migration task will be conducted directly. With the multicast migration and thread pool, VMs can be migrated in parallel, which greatly improves the efficiency of migration. As shown in Fig. 1, the main migration framework consists of the following components.

- *Controller:* Controller is mainly responsible for maintaining the mapping table.
- *Mapping Table:* Mapping table stores the mapping relationship between VM and destination host machine. VM migration refers to the mapping table information directly without calculation process.
- *Scheduler:* Scheduler is mainly run the VM placement strategy model based on comprehensive computation strength to determine the best destination host machine real-timely. Furthermore, it updates the information to the mapping table collaborative with Controller.
- *Sender:* According to the taks in the pool, sender calls the migration API to migrate VMs.
- *Task pool:* The migration request is broken down into a batch of migration task in task pool. Through the thread pool, VMs can be migrated in parallel while the resource consumption can be controllable.

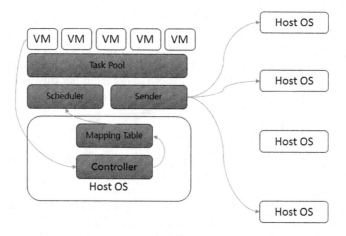

Fig. 1. Framework of multicast migration mechanism

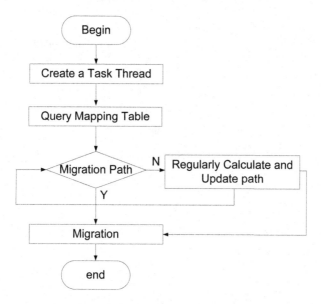

Fig. 2. Flow char of multicast migration mechanism.

Specific migration includes the follows processes as shown in Fig. 2.

1. VM migration task is sent.
2. In task pool, the corresponding multiple migration threads are created.
3. Controller finds the corresponding VM migration path in mapping table.
4. If the corresponding migration path exists, the migration path information will be sent to sender.
5. Sender executes the migration task and returns the result.

6. If there isn't the corresponding VM migration path in mapping table, the Scheduler will calculate the optimal migration path according to the VM placement strategy, and sends it to sender and updates mapping table.
7. Scheduler, mainly running virtual machine placement algorithm based integrated load, real-time host for the purpose of determining the optimal virtual machine and update the mapping table by Controller.

4   Implementation

In this paper, VM³ has been successfully implemented in the Inspur Incloud·Cloud Operating System(Incloud OS).

Incloud OS is the core production of the cloud computing solutions, which manages the virtualization platform to provide flexibility, on-demand virtual resource services and a full range of monitoring, while support security isolation multi-tenant resources management to provide safe and reliable resources services. In Fig. 3, it illustrates the architecture of Incloud OS.

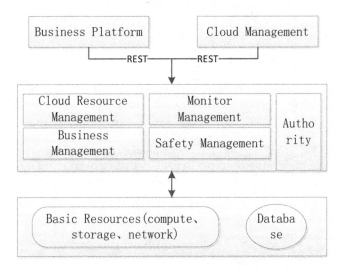

Fig. 3. Incloud OS architecture

VM³ has been successfully implemented in the intelligent scheduling module of cloud resource management platform, which is used to compute node load balancing, HA and VM migration. Moreover, intelligent scheduling module has been testified by many industry manufacturers.

5   Case Study

VM³ proposed in this paper is mainly to improve the efficiency and accuracy of VM migration. In this section, VM³ is mainly compared with the traditional VM migration. The experimental environment consists of the follows components.

- *Management node* mainly running WEB services, database, authentication, authorization, cloud resource management and other management services of cloud operating system, which is configured as a two-way servers with CenOS 6.0, Intel(R) Xeon(R) CPU, 16G memory, Mysql 5.1.42 database, OpenAM, etc.
- *Computing nodes* is mainly responsible for the VM resources available. There are four compute nodes, which is four-way servers of Inspur-iVirtual with Intel(R) Xeon R) CPU, 32G memory, which are virtualized as iVirtual developed by Inspur.
- *Storage* centralized storage IP-SAN, OCFS cluster file system, which provides 1 T storage space.
- *Network* provides Gigabit networks.
- *VM* consists of 2 CPU, 2G RAM, 120G hard drive, Windows XP system, etc.

One fixed computing node runs a static number of VMs, and other three nodes run several VMs randomly. The number of virtual machines on the fixed node is repeatedly adjusted, and the efficiency is compared with traditional VM migration. In Eq. 4, it defines the calculation for efficiency.

$$Efficiency = (SerialMigration - MulticastMigration)/SerialMigration \tag{4}$$

In the experiments, the values of several parameters in VM placement strategy based on comprehensive load are: $A = 0.4, B = 0.4, C = 0.2, D = 1, \rho = 0.5$. The experimental results are presented in Table 1.

Table 1. Experimental results

Number of virtual machine	Multicast migration	Serial migration	Efficiency promotion
1	3.0	3.11	3.54
5	12.41	15.20	18.36
10	25.13	33.0	23.85
20	44.00	62.38	29.46
30	60.66	95.93	36.77

From the experimental results shown in Figs. 4 and 5, the proposed VM^3 greatly enhance the efficiency of VM migration compared with the traditional migration. Furthermore, with the incasement of VM clusters, the migration efficiency is also improved.

Analyzing from the time complexity, assuming that the time complexity of a single VM migration in the serial migration is $O(1)$. Then the time complexity of VM cluster migration is $nO(1)$. The complexity of proposed VM^3 proposed is $O(1)$, which greatly enhances the migration efficiency.

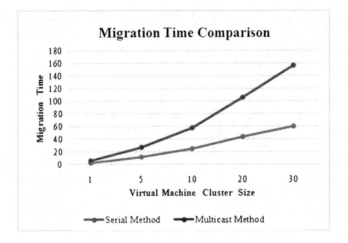

Fig. 4. Migration time comparison

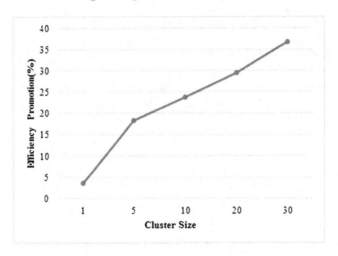

Fig. 5. Efficiency schematic

6   Conclusion

In this paper, we study the current development situation and existing problems of VM scheduling. For the lack of task model and dynamic usability evaluation techniques in migration, we propose VM^3, which consists of two parts, i.e. VM placement algorithm based on VM comprehensive load, and multicast migration mechanism. With VM^3, we can select the destination host with higher accuracy, and make it available to migrate VM in parrel. Through actual implementation and comparative experiments, it shows that VM^3 can greatly improve the efficiency and accuracy of VM cluster migration, and have a wide range of applications and applicability. However, VM³ can be improved for migration time forecast, which is our future work.

References

1. Vouk, M.A.: Cloud computing-issues, research and implementations. CIT J. Comput. Inform. Technol. **16**(4), 235–246 (2008)
2. Barham, P., Dragovic, B., Fraser, K., Hand, S., Harris, T., Ho, A., Neugebauer, R., Pratt, I., Warfield, A.: Xen and the art of virtualization. ACM SIGOPS Oper. Syst. Rev. **37**(5), 164–177 (2003)
3. Lowe, S.: Mastering VMware vSphere 4. Wiley, Indianapolis (2009)
4. Williams, D.E.: Virtualization with Xen: Including XenEnterprise, XenServer, and XenExpress. Syngress (2007)
5. Menasce, D., Bennani, M.N.: Autonomic virtualized environments. In: 2006 International Conference on Autonomic and Autonomous Systems, ICAS 2006, p. 28. IEEE (2006)
6. Zhao, W., Wang, Z., Luo, Y.: Dynamic memory balancing for virtual machines. ACM SIGOPS Oper. Syst. Rev. **43**(3), 37–47 (2009)
7. Song, Y., Li, Y., Wang, H., Zhang, Y., Feng, B., Zang, H., Sun, Y.: A service-oriented priority-based resource scheduling scheme for virtualized utility computing. In: Sadayappan, P., Parashar, M., Badrinath, R., Prasanna, V.K. (eds.) HiPC 2008. LNCS, vol. 5374, pp. 220–231. Springer, Heidelberg (2008)
8. Song, Y., Wang, H., Li, Y., Feng, B., Sun, Y.: Multi-tiered on-demand resource scheduling for vm-based data center. In: Proceedings of the 2009 9th IEEE/ACM International Symposium on Cluster Computing and the Grid, pp. 148–155. IEEE Computer Society (2009)
9. Resource management with VMware DRS. http://www.vmware.com/vmtn/resources/401
10. Hu, L., Jin, H., Liao, X., Xiong, X., Liu, H.: Magnet: a novel scheduling policy for power reduction in cluster with virtual machines. In: 2008 IEEE International Conference on Cluster Computing, pp. 13–22. IEEE (2008)
11. Angiuoli, S.V., Matalka, M., Gussman, A., Galens, K., Vangala, M., Riley, D.R., Arze, C., White, J.R., White, O., Fricke, W.F.: Clovr: a virtual machine for automated and portable sequence analysis from the desktop using cloud computing. BMC Bioinform. **12**(1), 356 (2011)
12. Lagar-Cavilla, H.A., Whitney, J.A., Scannell, A.M., Patchin, P., Rumble, S.M., De Lara, E., Brudno, M., Satyanarayanan, M.: Snowflock: rapid virtual machine cloning for cloud computing. In: Proceedings of the 4th ACM European Conference on Computer Systems, pp. 1–12. ACM (2009)

A Phased Workflow Scheduling Scheme
with Task Division Policy in Cloud Broker

Seong-Hwan Kim[(✉)], Kyung-No Joo, Yun-Gi Ha, Gyu-Beom Choi,
and Chan-Hyun Youn

Department of Electrical Engineering, KAIST, Daejeon, Korea
{s.h_kim, eu8198, milmgas, mosfetlkg, chyoun}@kaist.ac.kr

Abstract. In the science area, workflow management systems (WMS) coordinate collaborative tasks between researchers of many research organizations.
Also, WMS effectively compose the high performance computing system with
globally distributed computing resources. In addition, with the maturity of cloud
computing technology, many researches try to enhancing the economic feasibility and system tolerability. While executing a workflow application, a
workflow scheduler, which is in WMS, should recognize the dynamic status of
resources and decide to assign appropriate resource on each task. With the
negotiation procedure, users can ask for saving processing cost or shortening
completion time. However, satisfying these multiple objectives at the same time
is hard to achieve. Therefore, the existing workflow scheduling schemes try to
find the near optimal solution with heuristic approaches. In this paper, we
propose heuristic workflow scheduling scheme with petri-net workflow modeling, resource type mapping in accordance to workload ratio and policy based
task division to guarantee the deadline constraint with minimum budget
consumption.

Keywords: Workflow scheduling · Colored patri-net · Task division policy ·
Cloud computing

1 Introduction

In an aspect of modularization, automated processing, expandability, collaborative
works and ease of control and monitor, workflow is appropriate tool for modeling
complicated application. Especially, a scientific workflow is the computerized automation of a scientific process, in whole or part, which usually streamlines a collection
of scientific tasks with data channels [1]. Since the correct integration of these distributed services may require an efficient management scheme and tools, a well-
designed workflow management system in cloud is required to completely define,
manage, monitor, and execute scientific workflows through the execution of tasks
whose execution order is driven by a computerized representation of the workflow
logic. To process request of computing workflow from user, workflow scheduling
(resource planning), which allocate available computing resources to each workflow
tasks with amount and allocation time of resources, is required. However, it is difficult
to make optimal scheduling with consideration of multiple QoS (Quality of Service),

© Institute for Computer Sciences, Social Informatics and Telecommunications Engineering 2015
V.C.M. Leung et al. (Eds.): CloudComp 2014, LNICST 142, pp. 76–86, 2015.
DOI: 10.1007/978-3-319-16050-4_7

inter-task dependency and dynamic status of resources. In cloud environment, we should also consider the variation of resource capacity over time, the heterogeneity of resources and the VM (Virtual Machine) leasing cost model from cloud service providers. Because it is generally considered as NP-complete problem to solve multi object-workflow scheduling problem, many previous studies generally utilize heuristic strategies to acquire real-time decision with relatively high optimality [2].

Yu [3] proposed a workflow management system in grid with MDP (Markov Decision Process) based workflow scheduling scheme while guaranteeing the assigned deadline. By using the workflow partitioning strategy, they try to find optimal solutions (assign sub-deadline) on each partial task groups with MDP method. To achieve deadline guarantee, they consider critical path concept. By assembling local optimums on each partitioned task groups, they tried to find the global near optimum. However, since their algorithm can't consider complexity of cloud price policy, cost can be wasted in cloud environment. Although, MDP is calculated on partial task groups, MDP is relatively complex to compute.

In this paper, we propose heuristic workflow scheduling scheme with petri-net workflow modeling, resource type mapping in accordance to workload ratio and policy based task division by resolving problems in Phased Workflow Scheduling Scheme [4] to guarantee the deadline constraint with minimum budget consumption.

2   Workflow Scheduling in a Cloud Broker

In this paper, we consider Users, Cloud Brokers and Cloud Service Providers (CSP) as actor of our system framework. When user composite and request their own workflow instance to cloud broker with QoS constraints and budget contraction, it should be scheduled by Workflow Scheduling Engine (WSE) in cloud broker. Then, WSE should execute each task depending on scheduling decision in available cloud resources which are provided by CSP. With cooperation of Resource Provisioning Manager (RPM) which give abstraction to the VM leasing contraction, CSP cost policy and physical details of VMs, WSE can easily allocate tasks into proper VMs. RPM manages the Virtual Machine Pool (VMP) in cloud broker to provide resources into multiple application sets in efficient way. Because RPM makes reasonable contraction between multiple CSPs with the profiling and comparing manners, it is more efficient then 1:1 VM leasing contraction between applications and CSPs. Therefore, with the scheduling to find optimal resource planning to execute workflow and resource provisioning to make efficient proxy contraction, user doesn't need to consider the details of complex procedure to execute workflow after making contraction with cloud broker. Because billing contraction also contains service level violation penalty which is pay back cost from cloud broker when cloud broker can't satisfy service level, cloud broker should reject the contract when it is unable to achieve. There are many ways to set the violation penalty cost, but we will use linear penalty cost model [5] in this paper.

Figure 1 shows functional architecture of the proposed cloud broker. It simply has two core components – Workflow Scheduling Engine and Resource Provisioning Manager.

Chemical Service Client

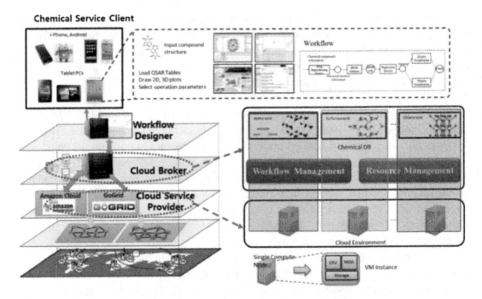

Fig. 1. Architectural model of the proposed cloud broker

Workflow Scheduling Engine (WSE). WSE provides unified user interfaces for creating, managing and executing workflow application service. User can compose the workflow instances with deployed services which are registered by participants formerly with service profiling data. When execution requests are given, the WSE should decide to assign appropriate resource on each task based on the scheduling scheme. Finally, with task dependencies, collaboration with RPM and resource mapping table, WSE can execute each tasks to the available VMP resources in order.

Resource Provisioning Manager (RPM). RPM manages virtual machine pool (VMP) as a logical container. The resources in the VMP represent the leased VMs from the underlying CSPs. Therefore, the RPM allocates or deallocates the resources in VMP based on its own resource leasing strategy. Also, RPM shares resources among various applications.

A problem which finds a schedule for a workflow $W = (P, Tr, A)$ to be executed within user-specified deadline D is defined as Workflow scheduling problem with deadline constraint. That is, deciding assigned computing resources-to-be set $R = \{R_1, R_2, \ldots, R_n\}$ and assigned time set $T = \{T_1, T_2, \ldots, T_n\}$ according to petri-net model is illustrated as the problem.

Cloud Virtual Machine Type is defined by combination of parameters which are time-invariant and continuously capable of being guaranteed by cloud service providers. (e.g. number of CPU cores: VT_c, clock rate of a CPU: VT_{hz}, memory size of the virtual machine: VT_m, storage size of the virtual machine: VT_s) In this paper, we only consider factors which are directly related with job processing time. Therefore, a Cloud Virtual Machine Type is illustrated as $VT_j = [VT_{c_j}, VT_{hz_j}, VT_{m_j}]$ and exists as a finite set $VT = \{VT_1, VT_2, \ldots, VT_m\}$. In addition, leasing cost per unit time for arbitrary virtual machine VT_j is defined as C_{VT_j}.

Application Profiling is the method to figure out expected execution time for a task t_i when it is processed on virtual machine type VT_j and manage the execution time data in the form of table. The row of table represents different task type $tt_k (= t_{i,type}, 1 \leq k \leq l)$ and the column represents virtual machine type VT_j Each execution time data $T_{VT_j}^{tt_k}$ is the average value acquired from enough times of repeated execution.

Also, we define cost model to figure out workflow processing cost using cloud resources. When denote VM usage time for the VM type VT_j as $T_{VT_j}^{tt_k}$, Then, execution cost required to process given workflow is described as following equation

$$execution\ cost = \sum_i C_{VT_j} \times T_{VT_j}^{tt_k}. \tag{1}$$

3   Phased Workflow Scheduling Scheme with Task Division Policy

In order to resolve the cost minimization while deadline-guaranteed workflow scheduling problem, we should pay the least at individual task processing by assigning appropriate resource. Also, the whole workflow schedule made by individual task scheduling should satisfy user-specified deadline. Kim [4] proposed phased workflow scheduling scheme. With the colored petri-net model, colored token which conducts different action on workflow topologies according to its color is defined to control the scheduling of given workflow topology. The scheme is composed with two phases: First one is Scheduling Phase, which decides the workload proportion and allocate sub-deadline into each task by backward token forwarding of scheduling token through petri-net. Second one is Execution Phase, assigns proper resource according to the load proportion of each task not to violate sub-deadline by forwarding execution token. As a result, the path which is in charge of the most portion of load in the workflow, namely, critical path is found out and delivered by the scheduling token. Because scheme use quietly simple and intuitive heuristic, it is fast enough to utilize in real-time workflow management system. Although this scheme takes advantage of static estimated task processing time, it is categorized as the dynamic scheduling as it carries out task scheduling according to the remaining service level indicator. Therefore, workflow management system can endure system fault from resources. However, when deadline which is shorter than the shortest estimated execution time of given workflow is required from user, it is not able to find a schedule which can satisfy user-specified deadline because of its finite resource set. Also, with the finite resource set, if processing delay exceed certain level, we can't guarantee the deadline, because we can't utilize better resources to compensate delays for processing remaining tasks.

To overcome the problems, we defined divisible task using the concept of arbitrarily divisible task. A task t_i which can be partitioned as they do not have any precedence relations and all elements in the task t_i are identical type of processing is defined as divisible task [6]. A divisible task t_i whose critical degree (cd), which is defined as the maximum number of partition of a task, is n can be divided into sub-tasks $[t_{i,1}, t_{i,2}, \ldots, t_{i,n}]$. For these divisible task, we can reduce job processing time by distributing partitions of tasks to multiple resources. Though task division makes workflow processing time reduced, task division is not always carried out as it is not appropriate to reduce required cost and processing time, namely, the goal of workflow scheduling problem. Therefore, we should determine when we have to proceed division based on processing time and required cost.

In this paper, we only consider half-load division to control scheduling complexity and size of historical data in low level. In addition, it is assumed that the load of each partitioned task is the same. Also, subtask type is defined by its size of load. r partial tasks gathers to compose subtask type $tt_{k,\{r\}}$ whose $cd(tt_{k,\{r\}}) = r$. Additional application profiling for all kinds of task bunches is required to measure execution time of each subtask type $tt_{k,\{r\}}$ on different resource type VT_j. Example of application profiling table is shown in Table 1.

Table 1. Example of application profiling for divisible task whose cd equals 8

	$tt_{k,\{8\}}$	$tt_{k,\{4\}}$	$tt_{k,\{2\}}$	$tt_{k,\{1\}}$
VT_1	$AP_1^{k,\{8\}} = T_{VT_1}^{tt_{k,\{8\}}}$	...	...	$AP_1^{k,\{1\}} = T_{VT_1}^{tt_{k,\{1\}}}$
VT_2	...	...	...	...
VT_3	$AP_3^{k,\{8\}} = T_{VT_3}^{tt_{k,\{8\}}}$	...	...	$AP_3^{k,\{1\}} = T_{VT_3}^{tt_{k,\{1\}}}$

Workflow Scheduling Phases

When a user submits a workflow execution request, then the cloud broker should map proper resources to tasks. We introduce the QoS constraints scheduling scheme which is used to schedule each task onto appropriate VM type. We assume that token forward and backward matrix is already extracted by analysis of workflow topology. Then we can move our token with multiplication of token status vector and token forward/backward matrix.

Phase I. Calculate the load rate r(p) for each task

We set the initial marking of token vector for first phase as $M = [0...01]$. Then the token moves through backward matrix along the workflow topology path reversely investigating each task's the load rate. The load rate $r(p)$ on a place p is the rate of the transition (task)'s relative load compared to relative load of its critical path.

$$r(p) = \frac{rl(p)}{cpl(p)}. \tag{2}$$

Also, relative load is defined as average execution time for a task on VM types:

$$rl(p) = \text{avr}_j\left(T_{VT_j}^{type(p^*)}\right) = \frac{1}{m} \cdot \sum_j T_{VT_j}^{type(p^*)}. \tag{3}$$

In addition, Critical path on a task is defined as set of following tasks which is composed of biggest relative load [7]. Then, we can figure out critical path load:

$$cpl(p) = f(x) = \begin{cases} \max_{p^{**}} cpl(p^{**}), & \text{if } p^{**} \text{ exist} \\ 0, & \text{otherwise} \end{cases}. \tag{4}$$

Because we assume that we already collected the application profiling matrix for all tasks on different VM type, we can calculate load rate on entire workflow in static way.

Phase II. Allocate sub-deadline and assigns proper resource according to the load proportion of each task

We set the initial marking of token vector for second phase as $M = [10...0]$. Then the token moves through forward matrix along the workflow topology path investigating each task's the sub-deadline and assigning cheapest VM which can guarantee sub-deadline. Sub-deadline is ways for guarantee the entire deadline. When we allocate sub-deadline properly, and if each task can guarantee the sub-deadline, we can achieve successful scheduling. Therefore, we allocate sub-deadline rationally based on remaining time (deadline D subtracted by current execution time $T_c(m)$) and load rate.

$$sd(p^*)\{= rl(p) \cdot (D - T_c(m)). \tag{5}$$

Then based on Application Profiling matrix, we can find cheapest VM which can execute task in sub-deadline, and can execute task into available VM with the support of Resource Provisioning Manager. When execution is over, token can be moved to next step.

When there are no available resource types to guarantee sub-deadline, it may cause deadline violation for entire workflow. Therefore, we token is not moved to next step and should apply task division policy in phase III.

Phase III. With the cost model check whether task division policy is necessary

As mentioned before, we should determine when we have to proceed division based on processing time and required cost. Also, we should consider the service level violation penalty on required cost. To determine profit in one dimension we define cost model to maximize profit while considering the cost and processing time. The profit Model for the scheduler is represented as follows:

$$P_t = B - C_l - C_p \tag{6}$$

In the formula above, P_t indicates Profit. B is budget which is supplied by user. C_l is cost for leasing VM(s) from cloud provider which is specified in (1). Penalty cost C_p, which is caused by SLA violation, is represented as follows:

$$C_p = \begin{cases} \alpha + \beta \cdot SV, & \text{if } SV > 0 \\ 0, & \text{otherwise} \end{cases} \tag{7}$$

$$SV = \begin{cases} ECT - D, & \text{if } ECT - D > 0 \\ 0, & \text{otherwise} \end{cases} \tag{8}$$

In Eqs. (7) and (8), variable SV indicates the degree of SLA violation. There are many models of violation penalty cost, but in this paper we use simple linear violation penalty model (7) [5]. As shown in (8), SV is described as subtraction deadline D from estimated completion time ECT.

We estimate SLA violation SV and SV' in a deterministic way. We define SV Estimation Token m_e in order to calculate penalty cost by proceeding them. Initially, the location of m_e is replicated from current execution token m. Also, each token save temporal current execution time $T_{tc}(m_e)$ which is replicated from current execution time $T_c(m)$. Then, by moving each token with forward matrix, calculating the estimated-sub-deadline, allocate temporal VM, cumulating the $T_{tc}(m_e)$ for each transition with the method in phase II until token reach the final place, we can get the estimated execution time $T_{tc}(m_e)$ in heuristic way.

Table 2. Algorithm of task division policy in workflow scheduler

Algorithm. Division Policy
Input: *workflow topology tp, workflow topology with half division tp', current execution token matrix m, current execution time $T_C(m)$, workflow deadline D, budget B, token forward matrix F*
Output: *Decision of division*

Copy execution token set m onto SV estimation token set m_e and copy current execution time $T_c(m)$ onto temporal current execution time $T_{tc}(m_e)$.
for workflow topology *{tp, tp'}*
  while m_e is not equal to $[0 \dots 0\ 1]$
    Let P= $\{p_1, p_2, \dots, p_n\}$ be places which has SV estimation tokens at current stage i and estimation token set at stage i as m_e^i
    for p = each element in P
      $sd(p^*) = rl(p) \cdot T_{tc}(D - m_e^i)$
      $p^*.temporal\_vm = VT_{\{j | T_{VM_j}^{type(p^*)} < sd(p^*), \min(C_{VT_j})\}}$
      Let $Tr = \{t_1, t_2, \dots, t_k\} =^* p$
      $T_{tc}(m_e^i) = T_{tc}(m_e^{i-1}) + \max_j \left(T_{t_j.temporal\_vm}^{type(t_j)}\right)$
    endfor
    $m_e^{i+1} = F \cdot m_e^i$ //token forwarding
  endwhile
  if $T_{tc}(m_e) - D > 0$
    $C_p = \alpha + \beta \cdot SV = \alpha + \beta \cdot (T_{tc}(m_e) - D)$
  else
    $C_p = 0$
  endif
  $C_l = \sum_i C_{t_i.temporal\_vm} \times T_{t_i.temporal\_vm}^{type(t_i)}$
  $P = B - C_l - C_p$
endfor
return $P_{tp} < P_{tp'}$ // If $P_{tp} < P_{tp'}$, return value is true. Otherwise return value is false

Then with the comparison of profit between the non-division case and division case (half division), we can determine the cost efficient decision. Therefore we should calculate profit P for non-division case and profit P' for division case. For calculating profit P' of division case, application profiling for divisible task (Table 1) will be needed.

If P < P', apply the half division and return to phase II. If division case not yet guarantee the deadline, division can be occurred recursively until task is no further divisible (critical degree equals 1). If P > P', allocate biggest VM to transition and return to phase II for forwarding to next step (Table 2).

4   Experimental Evaluation

4.1   Experiment Environment

The experimental environment consists of workflow designer, cloud broker, and OpenStack Cloud Infra as shown in Fig. 2. We composed three workflow topologies using workflow designer, and requested execution of one workflow within a certain deadline. The task request was sent to the cloud broker, and then a cloud broker did allocated each sub-task within the sub-deadline. The workflow management system used in the experiment was implemented for OpenStack cloud to run each sub-task.

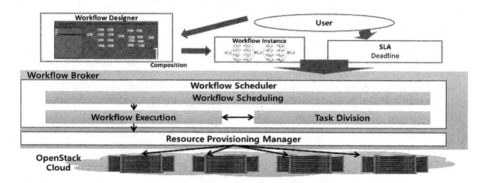

Fig. 2. Experimental environment

Three examples of workflow applications are shown in Fig. 3. Workflow type 1 (a) has some sequentially connected split-merge pairs that have some parallel tasks. Workflow type 2 (b) has little split-merge pairs. However, they have lots of parallel tasks. Workflow type 3 (c) are composed of hybrid structures. We used 4 kinds of task type in random distribution for each tasks.

4.2   Experimental Results and Discussion

We requested the execution of each workflow applications repeatedly with various SLAs (deadlines), and investigated the actual execution time and cost. Additionally, we

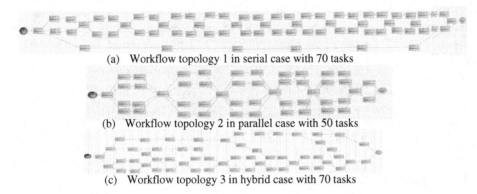

(a) Workflow topology 1 in serial case with 70 tasks

(b) Workflow topology 2 in parallel case with 50 tasks

(c) Workflow topology 3 in hybrid case with 70 tasks

Fig. 3. Three types of workflow topology used in experiment

calculated the difference between the given SLA and the actual execution time or cost to see how well each policy guaranteed the given SLA. Therefore, we should check whether the proposed scheme work properly so that the actual execution time follows

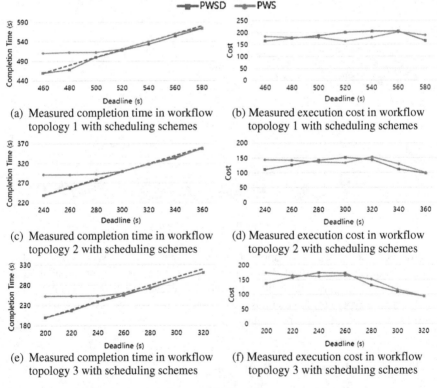

(a) Measured completion time in workflow topology 1 with scheduling schemes

(b) Measured execution cost in workflow topology 1 with scheduling schemes

(c) Measured completion time in workflow topology 2 with scheduling schemes

(d) Measured execution cost in workflow topology 2 with scheduling schemes

(e) Measured completion time in workflow topology 3 with scheduling schemes

(f) Measured execution cost in workflow topology 3 with scheduling schemes

Fig. 4. Experimental results with scheduling schemes (PWSD and PWS) on completion time and execution cost

the given deadline. Proposed scheme (PWSD) is compared with phased workflow scheduling without division policy (PWS) [4]. Because of the limitation on amount of cloud resources compared to the workload on each workflow instances, experiment was performed in emulation.

Figure 4 shows the experimental results according to the scheduling scheme. (a), (c), and (e) represent the actual execution time with different workflow types versus increment of deadline on PWSD and PWS scheme. Dotted lines is plotted to support comparison with the QoS (deadline) constraint. Line with circular points shows experimental result with PWS scheme and line with square points shows experimental result with PWSD scheme. We can find that three graphs show the similar result. When the deadline is too low, the deadline policy cannot meet the deadline in PWS although the broker allocates whole computing resource with large VM types. Therefore, there are some QoS violations in low deadline requirement. In this region, request should be rejected before it pass the admission controller. However, in case of PWSD, it guarantee the QoS region, which PWS can't guarantee, with task distribution and division policy. When the deadline is given adequately, the both scheme can schedule for adequate VM types with assurance of the requirement and might work in same way. In advance, (b), (d), and (f) show the execution costs of different workflow types when we change the deadline. In PWS scheme and, larger type VM are used frequently in order to meet deadline. Also because of violation penalty cost, the execution cost tends to be more expensive, when the deadline is small. However, in PWSD in the same manner, the execution cost does not increase because broker do not have to pay violation penalty. Because we do not consider the management load (split and merge) and data transmission delay between tasks, cost goes down with the profit from frequent task division.

In this experiments, we can conclude that the division policy schedules workflow with guaranteeing the deadline, while trying to use resources in efficient way. We checked this policy works well in various types of workflow.

5   Conclusion

We propose the adaptive workflow scheduling scheme based on the colored Petri-Net model which tries to schedule in the cheapest way while assuring the deadline. Our model uses the phased scheduling model. Therefore, it can schedule dynamically with low complexity. Also, we showed that our result ensures the deadline. Our work was to distribute sub-deadline to each tasks based on its importance compared to the rest of the workflow. We can extend this idea to distribute budgets to each tasks based on the same importance and make user to choose the policy they want. Further work will contain these extensions. Also, we can generalize the problem by using the utilization concept consisting of deadline and budget.

Acknowledgments. This work was supported by the ICT R&D program of MSIP/IITP [10038768, The Development of Supercomputing System for the Genome Analysis] and 'The Cross-Ministry Giga KOREA Project' of The Ministry of Science, ICT and Future Planning, Korea. [GK13P0100, Development of Tele-Experience Service SW Platform based on Giga Media].

References

1. Jeong, S., Jo, Y.M., et al.: A novel model for metabolic syndrome risk quantification based on areal similarity degree. IEEE Trans. Biomed. Engi. **61**(3), 665–679 (2014)
2. Ren, Y., Kim, S.-H., et al.: A cost-efficient job scheduling algorithm in cloud resource broker with scalable VM allocation scheme. KIPS Trans. Softw. Data Eng. **1**(3), 137–148 (2012)
3. Yu, J., Buyya, R., Tham, C.K.: Cost-based scheduling of scientific workflow applications on utility grids. In: First International Conference on e-Science and Grid Computing, pp. 8–147. IEEE (2005)
4. Kim, D.-S.: Adaptive workflow scheduling scheme based on the colored petri-net model in cloud. Master's thesis. KAIST, Daejeon, Korea (2014)
5. Wu, L., et al.: SLA-based resource allocation for software as a service provider (SaaS) in cloud computing environments. In: 11th IEEE/ACM International Symposium on Cluster, Cloud and Grid Computing (CCGrid), pp. 195–204. IEEE (2011)
6. Bharadwaj, V., et al.: Divisible load theory: a new paradigm for load scheduling in distributed systems. Cluster Comput. **6**(1), 7–17 (2003)
7. Kelley Jr., J.E.: Critical-path planning and scheduling: mathematical basis. Oper. Res. **9**(3), 296–320 (1961)

An Efficient Data Extracting Method Based on Hadoop

Lianchao Cao[✉], Zhanqiang Li, Kaiyuan Qi, Guomao Xin, and Dong Zhang

State Key Laboratory of High-end Server and Storage Technology,
System Soft Department of Inspur, Jinan 250101, China
{caolch,lizhanqiang,qiky,xingm,zhangdong}@inspur.com

Abstract. As an open-source big data solutions, Hadoop ecosystem have been widely accepted and applied. However, how to import large amounts of data in a short time from the traditional relational database to hadoop become a major challenge for ETL (Extract-Transform-Load)stage of big data processing. This paper presents an efficient parallel data extraction method based on hadoop, using MapReduce computation engine to call JDBC(The Java Database Connectivity) interface for data extraction. Among them, for the problem of multi-Map segmentation during the data input, this paper presents a dynamic segmentation algorithm for Map input based on range partition, can effectively avoid data tilt, making the input data is distributed more uniform in each Map. Experimental results show that the proposed method with respect to the ETL tool Sqoop which also using the same calculation engine of MapReduce is more uniform in dividing the input data and take less time when extract same datas.

Keywords: ETL · Hadoop · MapReduce · Big data · Range Partition

1 Introduction

Now, with the development of information technology, especially Internet technology, more and more data is generated, today's society is facing the era of big data. Data as the important asset and strategic resource in corporation, reflecting the growing number of economic value in the ear of big data. The construction of business intelligence and data warehouse system can provide comprehensive data sharing for enterprises, and help businesses make decisions. At present, the solutions for dig data focus on commercial solution and hadoop ecosystem solution [1–3]. Commercial solution has high performance, high integration, and easy to use features, but the diversity, flexibility and scalability of the member of current hadoop ecosystem is very attractive for SMEs(Small and Medium Enterprises), Hadoop ecosystem has become the preferred solution when they are face with big data. A major challenge of ETL technology is how to collect large amounts of data from different data sources in particular relational database into hadoop platform in a short time.

The distributed processing technology for the ETL process has high research value. Kettle [4,5] and Talend [6,7] is a similarly open-source ETL tool, can use multi-threaded parallel processing data method. However, these two methods to

© Institute for Computer Sciences, Social Informatics and Telecommunications Engineering 2015
V.C.M. Leung et al. (Eds.): CloudComp 2014, LNICST 142, pp. 87–97, 2015.
DOI: 10.1007/978-3-319-16050-4_8

integrate data into hadoop clusters with a lot of inconvenience, although they have developed their own big data expansion packages, but these expansion packages are only available for some particular hadoop version or enterprise version.

Making MapReduce [8,9] in the hadoop as ETL execution engine, and using JDBC or ODBC(Open Database Connectivity) interface can easily doing data extraction, clean and load operation parallel for relational database. Xiufeng Liu et al. presented A Highly Scalable Dimensional ETL Framework Based on MapReduce [10]. Using the MapReduce framework proposed solutions for different dimensions and facts, but this method did not give constructive suggestion for the problem of multi-Map segmentation of the input data of relational databases. For relational databases, it's need to segment data in database table when multiple Map extract data. Chen et al. [11] proposed a hadoop big table import programming model based on MapReduce. The segmentation algorithm of the big table in this model is first to statistic the total number of rows in the big table, then figure out the logarithmically step of the big table' total number of records by Map, get each Map's beginning line and interval length of extracting data. This method can ensure the workload of importing data by each Map is identical. The segmentation of Map input data in this method is similar to the query page of database, although each Map input data very uniform, this method less flexible, dependent on rowId data table for data segmentation, and this method's cost is large when extract data in order. Sqoop [12,13] is a commonly used ETL tool to call the MapReduce computation engine under hadoop ecosystem. For the data segmentation problem of giving each Map a data interval from relational database, Sqoop uses a canned query (select min(<split column>), max(<split column>) from<table name>) to determine boundaries for creating splits in all cases by default. To provide flexibility for using different queries based on distinct usages, a new boundary-query argument is provided to take any arbitrary query returning two numeric columns for the same purpose of creating splits. The Map input segmentation is highly flexible, but if the range of the selected field unevenly divided, prone to Map Data tilt at the time of extracting data, some Map may draw a lot of data entry, some may have little or even close to zero.

This paper presents an efficient parallel Hadoop-based data extraction method, mainly for relational databases, using MapReduce computation engine calls JDBC interface for data extraction. In order to solve the multi-Map data segmentation problem, this paper presents Map input dynamic partitioning segmentation algorithm based on data range –RPDS Algorithm, which reasonably divides data range of each Map input according to the data distribution, and effectively solves the problem of uneven distribution of Map input data in Sqoop. Experiments show that the method in this article keeps flexibility, and at the same time, can shorten the time of extracting data, and improve the Hadoop hardware resource utilization.

2   OverView

Figure 1 expresses the process of extracting data from the relational database to HDFS by using MapReduce calculating framework. Before extracting, choose a field in a relational database and find the minimum and maximum values of this field, then averagely cut the range formed by the minimum and maximum

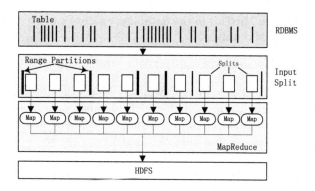

Fig. 1. Data Extracting Flow

into several Range Partitions, calculate weight value according to the number of data entries of each Range Partitions. Then calculate the number of Splits of each Partition according to weight value, the greater weight value, the greater the number of the divided Splits, all number of Splits add to the set number of Map. The calculated number of Splits of some Partitions is 0 for weight value too small, then you need to merge them into the Splits of other Partitions. Each Map corresponds to a Split range when extracting data.

Each Map executes a query to extract data via JDBC interface connecting RDBMS, boundary values for each Splits query as a filter condition, the data can be directly extracted to HDFS (HadoopDistributed File System) [1]. Before calculating the weights of each Partition, need to get data entries of each Partition, which is got by using multi-threaded parallel query via JDBC interface (Select Count (*) from <table name>). Since the database table primary keys and indexes can speed up queries of the database, this method takes full advantage of this feature, selecting the primary key or index field as a range segmentation field has a good effect.

3 RPDS Algorithm

3.1 Range Partitions

The effect of Range Partitions is generally obtaining the distribution of data in a database table, and then reasonably dividing input data according to the distribution of data.

Before data extraction must first select a database table field id and set the Range Partitions number M and Map number N. Then check the minimum

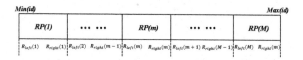

Fig. 2. Range Partitions

Min(id) and maximum Max(id) in the database, execute a query through JDBC interface in a relational database:

select max(id), min(id) from <table name>

Divide the queried id field range [Min(id), Max(id)] into M Range Partitions evenly. As shown in Fig. 2, divide id field range consisting of minimum Min(id) and maximum Max(id) into M Range Partitions and set 1 to M as the number of each Range Partition. Assume $T = \frac{Max(id) - Min(id)}{M}$, the m-th Range Partition interval denoted by $RP(m)$. the left and right boundary of the interval denoted by $R_{left}(m)$ and $R_{right}(m)$ respectively, when $1 \leq m < M$, $RP(m) = [R_{left}(m), R_{right}(m)]$, in which

$$R_{left}(m) = Min(id) + T * (m - 1) \text{ and } R_{right}(m) = Min(id) + T * m \quad (1)$$

when $m = M$, $RP(m) = [R_{left}(m), R_{right}(m)]$, in which

$$R_{left}(m) = Min(id) + T * (m - 1) \text{ and } R_{right}(m) = Max(id) \quad (2)$$

3.2 Input Splits

Step 1: Query Range Partition data rows
After getting Range Partition need to query their data rows $C_m (1 \leq m \leq M)$. Open M threads and execute parallel query.For the number m of Range Partition (when $1 \leq m < M$), the corresponding thread executes the SQL query in a relational database via JDBC interface:

select count(*) from <table name> where id $\geq R_{left}(m)$ and id $< R_{right}(m)$

when $m = M$, the corresponding thread executes SQL query in a relational database via JDBC interface:

select count(*) from <table name> where id $\geq R_{left}(m)$ and id $\leq Max(id)$

Assume as the number of obtained m-th Range Partition rows, the value of the total number C of extracted data table rows is:

$$C = C_1 + \cdots + C_m + \cdots + C_M, 1 \leq m \leq M \quad (3)$$

Step 2: Calculate the weight of Range Partition
This article take ratios of Range Partition and total number of rows of data as a value for each Range Partition weights w_m, that is, sum of weights of each Range Partition is 1, as shown in Eq. 4.

$$\begin{cases} w_m = \frac{C_m}{C}, 1 \leq m \leq M \\ w_1 + \cdots + w_m + \cdots + w_M = 1 \end{cases} \quad (4)$$

According to the above formula, the more Range Partition data rows, the greater its corresponding weight.

Step 3: Split Splits

Calculate the number of Splits of each Range Partition segmentation according to the weight of each Range Partition. Take the product $w_m N$ of weight w_m and total number N of Map as the divided number of Splits of each Range Partition, but $w_m N$ may be a decimal, so first allocate $INT(w_m N)$ Splits to m-th Range Partition(INT is rounded down). The remaining unallocated Splits is $N_o = N - \sum_{m=1}^{m=M} n_{int}(m)$.

For the mth Range Partition, the fractional part of $w_m N$ is $n_{dec}(m) = w_m N - INT(w_m N)$, the set of $\{ n_{dec}(1), \cdots, n_{dec}(m), \cdots, n_{dec}(M) \}$ ($1 \le m \le M$)is made up with M numbers decimals. To traverse this set and extract the front N_oth elements , each element which corresponds to the Rang Partition builds the K set . Let the set K to be $K = \{k_1, k_2, \cdots, k_{N_o}\}$, $k_x \in K$ and the Splits number which corresponds to the number k_x of Range Partition add one.

When Splits have been allocated, Range Partition will be splited by the number of Splits.

3.3   Range Partitions Merging

The number of Splits may be zero if the weight of Range Partition is much smaller, therefore, such Splits need to be merged to neighbor area in order to ensure all the datum can be extracted. The default method is to merge the zero Splits into the right Splits area, but sometimes it should be merged into left area which locates at the end of the Range Partition. The specific steps are:

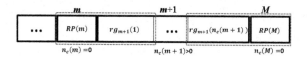

Fig. 3. Range Partition Merging

1. As Fig. 3 shows , if the mth Splits is zero and the right side is larger than zero($n_c(m)$ is equal to zero and $n_c(m+1) > 0$), the default measure is to merge the mth field into the right first field of $(m+1)$th, i.e. $rg_{m+1}(1) = rg_{m+1}(1) \cup RP(m)$.
2. If the mth Splits is zero and the left side is larger than zero($n_c(m)$ is equal to zero and $n_c(M-1) > 0$), the default measure is to merge the mth field into the left the rightest field of $(M-1)$th, i.e. $rg_{M-1}(n_c(M-1)) = rg_{M-1}(n_c(M-1)) \cup RP(M)$.
3. If several consecutive Splits digits are zero, we will merge them as one and then step to (1) or (2).

When Range Partition has been merged, the value field of the original database tables would transform into several relatively uniform Splits partitions. Every Splits has a Map. The filter condition for the select execution is the boundary value of Splits.

4   The Analysis of Time Complexity

RPDS algorithm of this paper has added the computation of Range Partition and the spliting of Splits compared with Sqoop algorithm. As it is shown at Table 1, let the C be the number of data table rows, M and N the total number of Map and Range Partition separately. If C is larger, the main increased time complexity of RPDS by contrast with Sqoop is caused by the selection of Range Partition rows, however, the computation of Range Partitions and Input Splits could be ignored. We use M threads to execute the selection of Range Partition rows, therefore, the cost will not be large if we set key or index as the split field. The cost of this part is within 2 seconds at experiment.

Table 1. RPDS algorithm and Sqoop algorithm time complexity analysis

Steps	Sqoop time complexitym	Ours time complexity
RDBMS:(Select min(id),Max(id) from <table name>)	O(C)	O(C)
Value field uniformly split	O(N)	
Computation of Range Partitions		O(M)
RDBMS:(Select count(*) from <table name where Conditions>) execution		Approximately O(C/M)
Computation of Input Splits		Approximately O(2M+N))

Sqoop is easy to happen uneven splited digits for input, the time of extraction data is determined by the maximum entries of map which have costed. While this cost of RPDS is relatively smaller because we split the input Map data uniformly.

5   The Analysis of Experiment

In order to verify this method, we have taken series experiments. The experiment is based on Hadoop enterprise Inspur In-Cloud CloudCanyon 2.0 and Oracle 11g. The hardware environment are: five faster 1.2 GHZ two road compute nodes, 76 total central processing units, 329 G memory, 1000M switch in cluster. The Hadoop configuration of Sqoop and this paper are the same. In order to guarantee the fair, the data tables which is used to test come from a real marketing system.

5.1   Range Partitions Merging

In order to test each Map data distribution, we get 4 tables to extract data from Oracle to Hadoop and take Sqoop algorithm and ours separately. The size and rows details of this 4 table as follow (Table 2):

Table 2. Size and rows of tables

Table Name	Size(GB)	Counts
Table-1	1.032	9,840,195
Table-2	4.567	28,812,669
Table-3	9.634	47,171,170
Table-4	17.457	80,992,567

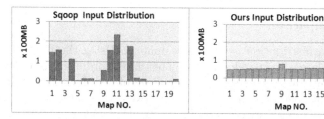

(a) Table-1 Comparison of the map input data distribution

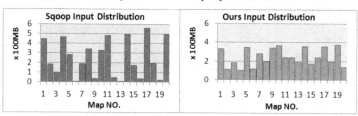

(b) Table-2 Comparison of the map input data distribution

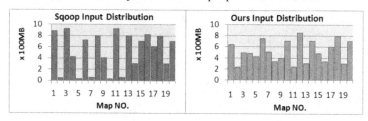

(c) Table-3 Comparison of the map input data distribution

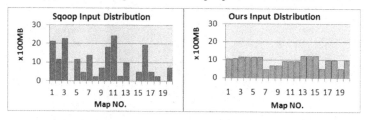

(d) Table-4 Comparison of the map input data distribution

Fig. 4. Comparison of the map input data distribution from Sqoop and our method

The Experiments use 20 Map to extract data, method of this article sets the number of Range Partition to be 20, both methods select the primary key of the table as splits field. After four tables extraction, distribution of the extraction data for every Map from Sqoop and this method is as shown in Fig. 4

Figure 4 left is the size distribution of reading data for each Map using Sqoop, the right is the size distribution of reading data for each Map using this articles method. As we can see from the figure, the distribution of input data is more uniform using our method, To use Sqoop, the distribution of input data is seriously unbalanced. The method here can make full use of the cluster resources.

5.2   Time Comparison

Because the data distribution is relatively uniform, Using the method of this paper to extract data will save a lot of time. The time recording of the experiment is as shown in Table 3, Fig. 5 shows a comparison of the time more intuitively. As can be seen, this method uses less time when extracting data. Compared with the Sqoop method, this algorithm increases the time of statistics for each Range Partition data rows, reduces the time of each Map data extraction. The reduced time is greater than the increased time, so the total time of data extraction will become less.

Table 3. Time recording of experiment

Table Name	Sqoop(Sec)	Ours(Sec)
Table-1	51.47	33.97
Table-2	97.89	86.1
Table-3	336.93	275.21
Table-4	1095.80	921.84

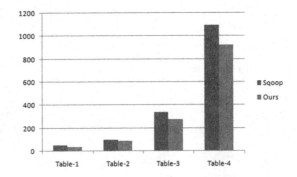

Fig. 5. Comparison of Sqoop method and our method

5.3   The Relationship Between the Number of Partitions and Data Distribution

In order to further verify how the number of Range Partition affects the uniformity of extraction data from each Map, this paper sets different Range Partition numbers to do experiments based on a table. The experiments have two groups, 10 Map and 20 Map. Figure 6 shows the comparision experiments of 10 Map, (a)(b)(c)(d)(e) show the distribution of map input data size when RP(Range Partition) is equal to 1, 4, 6, 7, 10 respectively. Figure 7 shows the comparision experiments of 20 Map, (a)(b)(c)(d)(e) show the distribution of map input data size when RP(Range Partition) is equal to 1, 5, 10, 15, 20 respectively. (f) of Figs. 6 and 7 is the Standard Deviation of Map input data according to different Range Partition numbers. From the Figs. 6 and 7, along with the increase of Range Partition values, Map input data distribution is more and more balanced, the Standard Deviation of Map input data is more and more small, the data skew is more and more unconspicuous.

Actually, calculating each Range Partitions rows and weight is measuring the distribution of the input data, then according to the distribution of the input data and Map numbers to split. The greater the Range Partition value is, the

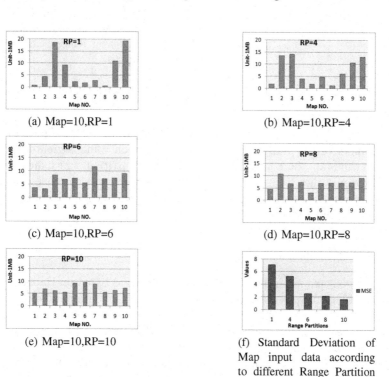

(a) Map=10,RP=1

(b) Map=10,RP=4

(c) Map=10,RP=6

(d) Map=10,RP=8

(e) Map=10,RP=10

(f) Standard Deviation of Map input data according to different Range Partition numbers

Fig. 6. Map input data distribution according to different RP values when Map is 10

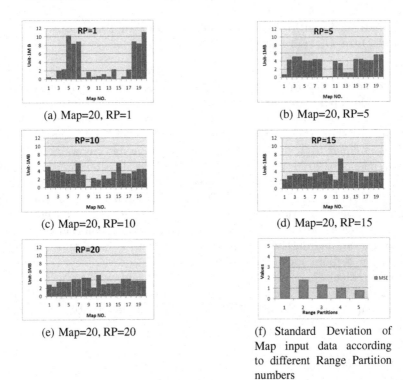

(a) Map=20, RP=1

(b) Map=20, RP=5

(c) Map=20, RP=10

(d) Map=20, RP=15

(e) Map=20, RP=20

(f) Standard Deviation of Map input data according to different Range Partition numbers

Fig. 7. Map input data distribution according to different RP values when Map is 20

more accurate measuring the distribution of the input data, but Split is limited by the number of the Map, when the Range Partition value is greater than the number of the Map, there must be merge of Range Partition, which lack of splits, with Split from other Range Partition. Merging more can also cause data skew. So in the process of extracting data, the recommended value of Range Partition is set to the number of the Map size.

6   Conclusions

This paper presents a parallel data extraction method based on Hadoop, which can efficiently use MapReduce compute engine to extract data parallelly from the relational database data. In order to avoid the data skew, this paper proposes an efficient data segmentation algorithm – RPDS, this method relies on the primary key of the database table or index field, adopts multi-thread method to rapidly implement the uniform segmentation of the input data. Experiments show that, relative to Sqoop method, the proposed method makes the Map input data segmentation more even, improves the resource utilization in the process of using MapReduce to extract data, at the same time shorten the time of extracting data. The Spark computing framework has faster computational efficiency than the MapReduce framework, future plan is to transplant this paper method to Spark computing framework, and do further optimization.

Acknowledgements. This work is supported by the Core Electronic Devices, High-end Generic Chips and Basic Software of National Science and Technology Major Projects of China,No.2013ZX01039002.

References

1. Ghemawat, S., Gobioff, H., Leung, S.-T.: The google file system. ACM SIGOPS Oper. Syst. Rev. **37**(5), 29–43 (2003). ACM
2. White, T.: Hadoop: The Definitive Guide. O'Reilly Media Inc., Sebastopol (2012)
3. Vavilapalli, V.K., Murthy, A.C., Douglas, C., Agarwal, S., Konar, M., Evans, R., Graves, T., Lowe, J., Shah, H., Seth, S., et al.: Apache hadoop yarn: yet another resource negotiator. In: Proceedings of the 4th Annual Symposium on Cloud Computing, p. 5. ACM (2013)
4. http://community.pentaho.com/projects/data-integration/
5. Casters, M., Bouman, R., Van Dongen, J.: Pentaho Kettle Solutions: Building Open Source ETL Solutions with Pentaho Data Integration. Wiley, Indianapolis (2010)
6. http://www.talend.com/products/talend-open-studio
7. Azarmi, B.: Talend for Big Data. Packt Publishing Ltd, Birmingham (2014)
8. Dean, J., Ghemawat, S.: Mapreduce: simplified data processing on large clusters. Commun. ACM **51**(1), 107–113 (2008)
9. Jain, N., Liao, G., Willke, T.L.: Graphbuilder: scalable graph etl framework. In: First International Workshop on Graph Data Management Experiences and Systems, ACM (2013)
10. Liu, X., Thomsen, C., Pedersen, T.B.: ETLMR: a highly scalable dimensional ETL framework based on mapreduce. In: Cuzzocrea, A., Dayal, U. (eds.) DaWaK 2011. LNCS, vol. 6862, pp. 96–111. Springer, Heidelberg (2011)
11. Chen, J., Le, J.: Programming model based on mapreduce for importing big table into hdfs. J. Comput. Appl. **33**(9), 2486–2489, 2561 (2013)
12. http://sqoop.apache.org/
13. Ting, K., Cecho, J.J.: Apache Sqoop Cookbook. O'Reilly Media, Inc., CA (2013)

Based Big Data Analysis of Fraud Detection for Online Transaction Orders

Qinghong Yang[1(✉)], Xiangquan Hu[2], Zhichao Cheng[1],
Kang Miao[2], and Xiaohong Zheng[3]

[1] School of Economics and Management, Beihang University,
No. 37 Xueyuan Road, Haidian District, Beijing 100191, China
rainbow.yang2013@gmail.com, chengzc@buaa.edu.cn
[2] School of Software, Beihang University, Xueyuan Road, No. 35 Northern
Shining Tower, 10th Floor, 1003, Haidian District, Beijing 100191, China
jxaal44081@163.com, 570662537@qq.com
[3] E-commerce China Dangdang Inc., Jingan Center, Dongsanhuan West Road,
Chaoyang District, Beijing 100028, China
zhengxiaohong@dangdang.com

Abstract. Fraud control is important for the online marketplace. This study addresses the problem of detecting attempts to deceive orders in Internet transactions. Our goal is to generate an algorithm model to detect and prevent the fraudulent orders. First, after analyzing the real historical data of customers' orders from Dangdang Website (http://www.dangdang.com. E-commerce China Dangdang Inc (Dangdang) is a leading e-commerce company in China. Dangdang officially listed on the New York Stock Exchange on December 8th, 2010, and is the first Chinese B2C e-commerce company which is completely based on online business to list on New York Stock.), we described characteristics related to transactions that may indicate frauds orders. We presented fraudulent orders characteristic matrix through comparing the normal and abnormal orders. Secondly, we apply Logic Regression model to identify frauds based on the characteristic matrix. We used real data from Dang company to train and evaluate our methods. Finally we evaluated the validity of solutions though analyzing feedback data.

Keywords: Internet translation · Fraud order · Big data · Fraud detection · Fraud prevention · Logistic regression

1 Introduction

Online transactions have been experiencing rapid growth over the past few years. Some marketplaces, such as Amazon[1] and Taobao[2], have reached great popularity and high level revenue, emerging as a very relevant model in the Business-to-Consumer (B2C) and Consumer-to-Consumer (C2C) e-commerce scenario [1]. It is convenient for people to purchase or return products through the Internet. On the other hand, huge

---

[1] http://www.amzon.com.
[2] http://www.taobao.com.

© Institute for Computer Sciences, Social Informatics and Telecommunications Engineering 2015
V.C.M. Leung et al. (Eds.): CloudComp 2014, LNICST 142, pp. 98–106, 2015.
DOI: 10.1007/978-3-319-16050-4_9

financial benefits and difficulties for network monitoring offers temptations and opportunities for criminal activities [2].

Many malicious persons are able to commit their crimes by stealing other consumer's accounts at unsuspecting websites and by conducting transactions using stolen payment account. Some fraud information is often ignored because of the existing disguise technologies, and financial losses are not detected until a long time has passed and significant damage has occurred. The fraud activity is usually undetected because of a lack of monitoring capability.

Given that online commerce is claiming a rapidly growing share of world business, customers have concern about security and privacy [3]. Detecting and preventing the fraud behaviors and build a secure.

In this work, we are concerned with frauds targeting online transactions, especially focus on detecting the Fraud orders. We extract the characteristic of fraud order through analyzing real historical big data from DangDang Weisite1, then we created a characteristics matrix for fraud detection. We improved the characteristics matrix through the machine learning method. Based on the characteristic matrix, We applied Logic regression model to identify frauds. Finally we evaluated the validity of solutions by analyzing feedback data.

The rest of this paper is organized as follows:

Section 2 summarizes the literature review and theoretical background (including Methodology/approach).

Section 3 introduces marketplace that support this work. Section 3 builts/structures/ creates fraudulent orders detection and build model. Section 4 shows results and application in transaction on time. Section 5 shows the Conclusions of this work.

2 Literature Review

Hogan summarized academic literature about fraud phenomena in 2008 [4]. These studies primarily focused on the fraudulent activities in accounting and auditing field during 1995–2006, and then on the accounting literature related to financial statement fraud [5].

Online transactions continue to increase, and so does the incidence of online fraudulent activity. However, loosely controlled market risk brings about more opportunity for online fraud. The reason that the online marketplace easily attracts fraud originates from a unique characteristic of Internet transactions [3]. Under considerable information asymmetry–the uncertainty of trader identity and the uncertainty of merchandise quality–online trade allows sellers or buyers to easily engage in opportunistic behavior [6]. Because online auction fraud is 20 times higher than traditional auction fraud [7], most owners of online auction sites have been working on improving security to protect their profits from fraud threats [8]. Therefore, when an online marketplace provides in-house security services along with basic transaction services, its decision on the preventative privacy controls is complicated by the issues of privacy concerns and the promotion of security services [9].

When it comes to the comprehensively counteract identity fraud, fraud prevention requires a three-part approach: prevention monitoring, detection, and incident response [2].

Several models have been designed to detect fraud in financial statements. Eining found that auditors using expert system discriminated better among situations with varying levels of management fraud risk and made more consistent decisions regarding appropriate audit actions [10]. Green and Choi used an artificial neural networks technique to detect fraud, with limited satisfactory results [11].

Select characteristics of order may indicate frauds evidence. Characteristics set can be applied logistic regression to both, improved and not improved [1]. Ohlson was the first academic researcher to apply Logistic Regression in the field [12]. In his work, not only he was able to detect what was the most important evidence for bankruptcy prediction, but also he was able to find fraud or error evidence since he observed that "the reports of the misclassified bankrupt firms seem to lack any warning signals of impending bankruptcy." Since then, many other studies have applied the method in fraud detection [13–15]. In particular, Viaene applied the method, in a pool of many other methods, for automobile insurance fraud data and concluded that "noteworthy is the good overall performance of the relatively simple and efficient techniques such as Logistic Regression…"

This study primarily focuses on how to detect fraudulent orders for internet transactions. Particularly, we pay attention on finding fraud orders before the transactions are conducted. Providing a security internet market environment may not only protect the benefits of users and the marketplace, but also improve marketplace reputation.

3   Build Fraud Orders Detection Model

We will discuss the procedure of building a fraud orders detection model and the technologies involved.

3.1   Definition of Fraud Orders

Fraud orders: Customers' online accounts are stolen and the thief uses stolen account balance to buy products. Customer service staffs usually check the orders and find that there are some abnormal features, or they get the complaint call or request email from customers.

The key idea of detecting and predicting fraud orders is to find the differences between normal and abnormal orders, and use these different features to distinguish between them. Extract the features of fraud order by person and have a basic knowledge and understanding.

Normally there are three steps in extracting fraud order features.

Step1, Obtain the initial fraud order information. Customer service staff have recorded all the complaints of customers about fraud order.

Step2, statistics of common information like order IP, receiver name, receiver address, receiver phone number and so on about every customer.

Step3, compare normal and abnormal orders, find features that are unique in abnormal orders.

3.2   Fraudulent Characteristic Statistics and Extraction

Initial statistics and analysis of data source. When facing strange data, the first thing to do is to complete some simple mathematical statistics to have a primitive cognition of the data and figure out what may be useful to detect fraud order.

Data source: "fraud order record until July 9th" given by algorithm engineer in DANG.

Data information: There are 2075 fraud orders and 1513 victim customers in total, then we find 14235 orders made by these customers in 2012.

An overview of all the features. We will define all the features used in this work. After checking the databases by users' name, address, phone number and so on. We can get 25 features of a customer (Table 1).

Table 1. All features defined

Feature name	Definition
us_name_cnt	The times of complaints of receiver name
sus_name_cust_cnt	How many customer ids the receiver name matches
sus_tel_home_cnt	The times of complaints of receiver home phone number
sus_tel_home_cust_cnt	How many customer ids the receiver home phone number matches
sus_tel_mobile_cnt	The times of complaints of receiver cellphone number
sus_tel_mobile_cust_cnt	How many customer ids the receiver cellphone number matches
sus_orderip_cnt	The times of complaints of receiver order IP
sus_orderip_cust_cnt	How many customer ids the receiver order IP matches
sus_addr_cnt	The times of complaints of receiver address
sus_addr_cust_cnt	How many customer ids the receiver address matches
sus_permid_cnt	The times of complaints of receiver permid
sus_permid_cust_cnt	How many customer ids the receiver permid matches
sus_email_cnt	The times of complaints of receiver email
sus_email_cust_cnt	How many customer ids the receiver email matches
usu_name_cnt	How many orders this customer id have made using this receiver name
usu_tel_home_cnt	How many orders this customer id have made using this home phone number
usu_tel_mobile_cnt	How many orders this customer id have made using this cellphone number
usu_email_cnt	How many orders this customer id have made using this email
usu_city_cnt	How many orders this customer id have made using this city id
usu_addr_cnt	How many orders this customer id have made using this address
is_bad_addr	Is the address a blurry address
total_price	The total cost of this order
Pay	How much money should the receiver pay for the order
pay_rate	The percentage of money the receiver should
hist_cnt_not_usu	All the orders this user has made

User name, address, IP and so on can be used as identities; some accounts may share the same address, IP, or other identities which means if one identity (like an address) has been part of a fraud order, all the accounts that use this address are suspicious. The first 14 feature are about complaint times of an identity like IP and how many customer ids the identity matches. One account would have a unique customer id. Features 15–20 are about how many orders an account has made using some identity; they are used to judge if this order is a fraud order because if then using many new identities are suspect.

We also build some rules according to the primitive analysis. If the receiver name, address, city are all not usually used by this account, we will consider it a fraud order. This rule is helpful; before the machine learning method is applied we can use this rule to decrease some fraud orders, and even after the machine learning antifraud system is built, we still keep this rule because it is useful.

3.3 Data Preparation and Preprocessing

After primitive analysis of the data, now we can decide that we will use machine learning algorithm which we will explain later. This step is about preparing the data source of machine learning method. We decide which databases will be our choice according to their content and how they are recorded, because there are many databases in Dangdang that are related to orders and customers. We should consider the scale of these databases, as this will affect the choice of machine learning algorithm, because some algorithm would be so slow when facing enormous input.

Data preprocessing is an important step in machine learning, because much of the data is not complete, not unanimous and sometimes contains noises that are invalid data. The quality of the data would affect the results of machine learning algorithm significantly. Data preprocessing commonly contains four steps: data cleaning, integration and alternation, stipulations of an agreement as well as conception layering [16]. Data cleaning includes: handling missing data, handling noises and handling not unanimous data. After data preprocessing, the data we have is clean and neat, and can be used in a machine learning algorithm.

3.4 Fraud Order Detection Model Base on Logistic Regression

The problem we are facing now can be defined as classification problem; that means we should classify an order into fraud order or normal order [17]. Classify problem are used in all kinds of fields, including finance, telecom, biomedicine, Internet and so on. And there are many kinds of algorithms to build a classify model, including logistic regression, neural network, decision-making tree and so on [18]. There are many norms to assess a classify model, and precision, recall and F1 are commonly used [19].

Logistic regression is appropriate for our need; it can give a possibility of an order being fraud order and it can also provide the degree of influences of each feature in the model. When we need a human recheck of predicted fraud orders, we can provide a reason why it's predicted as a fraud order like we classify it as fraud order because the receiver address isn't the usual one and the address is a blurry address, so the items in customer service can judge the order by checking if these reasons provided by the computer are reasonable.

Modeling: First we choose some features we think might be related to fraud order, and we use much data to train the logistic regression model to determine the influence of each feature, and the influence will be represented by a float number. After determining the influences, our model is easy to be used. We input all the features of an order, and we will get a possibility of this order being fraud order.

Target variable

$$Y = \begin{cases} \textbf{1 fraud account} \\ \textbf{0 normal account} \end{cases} \tag{1}$$

and we use account information as the features to predict this $(x = x_1, x_2, \ldots, x_p)$

Following are the formulas used in logistic regression.

$$P(Y = 1|x) = \pi(x) = \frac{1}{1 + e^{-g(x)}} \tag{2}$$

And $g(x) = \beta_0 + \beta_1 x_1 + \beta_2 x_2 + \cdots + \beta_p x_p$

We then need to decide a threshold of possibility, such as when the possibility is greater than 0.7, we can consider the order is fraud order. The threshold is determined by much examination; we compare the precision and recall of different thresholds and choose one we think is the best.

After all these steps are done, we will have a logistic regression model that is good to be used to detect a fraud order.

4   Results and Application

This chapter will collect the orders data operating real-time for 20 days of Dangdang from October 7, 2012 to October 27, 2012 as analysis object to model, and then compare the analysis results with the data of time when the orders were stolen to verify the validity of the model.

4.1   Variables Selection and Data Preparation

In Sect. 3.2, we have selected 25 variables. We have defined some artificial rules before logistic regression according to the statistical results.

Data cleaning also includes three types: missing values processing, noise data processing and inconsistent data processing. In the process of modeling, we take the methods of cross experiment, sampling, discretization to preprocess the data.

Cross validation: Among the given modeling sample data, taking the most samples to model, leaving small part of the samples to predict, then calculating the predicted error and recording the sum of their squares. The process goes on until all samples have been predicted just once. Adding each sample's predicted -error's Squares, which is called PRESS (Predicted Error Sum of Squares). S stands for dividing the data into S parts.

Data sampling: Data source is the collection of the order which is already known whether is stolen or not, selecting some orders randomly from the Fraud orders and normal orders, insuring the quantity proportion range from 1:5–1:9. Data sampling is artificially controlled.

Data discretization: Mapping the number which is originally continuously dispersed to the interval. For example, setting the amount to these intervals: 0–10 Yuan, 10–50 Yuan, 50–100 Yuan, more than 100 Yuan and so on. When the data is only related to their relative size but not their specific value, it can be discretized. Discretization is helpful to diagnose and describe the nonlinear relationship, and can effectively overcome the defects hidden in the data.

The discrete function we used

$$\ln(x + 1)/\ln2 \tag{3}$$

4.2   Modeling Process and Application

After statistics, we finally focused the following 6 key features can be really useful. We also define a new feature called blurry address. Definition of blurry address: satisfies at least one of the two following conditions. (1) ending by county, district, country, city, block, web bar, hotel and all other places that are not particular. (2) containing words like wait, contact, in front of, nearby and all other words that specify an odd way to get the stuff (Table 2).

Table 2. Key features of Fraud Order

Feature ID	Definition	P (thief| have this feature)
is_bad_addr	Is it a blurry address	0.610543
is_usu_city	Is this receiver city the usually city used by the customer	0.386541
is_usu_tel	Is the receiver telephone number usually used by the customer	0.302348
is_usu_name	Is the receiver name usually used by the customer	0.240243
is_usu_email	Is the receiver email usually used by the customer	0.316208

Selecting part of the characteristics and using R language to establish the logistic regression model to get the coefficient of the specific characteristic. Selecting part of the characteristics and using R language to establish the logistic regression model to get the coefficient of the specific characteristic.

4.3   Data Prediction Effect

Every Fraud order will cause losses to the consumer, so the model requires extremely high recall rate, it will bring the problem of lower accuracy, which we can solve with the measures of artificially examining.

Table 3. Results of the test 2

System model	Fraud order captured by API	All fraud order	Model recall rate
Online version	39	45	86.67 %

Prediction: Using coefficient and the corresponding characteristic of the order among the test set to calculate the probability of an order being Fraud order among the test set. Predicting whether the order is stolen through comparing with the specified threshold.

Data source: Using the first 6-months' data of 2012 to sample as training set, using the data of July and August as testing set (Table 3).

We applied this model in real on time online transaction. The model with a higher recall rate as well as artificially examining successfully reduces the number and the amount of Fraud orders.

5 Conclusions

In summary, this work primarily focused on the detection of fraudulent evidence concerning the online transactions, especially on Fraud orders. Online fraudulent customers can be divided into several categories: Hackers, malicious customers, dissatisfied customers and competitive sellers. All the cheating behaviors would finally be reflected in the purchase orders. We extracted the characteristics of cheating orders from the historical data of orders. Moreover, basing on the machine learning method, we improved those characteristics sets by applying Logistic Regression algorithm. Most likely we can distinguish whether customers' orders have the features of fraudulent orders or not. Finally, we verified the fraud order and dealt with them by marketplace's rules.

This model, which has been designed and applied in Dangdang with a higher recall rate as well as the artificial examination, has successfully reduced Fraud orders. So far, the recall rate of Fraud orders is 86.67 %.

For the online marketplace, providing a secure environment is necessary for its consumers. To help create a effective and efficient in online transaction, this work aimed to develop a detection method with higher accuracy and lower cost. In the future, we hope to apply other methodologies to identify and improve the accuracy of detecting fraud for online transactions.

Acknowledgments. The data of this work is provided by E-commerce China Dangdang Inc (http://www.dangdang.com). We thank Qiang Fu and QI Ju who are employees of Dangdang and for discussing the results with us. We thank Michael Wagner for revising the paper and editing the manuscript. We also thank, Jian Li, Jie Shen, Weiwei Yang and Daobo Wang, Who are the associate editor for providing a lot of helpful comments.

References

1. Maranzato, R., Pereira, A.: Fraud detection in reputation system in e-markets using logistic regression. In: SAC 2010, Sierre, Switzerland, 22–26 March 2010
2. Kim, T.K., Lim, H.J., Nah, J.H.: Analysis on fraud detection for internet service. Int. J. Secur. Appl. **7**(6), 275–284 (2013)
3. Shim, S., Lee, B.: An economic model of optimal fraud control and the aftermarket for security services in online marketplaces. Electron. Commer. Res. Appl. **9**, 435–445 (2010)
4. Hogan, C.E., Rezaee, Z., Riley, R.A., Velury, U.K.: Financial statement fraud: insights from the academic literature. Auditing J. Pract. Theor. **27**(2), 231–252 (2008)
5. Trompeter, G.M., Carpenter, T.D.: A synthesis of fraud-related resaerch. Auditing J. Pract. Theor. **32**(Supplement 1), 287–321 (2013)
6. Klein, B., Leffler, K.B.: The role of market forces in assuring contractual performance. J. Polit. Econ. **89**(4), 615–641 (1981)
7. Gavish, B., Tucci, C.: Reducing internet auction fraud. Commun. ACM **51**(5), 89–97 (2008)
8. Chang, W.-H., Chang, J.-S.: A novel two-stage phased modeling framework for early fraud detection. Expert Syst. Appl. **38**, 11244–11260 (2011)
9. Chang, J.-S.: An effective early fraud detection method for online auctions. Electron. Commer. Res. Appl. **11**, 346–360 (2012)
10. Eining, M.M., Jones, D.R., Loebbecke, J.K.: Reliance on decision aids: an examination of auditors' assessment of management fraud. Auditing J. Pract. Theor. **16**(2), 1–19 (1997)
11. Green, B.P., Choi, J.H.: Assessing the risk of management fraud through neural network technology. Audit J. Pract. Theor. **16**(1), 14–28 (1997)
12. Ohlson, J.A.: Financial ratios and the probabilistic prediction of bankruptcy. J. Account. Res. **18**, 109–131 (1980)
13. Lenard, M.J., Alam, P.: An historical perspective on fraud detection: From bankruptcy models to most effective indicators of fraud in recent incidents. J. Forensic Invest. Account. **1**(1), 1–27 (2009)
14. Lou, Y.-I., Wang, M.-L.: Fraud risk factor of the fraud triangle assessing the likelihood of fraudulent financial reporting. J. Bus. Econ. Res. **7**(2), 61–78 (2009)
15. Zhang, H., Lin, Z., Hu, X.: The effectiveness of the escrow model: an experimental framework for dynamic online environments. J. Organ. Comput. Electron. Commer. **17**(2), 119–143 (2007)
16. Lek, M., Anandarajah, B., Cerpa, N., Jamieson, R.: Data mining prototype for detecting e-commerce fraud. In: The 9th European Conference on Information Systems Bled, Slovenia, 27–29 June 2001
17. Lach, J.: Data mining digs. Am. Demographics **21**, 38–45 (1999)
18. Breiman, L., Friedman, J.H., Olshen, R.A., Stone, C.J.: Classification and Regression Trees. Wadsworth International Group, Belmont (1984)
19. Hosmer, D.W., Lemeshow, S.: Applied Logistic Regression. Wiley, New York, Chichester (2000)

Question Classification
Based on Hadoop Platform

XiangXiang Qi[1], Lei Su[1(✉)], Bin Yang[1], Jun Chen[2],
Yiyang Li[1], and Junhui Liu[2]

[1] School of Information Engineering and Automation, Kunming University
of Science and Technology, Kunming 650093, China
qixiangfighting@163.com, s28341@hotmail.com,
{yangbin0724,liyiyan001}@126.com
[2] School of Software, Yunnan University, Kunming 650091, Yunnan, China
timcj007@163.com, HanksLau@gmail.com

Abstract. The statistical supervised learning model for question classification needs a large amount of labeled training examples. However, labeled data are difficult to collected but unlabeled data are readily obtained. To solve the lack of labeled data, we utilize the method of transfer learning to build the learning model with the labeled and the unlabeled training examples. Based on the feature spaces of source and target domain, the common space are build. Then, those examples from source domain whose conditional probability is like to be similar to the target domain are selected into the common space. Therefore, the question classifier is trained by the labeled data in the source domain and the unlabeled data in the target domain. Meanwhile, the method of Map/Reduce based on the Hadoop platform is used to reduce the time complexity in kernel mapping. The subtasks are constructed for the mapping process and then the final result is obtained by assembling the subtasks. Experiments on question classification show that the proposed method could improve the classification accuracy. Furthermore, the learning model based on the Hadoop Platform could ask each computing resources to reduce the running time.

Keywords: Question answering · Question classification · Hadoop platform · Kernel mapping

1 Introduction

Question classification is an important part of Question Answering (QA), which is basic of formulating answer extraction strategy and accurately positioning the answer, the accuracy of classification directly affects the performance of question answering system. The question classification research mainly adopts the method of statistical learning at present, namely through the statistical learning of tagging question corpus, we can extract feature of expressing question types to build learning model and realize the recognition of the question types. Zhang and Lee [1] respectively introduce the machine learning algorithms of k-NN, Naive Bayes, Decision Tree and SNoW into question classification, the accuracy rate of classification reach 90 %. M.L. Nguyen et al. [2]

© Institute for Computer Sciences, Social Informatics and Telecommunications Engineering 2015
V.C.M. Leung et al. (Eds.): CloudComp 2014, LNICST 142, pp. 107–115, 2015.
DOI: 10.1007/978-3-319-16050-4_10

proposed the use of maximum entropy and boosting method with subtrees mined from training data as features and weak function. A. Moschitti et al. [3] employed tree structures based on shallow semantic encoded in predicate argument structures for question classification. It is important to note that the above methods are all based on the marked question corpora, by the training data to build model, which is then applied to the target domain. Most of the questions in real world have no the corresponding categories sign, which gives the application of traditional machine learning method a challenge. Look from another Angle, if there is a lot of training data under the different distribution, completely discarding these data is very regrettable. How to reasonable use of these data is a mainly problem in transfer learning. Transfer learning can transfer knowledge from the existing data, which is used to help the future study. This article focuses on how to combine transfer learning with question classification, using the unmarked data so as to improve the classification accuracy of question classification model.

At present, many effective transfer learning method have been put forward but they are all based on the following assumptions: the marginal distribution of data is directly related to the conditional probability in source domain and target domain, the assumption limits the application of transfer learning method in the source space and linear transformation. In order to broaden the application scope of transfer learning and reduce the limitation of assumptions, according to the paper [4], the source domain and target domain data are mapped to the public kernel space by kernel function, thus data distribution in two areas were in the same space, then selecting the same conditional probability sample in the source domain and target domain under the kernel space for model building so that we can achieve the goal of knowledge transfer.

Experimental data come from the 2 subclass of the online sports categories "football" and "basketball": a total of 75536 questions. Because of the question number is large, the experiment process uses the calculation method of traditional single node which not only consumes time but also cost is larger after error correction, so the paper adopts the present widely use of cloud computing technology Hadoop platform to carry on the calculation of the kernel mapping, due to the Hadoop platform adopts map/reduce style to carry out the scattered operation and the comprehensive of results, so it is necessary to improve kernel mapping algorithm in the hope of the accuracy of experimental results. This paper has carried on the summary to Hadoop platform in Sect. 2. Section 3 describes the application of the kernel mapping in domain adaptation; Sect. 4 is the design and implementation of kernel mapping in domain adaptation based on Hadoop platform; Sect. 5 is the result and analysis of the experiment.

2 Hadoop Platform

Hadoop is a platform suit for distributed computing and storing of big data, The Hadoop community expands unceasingly, and Hadoop itself has evolved into a collection which has many subprojects project, the most core part is used in the distributed storage of DFS (Distributed File System) File System and Map/Reduce computing architecture for distributed computing [5–7].

2.1   Hadoop Distributed File System (HDFS)

More and more data has beyond the management scope of single operating system in the Distributed computing environment, then a distributed document management system is needed to organize the scattered data on multiple machines, in the Hadoop is corresponding to the HDFS [5].

HDFS contains three parts: NameNode, DataNode, Secondary NameNode, The NameNode is the management node of the file system, It maintains the file directory tree of the entire file system, File/directory meta information and each file corresponding to data block list, Receive user operation request on file; The DataNode provide storage service on real file data, File stored in the form of block on the da-taNode; Secondary NameNode's main function is to maintain the integrity of the data, Download metadata information (fsimage, edits) from the NameNode, then the two merged, generating new fsimage, locally stored, and push it to the NameNode, At the same time, reset the NameNode edits (Fig. 1).

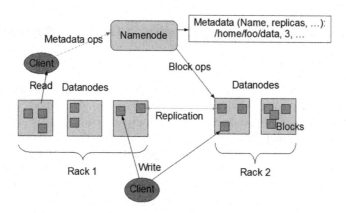

Fig. 1. The composition structure of HDFS

2.2   Distributed Computing Framework (Map/Reduce)

Map/Reduce is a kind of distributed computing model, Put forward by Google, which is mainly used in the search field, solve the problem of the calculation of huge amounts of data, Its architecture consists of two phases: Map and Reduce, Users only need to implement two functions of map() and reduce(), then distributed computing can be realized. Users submit the work to JobTracker, then The JobTracker assigned the task to TaskTracker, Performed by the TaskTracker, and is responsible for the start and follow up the implementation of tasks. The implementation process is as follows [5] (Fig. 2):

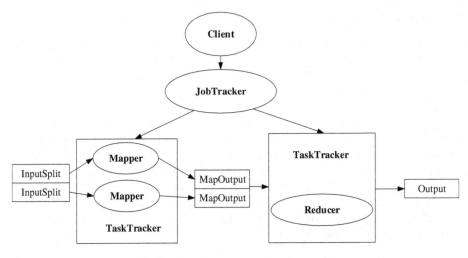

Fig. 2. Map/Reduce execution flow chart

3 The Application of Kernel Mapping in Domain Adaptation

3.1 Kernel Mapping

When a label sample number is less or more difficult to obtain, which limits the application range of the traditional monitoring machine learning method. The core idea of domain adaptation is using little or no label samples in source domain to enhance the learning accuracy in target field. Set $P_t(x, y)$ and $P_s(x, y)$ respectively represent the joint probability distribution of the sample in the target domain and the source domain. The supervised learning uses the large label samples in $P_s(x, y)$ and the small label samples in $P_t(x, y)$ to establish the learning model in view of target domain. However, the existing methods are based on the assumption that the edge distribution of data is directly related to the conditional probability in source domain and target domain, knowledge transfer can be carried out only in the case of $P_t(x, y)$ and $P_s(x, y)$ is similar, which limits the application scope of domain adaptation method in the source space and linear transformation.

Aiming at above problems, a lot of fruitful work is carried out [8]. According to the definition, $P(x, y) = r(x|y)q(x)$ where, $r(x|y)$ is the sample prior probability of the sample conditional probability $q(x)$. At present, work mainly can be carried out around two aspects: when $q_t(x)$ and $q_s(x)$ on the relevant samples are close on the relevant samples, $r_t(x|y)$ and $r_s(x|y)$ are similar in potential probability space; $q(x)$ is close to $r(x|y)$, all of these facts imply the above assumptions (t, s respectively represent the target domain and the source domain).

However, these assumptions may be too strict, in most cases, the edge and conditional probability distribution may be large difference in two domains. So no matter in the original data space, code space or the potential Dirichlet data space, the two assumptions are not satisfied. In this context, nonlinear transformation is considered, such as the kernel mapping reduces the limit of two assumptions. A suitable kernel function can map the input space data to the feature space of an easy operation [9], for example, Gauss kernel function not only has the effect of sample code, but also make the samples having the similar condition probability distribution in the mapping space to further make the structure of the domain adaptation simple.

3.2 The Application of Kernel Mapping Method for Question Classification

In order to combine the kernel mapping with domain adaptation and apply into question classification, according to the introduced method in paper [4], mapping the source domain and target domain to the public kernel space by using the kernel function, making the prior probability of samples in two domains similar; Then selecting samples that have the same conditional probability $r(x|y)$ in a public space to build learning model by using cluster evaluation standard to further carry out the knowledge transfer.

The paper adopts the Gaussian kernel mapping, suppose $\phi : f(x) \rightarrow h(x)$ is the objective function, which can transfer the samples from the conventional European Space to the reconfigurable Hilbert Space (Reproducing Kernel Hilbert Space) and adopt the way of sample inner product $K(x_i, x_j) = (\phi(x_i) \cdot \phi(x_j))$ to avoid direct mapping. Based on paper [10], set x_{ij} is the j-th sample in the i-th category, $\phi(v) \in h$ can be represented as:

$$\phi(\mathrm{v}) = \sum_{i=1}^{NC} \sum_{j=1}^{l_i} \alpha_{ij} \phi(x_{ij}) \tag{1}$$

Where, NC is the total number of categories; α_{ij} is the j-th group in $\alpha_i = \{\alpha_{i1}, \alpha_{i2}, \cdots, \alpha_{il_i}\}$, α_i is the coefficient of $\phi(x_j)$. The details of the decomposition process can be obtained in the paper [9].

After the above processing, mapping the source domain and target domain samples to public kernel space, ensuring the prior probability of sample is close. The conditional probability $r(x|y)$ of sample may still be different, so in a public space, adopt evaluation criteria based on cluster to choose samples, which have the same conditional probability in two domains.

The algorithm of selecting samples in kernel space is the adaptive correction clustering algorithm referred in paper [11]: Bisecting k-means. The causes of adopting clustering algorithm for the selection of samples is that the same conditional probability distribution of samples is similar, the clustering algorithm can get out of the same characteristics (or similar) of samples. The core of the adaptive clustering algorithm is that the square error of a cluster is greater than the sum of two sub-manifold error within the cluster, then the clusters are split into two sub clusters and achieve the characteristics of adaptive data distribution. The following is the core code of the Bisecting k-means:

Algorithm 1. Self-adapting Bisecting K-means

Input: Labeled Data: L

Output: Cluster Index of data in L: idx

$C=L$, idx={1,..........1}

for each C_i in C do

    Split C_i into two clusters C_i1 and C_i2 using K-means

    If Purity(C_i) $\leqq 0.7$ or Par(C_i,C_i1,C_i2)

    Then Replace C_i with C_i1 and C_i2,update idx

end for

Return cluster index of L

Where $Par(c, c_1, c_2) = ||se(c) - \sum_{i=1,2} se(c_i)|| c_1$, c_2 is two sub clusters of cluster C. $c_1 \cup c_2 = C$, $c_1 \cap c_2 = \emptyset$, $se(x)$ is the sum of the square error, $||x|| = \begin{cases} 1 \, x > 0 \\ 0 \, x < 0 \end{cases}$.

Samples is marked data in the cluster C_i, where, the mark is "+" and "−". $Purity(c_i) = max(\frac{"+"\in c_i}{|c_i|}, \frac{"-"\in c_i}{|c_i|})$.

Mapping the samples of different distribution in the source domain and target domain by using kernel function, using clustering algorithm to choose the same instances in source domain labels and the related cluster labels under the public kernel space to carry out the model training.

4   Kernel Mapping in Hadoop Platform

In the previous section, The principle of Kernel mapping in domain adaptation and the application of clustering algorithm in the sample selection are introduced, from its process, we are known that the different probability distribution samples deliver to the public kernel space by kernel mapping, then choosing the same conditional probability samples in kernel space to build model and applying into different fields, achieving the goal of knowledge transfer.

Due to the kernel mapping and sample selection process are independent, so parallel design is carried out in the experiment process as long as considering the design of Map and Reduce in two stages respectively.

Hadoop platform can distributed computing and multiple task execution, which thanks to its map/reduce execution flow, scattering operation into many subtasks by the map process, after calculating, the subtasks are carried out reduce process to get the final result.

Before the mapping, the various properties are took statute in sample, thus sample mean of X (x represents the sample set) is zero or $m_s = \frac{1}{l}\sum_{i=1}^{l} x_i = 0$ where l is the number of samples, so we can find a proper mapping space to employ kernel function calculation. So the property calculation and kernel mapping calculation are realized in the map logic.

After disposing, the different probability distribution samples are delivered to the public kernel space, the last mentioned Bisecting k-means algorithm should be re-writed. From more than 700 thousand samples, the same conditional probability $r(x|y)$ samples are selected, using the classification machine learning algorithm for model building.

5 Experimental Results Analysis

5.1 Hadoop Cluster Configuration and the Experimental Data

We use the Hadoop cluster composed of 7 computer to implement the Map/Reduce calculation Process mentioned above, one of the node as the NameNode, the rest 6 nodes are DataNode. The specific hardware configuration is as follows (Table 1):

Table 1. Each computer hardware configuration of Hadoop cluster

Node type	CPU	Memory
NameNode	Intel Core2 2.33 GHz	2 GB
DataNode	Intel Celeron 1.8 GHz	1 GB
DataNode	Intel Celeron 1.8 GHz	1 GB
DataNode	Intel Celeron 1.8 GHz	1 GB
DataNode	Intel Celeron 1.8 GHz	1 GB
DataNode	Intel Celeron 1.8 GHz	1 GB
DataNode	Intel Celeron 1.8 GHz	1 GB

The experimental data taken from Baidu Knows, selecting the category of "sports", Subcategory questions of "basketball" and "football", a total of 75536, which are consisted of 40000 "football" category and 35536 "basketball" category. Feature extraction method is *tf-idf*,Using supervised machine learning methods and transfer learning methods of Kernel mapping to do experiment.

The main idea of using supervised machine learning methods to knowledge transfer is: Training data source domain gets classifier model. The model will be applied to the target domain, Classifying target domain questions in order to achieve the goal of knowledge transfer. "Football" and "basketball" under the category data are divided into two parts, Included in the source domain and target domain respectively and there is no intersection. Data composition shown in Table 2:

Table 2. Experimental data of supervised machine learning methods

Data set	Question number	Data composition		Category
		Football	Basketball	
DataSource-A	50536	25000	25536	Football/Basketball
DataSource-B	50536	15000	35536	Football/Basketball

5.2 Domain Adaptation Based on Kernel Mapping

Traditional supervised machine learning must be make sure the different categories label, Sample data allowed the category labels based on the kernel mapping, The experimental data of this method has a label (Football) or not.

Questions after word segmentation by LTP Platform [12] adopting the method of *tf-idf* to build characteristic vocabulary in the process of the experiment. Select top 1000 dimension feature and take the question into VSM format. The baseline learning model is SVM. After 10 times of iterative computation, the result is as follows (Table 3).

Table 3. Results of experiments

Method of learning model	Classification accuracy	
	A → B	B → A
Supervised learning	66.82 %	63.66 %
Kernel mapping	74.13 %	65.49 %

The experimental results show that: In the case of feature dimension, Using conventional method of training sample selection model of knowledge transfer, Because label data has considerable proportion of unlabeled data in the data set A, The effect of area A transfers to the area B is better than area B transfers to the area A; Adopting the chi improve *tf-idf* features extraction method can enhance the accuracy in knowledge transfer.

Compared to traditional supervised machine learning methods, using a small amount of tag data can achieve good effect of transfer by kernel mapping, save the calculation time and category with resources compared to the supervised machine learning method.

6 Conclusion

The main purpose of the domain adaptation is the use of domain knowledge, using less marked samples to obtain better performance classifier in the similar domain. Compared to the traditional supervised machine learning method, the method of kernel mapping has full use for the unmarked samples, you don't need to take the time to mark the samples who do not help or less help for further training, which can avoid the waste of resources so as to effectively reduce the cost to obtain the training samples. On the basis of the current work, the algorithms in this paper still have a lot to improve. First of all, the parallel algorithm design of machine learning do not consider in this paper, just copy the complete code to TaskTracker for execution; Second, in the selection process of the same conditional probability samples in the kernel space, using the way of the iterative calculation to gradually narrow error for the choice of samples on reduce nodes, so there may be no solution, namely the similarity result is just near to threshold but unable to get the final result, what is more, the questions dimension is 1000, where there are a large number of zero elements in scatter matrix, solving the problem of sparse matrix to improve the classification accuracy also plays a key role. So we still should study for the above problems in order to build more effective question classification model.

Acknowledgment. This work was supported by the National Natural Science Foundation of China (No. 61365010), Yunnan Nature Science Foundation (2011FZ069), Yunnan Province Department of Education Foundation (2011Y387).

References

1. Zhang, D., Lee, W.S.: Question classification using supports vector machines. In: Proceedings of the 26th Annual International ACM SIGIR Conference on Research and Development in Information Retrieval, Toronto, Canada, pp. 26–32 (2003)
2. Nguyen, M.L., Nguyen, T.T., Shimazu, A.: Subtree mining for question classification problem. In: Proceedings of the 20th International Conference on Artificial Intelligence, Hyderabad, India, pp. 1695–1700 (2007)
3. Moschitti, A., Quateroni, S., Basili, R., Manandhar, S.: Exploiting syntactic and shallow semantic kernels for question/answer classification. In: Proceedings of the 45th Annual Meeting of the Association of Computational Linguistics, Prague, Czech, pp. 776–783 (2007)
4. Zhong, E., Fan, W., Peng, J., et al.: Cross domain distribution adaptation via kernel mapping. In: Proceedings of the 15th ACM SIGKDD International Conference on Knowledge Discovery and Data Mining, Paris, pp. 1027–1036 (2009)
5. Pang, X.: Research on Classification Algorithm Based on Active Learning SVM in Hadoop Platform. Master dissertation, South China University of Technology (2011)
6. Chen, M., Mao, S., Liu, Y.: Big data: a survey. ACM/Springer Mob. Netw. Appl. **19**(2), 171–209 (2014)
7. Chen, M.: NDNC-BAN: supporting rich media healthcare services via named data networking in cloud-assisted wireless body area networks. Inf. Sci. **284**(10), 142–156 (2014)
8. Sinno Jialin Pan and Qiang Yang: A survey on transfer learning. IEEE Trans. Knowl. Data Eng. **22**(10), 1345–1359 (2010)
9. Baudat, G., Anouar, F.: Generalized discriminant analysis using a kernel approach. Neural Comput. **12**(10), 2385–2404 (2000)
10. Schölkopf, B., Herbrich, R., Smola, A.J.: A generalized representer theorem. In: Helmbold, D.P., Williamson, B. (eds.) COLT 2001 and EuroCOLT 2001. LNCS (LNAI), vol. 2111, pp. 416–426. Springer, Heidelberg (2001)
11. Ren, J., Shi, X., Fan, W., et al.: Type-independent correction of sample selection bias via structural discovery and re-balancing. In: Proceedings of the 2008 SIAM International Conference on Data Mining, pp. 565–576 (2008)
12. Che, W., Li, Z., Liu, T.: LTP: a Chinese language technology platform. In: Proceeding of the 23rd International Conference on Computational Linguistics, Demonstrations Volume, 23–27 August 2010, Beijing, China, pp. 13–16 (2010)

A Dynamic and Static Combined Replication Management Mechanism Based on Frequency Adaptive

Zhenli He[1](✉), Hua Zhou[1], Long Hu[2], Junhui Liu[1], and Lei Su[3]

[1] School of Software, Yunnan University, Kunming 650091, Yunnan, China
{hezhenli1987,HanksLau}@gmail.com, hzhou@ynu.edu.cn
[2] Embedded and Pervasive Computing Lab,
School of Computer Science and Technology,
Huazhong University of Science and Technology,
1037 Luoyu Road, Wuhan 430074, China
longhu.cs@gmail.com
[3] School of Information Engineering and Automation,
Kunming University of Science and Technology, Kunming 650093, Yunnan, China
s28341@hotmail.com

Abstract. In recent years, academia vigorous a research campaign about cloud computing since its rise, where replication management mechanism is one of its hotspot issue. More and more scholars pay attention to the redundant replica policy of cloud computing. That whether the replication management mechanism is good or not decides the experience of user, the expand ability of the system and the efficiency issue directly. In this paper, a series of static and dynamic replication management mechanism that have exist are discussed. In addition, on this basis a dynamic and static combined replication management mechanism based on frequency adaptive is proposed.

Keywords: Cloud computing · Replication management · Dynamic and static combined · Frequency adaptive · Modeling

1 Introduction

In recent years, file replication management mechanism have been paid more and more attentions because of the rapid development of cloud computing [1]. The servers used in cloud computing are all super-large scale [2]. Take Google as an example, Google cloud computing already have more than one million servers [3]. The shutdown of servers and the damage of hardware of system (such as hard disk drive) should be take as a common state under the condition of such a super-large scale servers [4]. Therefore, what policy should be used to realize a replication management mechanism that have a fault-tolerant ability and a high efficiency [5] is a research hotspot.

In a distributed file system, one file can have several file replicas saved in other sites. However, data synchronization between each file replica will be involved, because distributed file system have consistency requirements for file replicas. That is why the larger scale of the system is the more complex the internet environment. If the number of file replicas is increasing by unlimited number, the cost of system cost by data synchronization machine will increase rapidly. Meanwhile, if file replicas have been stored in a wrong site, the file request will be satisfied only after flowing through multiple nodes and generate a big operating delay.

Therefore, the number and site of replicas is the entry point of replication management mechanism in a distributed file system. The number of replicas have decided the usability [6] and the fault-tolerant ability [6] of system. While the site of replicas has decided the system performance. So the number and the site of replicas are given by using different policies in a lot of file replication management mechanism.

For the static replication management mechanism, the advantage of it is that it can provide serves of different securities to match different standards to charge the users. But this mechanism may lead to an overweight burden of nodes. Because the majority of file operations are concentrate on a few nodes of system, and the system performance will be affected. For the dynamic replication management mechanism [8], its advantage is that it will adapt to the change of system when the scale of system is expanding. But for the centralized dynamic replication management mechanism, though it's easy to achieve it will become a bottleneck that will restrict the system performance because the operations of file replicas are under the charge of one single node, for the reason that it should have a comprehensive recognition to every file replica. But for distributed dynamic replication management mechanism, though it's more complex, it has no this restriction.

In this paper a dynamic and static combined replication management mechanism based on file access frequency has been proposed. It can provide serves of different security level based on users' request, on operation state of system, and on the access frequency of file. On the basis of static policy, distributed management mechanism is used to modify the number and site of replicas. By this mechanism, we can adapt to the change of system and the request of users more flexibly, under the condition of a guaranteed system performance a flexible replication dynamic management can be operated.

2   Related Works

There are many different kinds of implementations for distributed replication management mechanism [7].

Khaneghah Ehsan Mousavi, et al. pointed out that enlargement of the gap between data processing and I/O operations throughput will bound the system performance to storage and retrieval operations and remarkably reduce the overall performance of high performance computing clusters [9]. They proposed a mechanism that estimates the required number of replicas for each file based on its popularity. In the mechanism, two agents are responsible for estimating replication factor and performing file replication. RFEA estimates the required number of replicas for each file and RFSA adapts this number to the remaining storage space of cluster. RFEA and RFSA are implemented as a multi-thread program which runs on the NameNode in a Hadoop cluster.

Xin Sun, et al. pointed out that most replication methods lead to high overhead for unnecessary file replications and consistency maintenance [10]. They proposed a dynamic minimum access cost based MAC replication strategy. The MAC replication strategy takes into account the access frequency, the status of the network connection and average response time to perform optimal replication. It first selects the popular files, calculated the average response time to determine which logical resource should be replicated. Then calculates an appropriate site to replicate for better shortening the response time of the data resource.

Hegde S have compared many kinds of models of replication management mechanism through different aspects [11]. Some models are complex to achieve and the computing complexity will increase rapidly when the scale of system is expanding. So the degree of complexity of replication management mechanism should be controlled in a rational extent.

3   The Model for Adaptive Replication

According to what has been discussed above, in this paper the file replication management mechanism take the form that dynamic and static are combined. File replicas with fixed site and number will be established the time the files entering the system firstly to ensure the usability and the fault-tolerant ability of the system. At the same time, replicas will be added or deleted at a proper site by using distributed dynamic replication management mechanism when the system is operating. In order to ensure the system performance the replica established by using static policy can not be deleted.

A. The Adaptive Replication Policy

This policy refers to distributed dynamic replication management mechanism. In order to reduce the cost of system, we hope only the nodes that have file replicas need to estimate whether the file replica should be added or deleted on the nodes according to the condition it master, and does not need to er to the other nodes in the system.

We make an appoint as following:

- There are N mainframes in the whole system, $Node_x$ presents the x_{th} mainframe, $x \in N$.
- Assume there are n replicas saved at n replica nodes in file F, then we set the replication degree of file F is n.
- There are two operations for file replicas in a system, and they are writing and reading. Among them reading just refers to one replica node, writing needs to update all of the file replicas because of the consistency requirements of replicas.

- The route algorithm of the system follows the principle of read the nearest, that is to say if there is not a file replica needed exist on the node, then search it on the node that is nearest.
- Each replica node i of file F maintains a series of counters: R_{inside}, $R_{outside-x}$, W_{inside}, $W_{outside-x}$. In a period of time t, R_{inside} is the frequency of reading requirement to the file replica on this node. $R_{outside-x}$ is the frequency of reading file replicas that $Node_x$ has required. W_{inside} is the frequency of writing operation to file replica on this node. $W_{outside-x}$ is the frequency of updating the file replica that $Node_x$ has required.
- Assume a is the cost of a node without replicas reading the file from other nodes. b is the cost of updating a file replica non-local by writing operation.

According to the appoint above, if a $Node_x$ has replicas the cost of system cost by replicas can deduced as:

$$Cost = 0R_{inside} + \sum_{i=1}^{N} R_{outside-i}a + \sum_{i=1}^{N} W_{outside-i}bn + W_{inside}b(n-1) \quad (1)$$

Actually, reading operation to file replica inside node will not produce any network transmission. Non-local node will produce a cost a when operate reading operation to file replica. Non-local node will produce a cost b when operate writing operation to file replica and produce a cost $(n-1)b$ to update $n-1$ replicas left. The $n-1$ replicas are needed to updated the time operate writing operation to the file replicas inside node and it will produce a cost $(n-1)b$.

On the $Node_x$ we add a replica of this file ($y \in N$), the replication degree of file F will change to $(n+1)$, $Node_y$ will operate reading operation directly without through $Node_x$. Actually, if the access pattern for a file is not change too much in a period of time, then we can consider the frequency of reading requirement to the file replica inside this node is still R_{inside}, the frequency of writing requirement is still W_{inside}. But $R_{outside-y}$ will become the frequency that local node read the file replica on $Node_y$. So $R_{outside-y}$ is beyond calculation range. Similarly, $W_{outside-y}$ is beyond calculation range. Meanwhile, n replicas are needed to update since $W_{outside-y}$ becomes the frequency that local node operate writing operation on the file replica on $Node_y$. The total cost been produced is $W_{outside-y}bn$. So the cost of the system is as follow:

$$Cost_A = 0R_{inside} + \sum_{i=1,i\neq y}^{N} R_{outside-i}a$$

$$+ \sum_{i=1,i\neq y}^{N} W_{outside-i}b(n+1) + W_{inside}bn + W_{outside-y}bn \quad (2)$$

According to formulas (1) and (2) the judge condition of adding a replica on $Node_y$ by $Node_x$ is $Cost_A < Cost$. Plug this into formula and simplify it, we can get:

$$R_{outside-y}a > W_{inside}b + \sum_{i=1,i\neq y}^{N} W_{outside-i}b \quad (3)$$

Consider formula (3) as a judge condition is very complex in a actual system. Because the frequency of writing operation of nodes outside should been accumulated in each judgment.

As $\sum_{i=1,i\neq y}^{N} W_{outside-i} b < \sum_{i=1}^{N} W_{outside-i} b$, so formula (3) is work when formula (4) is work:

$$R_{outside-y} a > W_{inside} b + \sum_{i=1}^{N} W_{outside-i} b \tag{4}$$

If we set $W_{outside}$ as the total frequency of updating file replicas on $Node_x$ required by nodes outside, formula (4) can be simplified as:

$$R_{outside-y} a > W_{inside} b + W_{outside} b \tag{5}$$

No matter update the file F by reading the file or writing on the file, the data presents the size of file F is needed to transport to network transmission. So for the sake of simplicity, we assume $a \approx b$, we can get as follows:

$$R_{outside-y} > W_{inside} + W_{outside} \tag{6}$$

So the formula of judging condition of adding a replica on $Node_y$ by $Node_x$ is formula (6).

If $Node_x$ delete local replicas, the replication degree of file F will become $(n-1)$. Actually, if the access pattern for a file is not change too much in a period of time, then we can consider the frequency of reading requirement to this file replica inside $Node_x$. R_{inside} will turns to be the frequency of reading file replica on other nodes required. The frequency of requirement W_{inside} will turns to be the frequency of updating file replica on other nodes required. Then the cost of this system will be:

$$Cost_B = R_{inside} a + \sum_{i=1}^{N} R_{outside-i} a + \sum_{i=1}^{N} W_{outside-i} b(n-1) + W_{inside} b(n-1) \tag{7}$$

From formulas (1) to (7) the judging condition of deleting local replica decided by $Node_x$ can be obtained: $Cost_B < Cost$. Plug this into formula and simplify it, we can get:

$$R_{inside} a < \sum_{i=1}^{N} W_{outside-i} b \tag{8}$$

Similarly, we can get:

$$R_{inside} < W_{outside} \tag{9}$$

So the judging condition of deleting local replica decided by $Node_x$ is formula (9).

B. The Scanning Cycle Policy

According to the adaptive replication policy, the node with replica can judge when to add or delete a replica according to its counter. But it's still need a scanning cycle to control it, and the node with replica will scan and make the judgment after a circle. Thus it refers to the problem of choosing the scanning circle.

To solve this problem, the scanning cycle policy is introduced. We hope scanning circle which can be shorten by node automatically when the frequency of a file replica is increasing at the time of accessing the node. When the frequency is decreased, the scanning circle can be lengthen by the node automatically. The advantage of it is that when a file is been accessed for many times, a mass of files will centralize on the node of system that saved the file replica. It will lead to the burden of the node be overweighted and the system performance will be affected. At this time shorten the scanning circle will make the node to reflect as soon as possible. Make sure it is needed to add replicas on other nodes and delete local replica to adapt to the new access pattern to ensure its performance. But when the frequency of accessing the file is decreasing, the lower the frequency is the less effect to the node of system cost by replicas of this file. At this time, lengthen the scanning circle, the scanning frequency of the node will decreasing, and the load will decrease.

To describe this policy, add some appoints on the basis of article above:

- Assume the initial scanning circle is T_1 when the system has been initialized.
- Assume the scanning circles of replica on $Node_x$ in file F can make up a circle array T_1, T_2, T_3, ... T_m, ... T_n, we set A_m as the accessing frequency the file replica received in scanning circle T_m. That is to say:
  $A_m = R_{inside} + \sum_{i=1}^{N} R_{outside-i} + W_{inside} + \sum_{i=1}^{N} W_{outside-i} = R_{inside} + R_{outside} + W_{inside} + W_{outside}$
- If we establish a coordinate axis, set x axis as time, and set y axis as accessing frequency, we can get the Fig. 1.

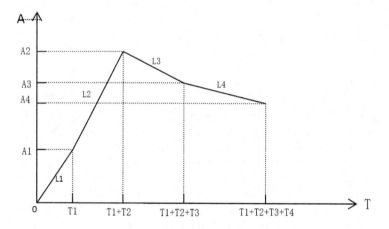

Fig. 1. The relationship between A_m and T_m.

From the coordinate axis we can know, if we take segments L_1, L_2, L_3, L_4 as judgment standard, when the slop value is a positive number it means to the accessing frequency is increasing in this circle. When the slop value is a negative number it means to the accessing frequency is decreasing in this circle. And the slop value shows the magnitude of increasing or decreasing of accessing. According to the appoints above, after $Node_x$ has been initialized, the scanning circle of a replica in file F is T_1, when T_1 is ending the access frequency of file replica is A_1, the degree the access frequency is:

$$D_1 = \frac{A_1 - 0}{T_1} \tag{10}$$

The formula changed further more:

$$D_i = \frac{A_i - A_{i-1}}{T_i}, i = 1, 2, 3...n \tag{11}$$

When D_i is a positive number it presents the degree of increase of access frequency in circle T_i. When D_i is a negative number it present the degree of decrease of access frequency in circle T_i.

According to our idea, the node will shorten the scanning circle automatically when the frequency of accessing the file replicas of a node. But the node can lengthen the scanning circle automatically when this frequency is decrease. So we set increment t as the unit interval of modifying the scanning circle.

What we can get is that:

$$T_i = T_{i-1} - D_{i-1}t, i = 2, 3, 4...n \tag{12}$$

Plug formula (11) into formula (12):

$$T_i = T_{i-1} - \frac{A_{i-1} - A_{i-2}}{T_{i-1}}t, i = 2, 3, 4...n \tag{13}$$

Scanning frequency can be changed automatically according to formula (13), the adaptability will been strengthen.

C. The Selection Policy

According to what has been discussed above, $Node_x$ can tell when to add or delete file replica. To delete local replicas, only R_{inside} and $W_{outside}$ are needed to be judged. But to add a file replica on a node, which node should add new replica should be confirmed firstly. In the article above, $Node_x$ decides to add a replica on $Node_y$ is what has been limited by the article. Actually, $Node_x$ needs to tell which node should add a replica, this refers to the chosen of nodes.

We observe formula (6) again, and we can tell whether $Node_y$ needs to add a replica, the main element is $R_{outside-y}$. We can know it clearly that $Node_x$ can choose to read the node outside that have required most primarily. And then we can tell which node is in great need of copying file replica.

Under the condition of a large scale system, the quantity of the nodes that require to read $Node_x$ may be very big. Therefore, it is inadvisable to scan all the nodes that have make a reading requirement to tell whether the replica should be added. In addition, if we scan all nodes outside, may cause to a replica been continuously created and deleted, and then system thrashing will be produced. So we make a rule that the node tell whether it's necessary to add a file replica on a node outside can only according to the frequency of read requirement to the node from the nodes outside by the order. The time obtaining a node fit to formula (6) the scanning is stop, and wait for the next scanning circle.

4   The Adaptive Replication Algorithm

According to our policy, establishing file replicas of a fixed site and number in static replication management mechanism is according to the security of users, and their personalized requirements when the file entering the system, and ensure the usability and fault-tolerant ability of system. Then using distributed dynamic replication management mechanism to add or delete replica at a proper site in the process of the operation of the system. But can't delete the replicas established by using static policy, and ensure the system performance. Therefore, the lower limit of the number of replicas is determined according to the security and the personalized requirements of the users. No matter how the replicas change later. The file replicas cannot added unlimited. So we must set an upper limit for it according to the actual circumstances of the system.

According to what have been discussed above, we make definitions as follows:

- Defining the replication degree of a file replica as N_{min} according to the requirement of security and personalized from users.
- Defining the maximum replication degree of file replica as N_{max} in the whole system.

The replication degree of file replica is as formula (14)

$$N_{min} \leq N \leq N_{max} \tag{14}$$

Similarly, scanning circle could not increase or decrease unlimited, in order to avoid the cycle is too short or too long, you should also set a range for it, we set upper and lower limits as T_{min} and T_{max}, each cycle length T should within this range, that is to say:

$$T_{min} \leq T \leq T_{max} \tag{15}$$

The algorithm is executed in any one node in the system, each node has a set of counters for reading and writing, and a counter for scanning cycle. Therefore, we can list the main steps of The Adaptive Replication) Algorithm as follows:

1. Nodes wait for the timer of scanning cycle expires. If the system is initialized, the cycle is T_1.
2. $Node_i$ traverses all of its file replicas when the scanning cycle is times out. For each file, calculate it by reading or writing on the counter, traverse it according to the frequency of read requirement to the node from the nodes

outside by the order. Stop traversing when obtained the first $Node_y$ that matches formula (6) and judge formula (14). if the number of replicas of file does not meet the upper limit, add replicas of $Node_y$. Otherwise do not add one.

3. At the expiry of the scanning cycle, $Node_i$ traverse all of its own file replicas. For each file calculate it by using formula (9) by reading or writing on the counter. Judge formula (14) immediately if it's right. If it doesn't reach the lower limit of the number of replicas, then delete the replicas of this file. Otherwise do not delete the replicas.

4. When the step 2, 3 are finished, update the scanning cycle of this node according to formula (13). While the scanning cycle updated does not comply with formula (15), stop updating the scanning cycle.

5   Validation

To verify the replication management mechanism proposed in the previous chapter, now we use an experiment to be calculated.

We choose 20 distributed computers combined into a network and uses a file to test. For comparison, we used the other two mechanisms, namely the static replication management mechanism and the dynamic management mechanism with fixed scan time.

The parameters are set as follows:

$$T_1 = 20, N_{min} = 3, N_{max} = 5, T_{min} = 10, T_{max} = 600$$

The number of file replicas fixed to 3 when use static replication management mechanism, and the scanning circle is 20 s when use the dynamic management mechanism with fixed scan time. Request access to all nodes in accordance with "the nearest reads" principle to operate locally or at the most recent copy. After running test system for some time, statistics the operation count both the read operation for the file from remote node and the synchronization operation for the file (Table 1).

Table 1. The experimental result

Mechanism types	Operands
Static replication management mechanism	34,246
Dynamic management mechanism without fixed scan time	29,263
Static and dynamic combined replication management mechanism	19,896

From the results, we can see that the proposed adaptive static and dynamic combined replication management mechanism greatly reduced for 58 % of operands for the static replication management mechanism, and reduced for 68 % of operands for the dynamic management mechanism with fixed scan time.

6   Conclusion

This paper have discussed a kind of adaptive static and dynamic combined replication management mechanism based on file replica access frequency, aiming at solving a series of problems exist in the static replication management mechanism and the dynamic management mechanism. Increase the expandability and system performance.

Acknowledgements. This work was supported by the National Natural Science Foundation of China (No.61365010). This work was also supported in part by China National Natural Science Foundation under Grants 61300224, the International Science and Technology Collaboration Program (2014DFT10070) funded by China Ministry of Science and Technology (MOST), Hubei Provincial Key Project under grant 2013CFA051.

References

1. Armbrust, M., et al.: A view of cloud computing. Commun. ACM **53**(4), 50–58 (2010)
2. Zhang, Y., et al.: CAP: crowd activity prediction based on big data analysis. IEEE Netw. **28**(4), 52–57 (2014)
3. Weiss, A.: Computing in the clouds. Networker **11**(4), 16–25 (2007)
4. Liu, P.: Cloud Computing, 2nd edn. Electronic Industry Press, Beijing (2011)
5. Wang, P.: Key Technologies of Cloud Computing and Its Application. Post & Telecom Press, Beijing (2010)
6. Vouk, M.A.: Cloud computing-issues, research and implementations. J. Comput. Inf. Technol. (CIT) **16**(4), 235–246 (2008)
7. Venugopal, S., Buyya, R., Ramamohanarao, K.: A taxonomy of data grids for distributed data sharing, management, and processing. ACM Comput. Surv. (CSUR) **38**(1), 3 (2006)
8. Chang, R.S., Chang, H.P., Wang, Y.T.: A dynamic weighted data replication strategy in data grids. In: IEEE/ACS International Conference on Computer Systems and Applications (AICCSA), pp. 414–421. IEEE (2008)
9. Khaneghah, E.M., et al.: A Dynamic replication mechanism to reduce response-time of I/O operations in high performance computing clusters. In: International Conference on Social Computing(SocialCom), pp. 738–743. IEEE (2013)
10. Xin, S., et al.: Dynamic data replication based on access cost in distributed systems. In: International Conference on Computer Sciences and Convergence Information Technology. IEEE (2009)
11. Hegde, S.: Replication in Distributed File Systems. Department of Computer Science 3(06), University of Texas at Arlington (2011)

A Distributed Business Process Collaboration Architecture Based on Entropy in Cloud Computing

Qi Mo[1], Fei Dai[1(✉)], Rui Zhu[1], Jian Da[2], Leilei Lin[1], and Tong Li[1]

[1] School of Software, Yunnan University, Kunming 650091, China
moqiyueyang@163.com, {59671019,522015032,
370145235}@qq.com, tli@ynu.edu.cn
[2] Department of Information Engineering, Huai'an Senior Vocational
and Technical School, Huai'an 212901, China
5550129@qq.com

Abstract. Business process collaboration enable organizations to communication, interact and cooperate with each other to achieve specific business goals. Currently, the research work on business process mainly focus on the modelling and analysis for their organization structure or interactive relationship. This paper study business process collaboration from the view of software architecture, a distributed architecture called "agent end + stockholder end" is proposed, by analyzing the collaboration architecture finds, in the case of the participation organizations are given, determining the agents in collaboration and the participation organizations in every management region becomes the key for effective collaborating. For this reason, with the help of fuzzy cluster to determine the membership matrix and clustering centers firstly in this paper, then the best number of agent is determined through agent entropy, and thus the set of participation organizations in every management region are determined. Experiment results show that the method proposed in this paper is feasible and effective.

Keywords: Cloud computing · Software architecture · Business process collaboration · "agent end + stockholder end" · Entropy

1 Introduction

With the development of economic globalization and the advancement of enterprises' information, the manage models of enterprises has taken place a great change, the business of enterprises have changed form a signal goal oriented represents an independent model to the model that represents multi-goals cooperation crossing organizational boundaries [1]. In the context of modern business, especially with the

This work was financially supported by the National Natural Science Foundation of China (61262024,61379032,61462095), Yunnan Natural Science Foundation (2012FD005), Science Research Foundation of Yunnan Department of Education (2013Y365) and Open Foundation of Key Laboratory for Software Engineering of Yunnan Province (2012SE307).

© Institute for Computer Sciences, Social Informatics and Telecommunications Engineering 2015
V.C.M. Leung et al. (Eds.): CloudComp 2014, LNICST 142, pp. 126–134, 2015.
DOI: 10.1007/978-3-319-16050-4_12

development of cloud computing and Big Data [19, 20, 21], there is not an enterprise is isolated. An enterprise as a participant participates the business collaboration, and they interact with others to complete the particular business function in the process of collaboration. Business process is an important research field in industry information system [2, 3], a business process is used to describe the activities in an organization and the relationships among organizations in order to achieve the given business goal [4]. With regard to the cross-organizational business process, because of involving many organizational process units, crossing the boundaries of organizations, in the cross-organizational enterprise information system [5, 6, 7, 8] and the context of e-commerce [9], it focuses on the flow relationship between business function and manufacturer activities. Its main task is to via the information systems respectively, different enterprises can cooperate and collaborate conveniently in business [10] used to complete specific business goal, it plays a more and more important role in the context of business.

Currently, researches on business process collaboration mainly focus on modeling. Namely through some formal methods, i.e., Petri Net, CCS(A Calculus of Communicating Systems), Pi Calculus and so on, to model the structure and interactive behaviors of cross-organizational business process collaboration, then verifying some properties of established model, such as Sound, Consistent and so on. [12] proposes IOWF(International Organization Workflow) used to model the Inter-organizational Workflows based on WF-net(Workflow Net) and Colored Petri Nets; [13] proposes a method to model the business process of Web Service form internal and external view; [14] proposes to use WF-net to describe the private process inside an organization and providing interactive interfaces for external environment, then using Interaction-Oriented Petri Nets model to define the interactive relationship between organizational business processes based on WF-net, [15] proposes the Open Workflow Nets to model cross-organizational business process, and then supporting a design by contract; [16] proposes a method that combines Petri Net and Pi Calculus, proposing to model local flow of business process based Petri Net and model interactive behaviors of business process based on Pi Calculus; [17] proposes a model called OTRM-Net and used to describe the task coordination patterns and disposal process in the emergency response systems formally.

The typical researches above belong to the range of modeling for organization structure in business process collaboration, there are rare literatures discuss the business process collaboration from the view of architecture. Therefore, an architecture called "agent end + stockholder end" is proposed, and discusses the method for determining agents in this architecture and organizations partition. The main contributions cover:

(1) This paper propose a new distributed business process collaboration architecture called "agent end + stockholder end" and define it formally, which can discuss business process collaboration form macroscopic view.
(2) For this distributed collaboration architecture, in the case of the participation organizations are given, how to determine the agents in collaboration and the participation organizations in every management region becomes the key for efficient collaborating. For this reason, this paper uses fuzzy cluster to determine the membership matrix and clustering centers firstly, then the best number of agent determined through agent entropy, and then the set of participation

organizations in every management region are determined, which can conduct the structure for collaboration applications.

The rest of this paper is organized as follows. Section 2 discusses the system architecture for business process collaboration; Sect. 3 discusses the method for determining agents in this architecture and the method for organizations partition based on entropy and Fuzzy Cluster; Sect. 4 is the experiment and results discussion; Sect. 5 concludes and presents our future work.

2   System Architecture for Business Process Collaboration

Business process collaboration has two obvious characteristics: (1) the autonomous character of participation organizations. The participant organizations has the right of control for resources provided by themselves, the authority for accessing resources determined by organizations and organizations determines whether join or quit the business process collaboration. (2) goals drive. In the time of some specific business goals are needed to complete, some organizations are needed to select dynamically in cooperation with each other to complete some specific business goals timely. The characteristics above possessed by business process collaboration can be used for autonomous character of services provided by organizations and has a full right of control for their resources. At the same time, business process collaboration asks for combining organizations to achieve some specific business goals, however, the dynamics caused by the autonomous character of organizations may lead to complete business goals unsuccessfully. So in the basis of the autonomous character of organizations guarantees, there are some man or organizations select members dynamically and some constraints and control strategies are settled to complete some specific business goals. At the same time, there is a mechanism which can make perception and reaction timely when the organization members change in the process of collaboration,

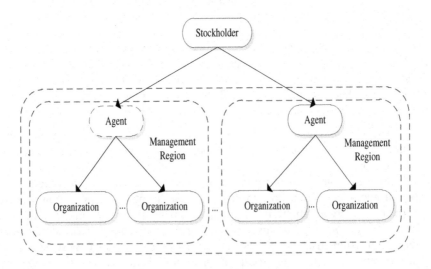

Fig. 1. Business process collaboration architecture

and make some adjustments to business process collaboration to keep it in operation sostenuto. In this paper, this type of the man or organizations is called stakeholder. At the same time, for alleviating the load of communication and monitoring of stockholder in collaboration process, several agents are established using for cooperating work of stockholder to collaborate efficiently. The conceptual model of business process collaboration architecture in this paper is shown in Fig. 1.

From the Fig. 1, we can see that the business process collaboration architecture, namely "agent end + stockholder end" is a model with three levels. The lowest level is organization level, some diversities exist among participation organizations, the whole collaboration process is composed by organizations and the communications among organizations; the middle level is agent level, for a category of similar organizations, there is an agent in charge of monitoring the operation situations of this category of organizations and a management region is produced, and when an organization can't provide services sequentially, the agent reports to stockholders timely; the top level is stockholder level, though the communications between the agents, the stockholder can learn the changes of organizations and react, also can monitor the operation situations of agents.

2.1 The Formal Definition for Business Process Collaboration Architecture

Definition 1 (Organization). Let $org_1, \ldots, org_n$ are the all organizations in business collaboration, the set $Org = \{org_1, \ldots, org_n\}$ is called organization region in business process collaboration, for $\forall org_i \in Org$ can be defined formally as a two-tuples $Org_i = (id, I)$, where,

(1) *id* is used to identity an organization uniquely in collaboration process;
(2) the set $I = \{I_1, \ldots, I_m\}$ is m-dimension measurement index, its measurement value are $v_1, \ldots, v_m$, and every element I_i is called decision factor, which is used to determine this organization belongs to.

Definition 2 (Agent). Let $agent_1, \ldots, agent_n$ are the all agents in business collaboration, the set $Agent = \{agent_1, \ldots, agent_n\}$ is called agent region in business process collaboration, for $\forall agent_i \in Agent$ can be defined formally as a three -tuples $agent_i = (id, Org, R)$, where,

(1) *id* is used to identity an agent uniquely in collaboration process;
(2) the set $Org = \{org_1, \ldots, org_m\}$ is the set of similar organizations which the number is m, called a management region;
(3) $R \subseteq agent_i \times Org \cup Org \times agent_i$ is "agent-organization" flow relationship.

Definition 3 (Business Process Collaboration Architecture). Let the set $Org = \{org_1, \ldots, org_n\}$ and the set $Agent = \{agent_1, \ldots, agent_n\}$ are organization region and agent region respectively in business process collaboration, then the whole of business process collaboration architecture can be defined formally as a three-tuples $BPA = (stockholder, Org, Agent, R)$, where,

(1) *stockholder* is stockholder;
(2) $R \subseteq Agent \times stockholder \cup stockholder \times Agent$ is "stockholder–agent" flow relationship.

3 Agent Determination and Organization Partition Based on Entropy and Fuzzy Cluster

From the Sect. 2 above, we can know that for the specific business goals, different organizations combine to achieve the solution for problems in the way of collaboration in the business process collaboration architecture. Because of the autonomous character of participation organizations, which needs corresponding man or organization, namely stockholders, to select members dynamically and some constraints and control strategies are settled to complete some specific business goals successfully. In one process of collaboration, there are a large number of organizations, for alleviating the load of communication and monitoring of stockholder, it is reasonable to set several agents using for cooperating work of stockholder in collaboration architecture. In the specific architecture, to processed with the collaboration work effectively, agent determination and organization partition become a key issue in the design of business process collaboration architecture, namely in the case of the participation organizations are given, how to determine the agents and the participation organizations included in every management region.

3.1 Fuzzy Cluster for Participation Organizations

In this paper, fuzzy cluster is used to get the membership matrix and clustering centers in the case of the number of agents C ($2 \leq C \leq N$, N denotes the number of participation organizations) is given, and the membership matrix and clustering centers are the basis for agent determination and organization partition based on entropy in next section. So algorithm 1 is proposed to get the membership matrix and clustering centers.

Algorithm 1. Obtaining the membership matrix and clustering centers
Input: the set of participation organizations $Org = \{org_1, \ldots, org_n\}$, the number of agents C ($2 \leq C \leq N$), fuzzy-weighted coefficient m, Matrix A and iteration stop threshold value ε;
Output: the set of membership matrix M and the set of clustering centers C.
Step 1. Structuring the measure index matrix K for the set of participation organizations $Org = \{org_1, \ldots, org_n\}$, for $\forall$ v_{ij} in K, taking a normalization, namely, when v_{ij} is positive increment dimension value, such as validity, reliability and so on, processing it by formula $v'_{ij} = \frac{v_{ij} - r^j_{min}}{r^j_{max} - r^j_{min}}$, while the v_{ij} is positive decrease dimension value, such as response time, cost and so on, processing it by formula $v'_{ij} = \frac{v_{ij} - r^j_{min}}{r^j_{max} - r^j_{min}}$, while the v_{ij} is positive decrease dimension value, such as response time, cost and so on, processing it by formula $v'_{ij} = \frac{r^j_{max} - v_{ij}}{r^j_{max} - r^j_{min}}$, obtaining the normalization matrix K' lastly.

Step 2. For the number of agents C $(2 \le C \le N)$, clustering it by applying the fuzzy C-mean cluster algorithm [17], when ε satisfies, the algorithm stops and records the membership matrix and clustering centers to C.

Step 3. For every C, outputting the membership matrix and clustering centers.

3.2   Agent Determination and Organization Partition Based on Entropy

In the information theory, information entropy is used to measure the uncertainty of event, we can obtain information content after the event occurs. Information content denotes the information entropy before the event occurs minus the information entropy after the event occurs.

For the discrete and immemorial information source, if the space of probability is $[X, P] = [x_k, p_k | k = 1, 2, .., N]$, then the uncertainty of information source denotes $H(X)$, namely the entropy of information source X, its calculation formulate is $H(X) = \sum_k p_k \log \frac{1}{p_k}$.

Let the C is the number of agents and U is the membership matrix obtained by algorithm 1, then agent entropy $H(C)$ is defined as follows,

(1) when $\mu_{ij} \ne 0$, then $H(C) = -\frac{1}{N} \sum_{i=1}^{C} \sum_{j=1}^{N} \mu_{ij} \ln(\mu_{ij})$;

(2) when $\mu_{ij} = 0$, then $H(C) = 0$.

Theorem 1. agent entropy has some properties as follows:

(1) $0 \le H(C) \le \ln(C)$;
(2) when U is hard partition, $H(C) = 0$;
(3) when $\mu_{ij} = 1/C$, $H(C) = \ln(C)$.
     Proving this theorem is very simply, it is limited to the length of this article, so the process omits.

For the different C, there is different agent entropy $H(C)$, if there is a C^* can lead to minimum $H(C)$, then C^* is the best number of cluster, combining with the membership matrix and clustering centers obtained by algorithm 1, thus the agents and the participation organizations included in every management region can be determined in the collaboration architecture. So algorithm 2 is proposed for this purposes.

Algorithm 2. Determining the agents and the organizations partition
Input: the number of agents C $(2 \le C \le N)$, the set of membership matrix $M = \{A_1, \ldots, A_C\}$ and the set of clustering centers $C = \{B_1, \ldots, B_C\}$;
Output: the set of agents $Agent = \{agent_1, \ldots, agent_k\}$ and the set of organizations in every management region $Org = \{Org_1, \ldots, Org_k\}$.
Step 1. Computing the agent entropy according to the corresponding membership matrix to C obtains the set of agent entropy $AE = \{ae_1, \ldots, ae_k\}$;
Step 2. Taking a normalization to AE, namely $AE' = \{ae_1/\ln(C_1), \ldots, ae_k/\ln(C_k)\}$;
Step 3. Outputting $C_i = \arg \min_i AE'$, and the corresponding clustering centers and the set of cluster to C_i.

4 Experiment and Analysis

For illustrating the effectiveness of the method proposed in this paper, supposing there are sixty eight organizations $Org = \{org_1, \ldots, org_{68}\}$ in a supply chain. Generally, the measure indexes of organizations can be obtained by two way: (1) the data collected in practice. (2) the data is generated randomly by computer simulation. In this paper, we adopt the second way, and for the simpleness, supposing every organization has only two measure indexes. Algorithm 1 and algorithm 2 are realized by Matlab, and the fuzzy-weighted coefficient is 2, matrix A is unit matrix and iteration stop threshold value is $\varepsilon = e^{-5}$.

Table 1. The relationship among C, H(C), H(C)/lnC and PI

C	H(C)	H(C)/ln(C)	PI
2	0.2878	0.4152	0.8319
3	0.2878	0.4152	0.7919
4	0.2878	0.4152	0.7257
5	0.2878	0.4152	0.7039
6	0.2878	0.4152	0.7523
7	0.2878	0.4152	0.8066
8	0.2878	0.4152	0.8596
9	0.2878	0.4152	0.8336
10	0.2878	0.4152	0.8007

4.1 Results Analysis

The number of agents C, the agent entropy $H(C)$, normalization agent entropy $H(C)/\ln C$ obtained by algorithms 1 and 2 is shown in Table 1. It is limit to the length of this paper, only the front of 10 items is listed, because of the rest of items' $H(C)/\ln C$ all less than $H(8)/\ln 8$, which is not affect the discussion below so omits. The partition index(PI) [18], which is a valid index in fuzzy cluster also is listed in Table 1, only the front of 10 items is listed, because of the rest of items' PI all greater than $PI(C = 8)$, so omits.

Table 2. The relationship between organizations and region

Management region	Participation organizations
1	org_{16}, org_{17}, org_{18}, org_{19}, org_{20}, org_{21}, org_{22}, org_{23}, org_{24}
2	org_8, org_9, org_{10}, org_{11}, org_{12}, org_{13}, org_{14}, org_{15}
3	org_{33}, org_{34}, org_{35}, org_{36}, org_{37}, org_{38}, org_{39}, org_{40}, org_{41}
4	org_{60}, org_{61}, org_{62}, org_{63}, org_{64}, org_{65}, org_{66}, org_{67}, org_{68}
5	org_1, org_2, org_3, org_4, org_5, org_6, org_7
6	org_{42}, org_{43}, org_{44}, org_{45}, org_{46}, org_{47}, org_{48}, org_{49}, org_{50}, org_{51}, org_{52}
7	org_{53}, org_{54}, org_{55}, org_{56}, org_{57}, org_{58}, org_{59}
8	org_{25}, org_{26}, org_{27}, org_{28}, org_{29}, org_{30}, org_{31}, org_{32}

Form the Table 1, we can know that when $C = 8$, the $H(C)/\ln C$ gets the minimum value, so we can get the conclusion that $C = 8$ is the best number of agents. Comparing with the PI, we can see that when $C = 8$, the partition index get the maximum value, so a conclusion can be drawn that the method proposed in this paper is valid.

$C = 8$ is the best number of agents which got by analysis in Table 1, so according to algorithm 2, the participation organizations included in every management region can be obtained and is shown in Table 2, thus the collaboration architecture of this supply chain is determined.

5 Conclusions and Future Work

Currently, the researches on business process mainly focus on the modelling and analysis for their organization structure or interactive relationship, there are rare literatures pay attention to the business process collaboration from the view of architecture. Therefore, an architecture called "agent end + stockholder end" is proposed, and then the agents in collaboration architecture and organizations partition is determined though information entropy and fuzzy cluster, which can discuss business process collaboration form macroscopic view and conduct the structure for collaboration applications.

Future work involves two aspects as follows: (1) the formal description and verification for this collaboration architecture; (2) discussing the schedule issues specifically based on collaboration architecture.

References

1. Lu, Y.-h., Ming, Z., Zhang, L.: Collaboration patterns of business process (in Chinese). J. Comput. Integr. Manuf. Syst. **17**, 1570–1579 (2011)
2. Rosa, M.L., ter Hofstede, A., Wohed, P., Reijers, H., Mendling, J., van der Aalst, W.: Managing process model complexity via concrete syntax modifications. J. IEEE Trans. Industr. Inf. **7**, 255–265 (2011)
3. Rosa, M.L., Wohed, P., Mendling, J., ter Hofstede, A., Reijers, H., van der Aalst, W.: Managing process model complexity via abstract syntax modifications. J. IEEE Trans. Industr. Inf. **7**, 614–629 (2011)
4. Workflow Management Coalition: 'Workflow management coalition terminology and glossary'. http://www.wfmc.org/
5. Li, S., Xu, L., Wang, X., Wang, J.: Integration of hybrid wireless networks in cloud services oriented enterprise information systems. J. Enterp. Inf. System **6**, 165–187 (2012)
6. Wang, K., Bai, X., Li, J.: C. Ding.: A service-based framework for pharmacogenomics data integration. J. Enterp. Inf. Syst. **4**, 225–245 (2010)
7. Xu, L.: Enterprise systems: State-of-the-art and future trends. J. IEEE Trans. Indust. Inf. **7**, 630–640 (2011)
8. Zdravković, M., Panetto, H., Trajanovic, M., Aubry, A.: An approach for formalizing the supply chain operations. J. Enterp. Inf. Syst. **5**, 401–421 (2011)
9. Guo, J., Xu, L., Gong, Z., Che, C.-P., Chaudhry, S.: Semantic inference on heterogeneous E-marketplace activities. J. IEEE Trans. Syst. Man, Cybern. Part A: Syst. Hum. **5**, 401–421 (2012)

10. Guo, J.: Collaboration role in semantic integration for electronic marketplace. J. Int. J. Electron. Bus **8**, 528–549 (2010)
11. van der Aalst, W.M.P.: Modeling and analyzing interorganizational workflows. In: 1st International Conference on Application of Concurrency to System Design, pp. 262–272. IEEE Press, Washington, DC (1998)
12. Li, X.-T., Fan, Y.-S.: Analyzing compatibility and similarity of web service processes (in Chinese). Chin. J. Comput. **32**, 2429–2437 (2009)
13. Ji-Dong, G.E., Hu, H.-Y., Zhou, Y., Hu, H., Wang, D.-Y.: A decomposition approach with invariant analysis for workflow coordination (in Chinese). Chin. J. Comput. **35**, 2169–2181 (2012)
14. van der Aalst, W.M.P., Lohmann, N., Massuthe, P., Stahl, C., Wolf, K.: Multiparty contracts: agreeing and implementing inter-organizational processes. Comput. J. **53**, 90–106 (2010)
15. Zhang, L., Lu, Y., Xu, F.: Unified modelling and analysis of collaboration business process based on Petri nets and Pi calculus. J. IET Softw. **4**, 303–317 (2010)
16. Zeng, Q.-T., Lu, F.-M., Liu, C., Meng, D.-C.: Modeling and analysis for cross-organizational emergency response systems using Petri nets (in Chinese). Chin. J. Comput. **36**, 2291–2301 (2013)
17. Bezdek, J.C.: Pattern Recognition with Fuzzy Objective Function Algorithm. Plenum Press, New York (1981)
18. Pedrycz, W.: Knowledge-Based Clustering: From Data to Information Granules. Wiley Press, Hoboken (2005)
19. Zhang, Y., Chen, M., Mao, S., Hu, L., Leung, V.: CAP: crowd activity prediction based on big data analysis. J. IEEE Netw. **28**, 52–57 (2014)
20. Chen, M., Mao, S., Zhang, Y., Leung, V.: Big Data: Related Technologies, Challenges and Future Prospects. Springer, New York (2014)
21. Chen, M., Mao, S., Liu, Y.: Big data: a survey. J. ACM/Springer Mob. Netw. Appl. **19**, 171–209 (2014)

DSBAF: Running My Web Services in Your WS Environment

Junhui Liu[1,2], Zhenli He[1,2], Di Jiang[1,2], and Lei Su[1,2(✉)]

[1] School of Software, Yunnan University, Kunming 650091, Yunnan, China
[2] Kunming University of Science and Technology, Kunming 650093, China
s28341@hotmail.com, hezhenli1987@qq.com,
{HanksLau, alexjiang.yn}@gmail.com

Abstract. SaaS is the research hotspot of cloud computing in the software application layer. With the wide application of Web services composition technology, Web services interaction becomes more and more complex, while the static Web service behavior adaptation method is difficult to support complex behavioral adaptation between Web services. This paper presents a behavior adaptation model BAM and adaptation framework DSBAF with dynamic Web service behavior adaptation. The method which complete Web service adaptation by the engine driven execution unit with behavioral adaptation separate modeling and dynamic loading the adapter framework model is able to dynamically complete Web service adaptation; Furthermore, the use of behavioral adaptation model can build a virtual service on DSBAF at run time, which will make our Web service operate in the external environment.

Keywords: SaaS · SOC · Service adaptation · Static adaptation · Dynamic behavior adaptation

1 Introduction

With the rapid development of cloud computing, the enterprise more and more widely accept cloud computing and business function built above the cloud services. Cloud computing deem that all resources are in service [1], which performance for the software as a service (SaaS) [2] in the software application layer. SaaS is calculated using Service Oriented on the concrete implementation(Service - Oriented Computing, SOC) [3], which use serve as the basic unit of building software, and through the Service composition to achieve the software application of rapid low cost under the heterogeneous environment. At present, Web service has become the fact standards of the Internet service encapsulation and the best implementation framework of SOC. And the Web service has characteristics of heterogeneity, dynamic, distributed and the continuous changes of specific software function in the Web services encapsulate make the synergistic interaction between Web services becomes exceptionally complex, how to ensure correct solid interaction between Web services becomes the key to promote a SaaS application and implementation. Web service adapter technology provides a feasible solution to solve the problem, it can make the service that originally not correct coordinated correctly complete the work together under the intervention of service

© Institute for Computer Sciences, Social Informatics and Telecommunications Engineering 2015
V.C.M. Leung et al. (Eds.): CloudComp 2014, LNICST 142, pp. 135–144, 2015.
DOI: 10.1007/978-3-319-16050-4_13

adaptation. At the same time, along with the application of Web service composition, service behavior interaction and cooperation become increasingly complex. Currently, widely use the static service behavior adaptation mechanism is difficult to support complex behavioral adaptation between services. Service behavior adaptation framework for complex service behavior of dynamic and flexible is of great significance to further promotion of the implementation and application of SaaS.

2 Related Work

Web service adaptation [4] refers to making a Web service can present the desired service after adapter encapsulation through an adapter, and the adapter as the intermediary between the two Web services making the two incompatible Web services can work coordinately [5]. At this stage, the research based on Web service adaptation is mainly focus on the grammar adaptation, behavior adaptation, semantic adaptation and non-functional adaptation [6]. Grammar adaptation construct service interface model from the grammar, which resolve the mismatch problem of service in the method name, the parameter name, type name, complex type data structure, the types of method, parameter type, abnormal type, the parameter sequence and number of parameters such as inconsistent situations; Interaction between behavioral adaptation for service build service interface model, solve the mismatch problems of service in the message interaction sequence inconsistency, redundancy and information loss case; Semantic adaptation will understand service interface semantic as ontology, it build the service interface model based on ontology concept, and solve the mismatch problems of service semantic description which is not consistent or services do not fully meet the demand of system caused, such as the conceptual approximation, conceptual contain and conceptual equivalence; Nonfunctional adaptation, also called the quality adaptation, quality attributes building service interface model based on service, solving the mismatch problem during services in safety, persistence, transaction, reliability and performance of such inconsistency case. This paper is aimed at the behavioral adaptation of Web service.

The industry proposed many solutions in terms of Web service behavior adaptation. In [7, 8], Brogi et al. propose the adaptation method based on the service execution path, we used the YAWL service modeling. In [9], Massuthe proposes pattern matching method based on automation theory. This method has made a lot of simplification, the service behavior is difficult to apply in actual adaptation process. In [10], Massuthealso put forward a kind of pattern matching method. What is different is that the method uses extended Petri net, namely, Open workflow nets modeling for service behavior to describe the external interface of the service. In [11], also is based on the thought pattern matching, but only for finite state service. In [12] Gierds proposes a method for generating the adapter based on the transformation rules. The method can be applied to any service adaptation in theory. In [13], presented a service whose adapter is generated by using mismatch tree, and eliminating the service interface and the agreement does not match. In [14], Sinha proposes the method that generating adapter by model test, this method determines the existence of the adapter using the tableau based on algorithm, and if there exists an adapter, then automatically generate adapter's custom fairness constraints.

According to the researches above, behavioral adaptation of Web service focused on the analysis of the service behavior of static and adaptation issues. The static behavior of a Web service adaptation considers almost all of the operating conditions of system at the system design stage, modeling for Web service behavior and the process of their interactions, and building the adapter after analyzing the mismatching points of Web service interaction according to the model. In the current dynamic and changeable Web service application environment, mainly exist the following problems:

(1) Failing to support the dynamic evolution or update of Web services. Static Web service adaptation method is set ahead of the Web service operation, Unable to adjust dynamically at runtime. On the one hand, the system design is not able to consider all possible operating conditions, if there's an unexpected situation in the process of design, it will lead to the exception of system during operation; on the other hand, SOC attach great importance to the synergistic combination of characteristics and replaceable characteristics among the services. For real-time demand of the users, we can complete the goal function by using Web services dynamic combination, the user's demand changing and the system all the time in the evolution of the dynamic or update, how to maintain the adapter synchronous evolution or update and the consistency of the system operation is unable to solve by static adaptation method.

(2) The complexity of the complex service adaptation is too high and cost too much. For simple Web services, it contains only the temporal logic behavior of order, single path, analysis and adaptation by using static adaptation method, which the process is simple. However, with the service behavior tends to be complex, it will be a heavy task that analyzing and making sure all possible path. In addition, the static adaptation method system mostly is a conceptual model now, which lacks of concrete frame in the specific application process.

3 Dynamic Web Service Behavior Adaptation

Dynamic Web service behavior adaptation will delay the service behavior, compatibility analysis and adaptation of design stage to operation stage, and can change dynamically adaptation at runtime. The essence of dynamic behavior of a Web service adaptation is the design and implementation of a generic adaptation framework, which mapping the service agreement and protocol interface of two services as input, and by the engine dynamically creating and managing the behavior adaptation execution unit of the two service. Behavioral adaptation execution unit is a general intelligence unit, which can dynamically load behavior adaptation model and avoid the type expansion of adapter, at the same time, it can dynamically perceive, dynamically receive, process and forward service message. Behavioral adaptation model modeling for complex service adaptation, which covers the complex service adapter logic and service composition, and has the ability of dynamically update and replace. From this, we can see that the key of dynamic behavior of a Web service adaptation are two parts which are of behavioral adaptation model and adaptation framework.

3.1   Behavior Adaptation Model (BAM)

Web services with uniform behavior in the external message communication have encapsulated the realization of the concrete function. From the generalized Web service matching point of view, we can undertake message transformation, external perform logic and composite service behavior operations. Behavioral adaptation model (BAM) will match the various behaviors in the process of abstraction for three main bodies of Behaviors, Behavior Actions and Operation, which modeling by its behavior scene. As shown in Fig. 1:

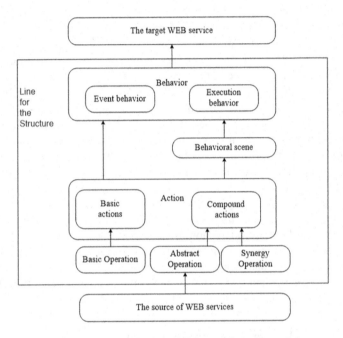

Fig. 1. Behavior adaptation model structure

(1) BAM behavior modeling service behavior can be divided into two types: event behavior and executing behavior. Execution behavior describes the logic in the collection of service adapter, which is performed a process execution according to certain strategy. Event behavior describes the place collection in the service adaptation, occurrence is produced within the framework and have influence on the service adapter. Event behavior and execution behavior are described in the operation, they are associated with specific specification, executing code values as well as the service interface, and modeling in the behavior scene;

(2) Action is the foundation behavior unit of BAM and the basis of the behavior semantics. Action can accomplish a behavior directly, but also can through multiple action cooperate complete a complex behavior. Action is divided into basic actions and composite actions, basic action execution framework itself provides basic moves support behavior, such as the Exception Action, Variable

Action, the Message Action, etc.; Composite action is the action of pointing to Web services composition and formation, which contains a specific Web service object and the behavior concept in relations, and It consists of the abstract operation and cooperative operation;

(3) Basic operation is support to basic actions, abstraction and collaborative operation together support actions. Abstract operation is an abstract for concrete implementation operation, it describes structured interface information of operation and corresponds to the concrete realization of atomic operation service; Collaborative operation is build on the basis of the actions in the form of action scene, which contains basic, abstract and other collaborative operations, at the same time, collaborative operations have consistent structured interface information with abstract operation;

(4) Behavior scene is behavior actions container, which explains a series of actions of adaptation behavior, and describes an implementation process of adaptation, it modeling with the perspective of behavior process, and provide the execution environment for the Action. Behavior scene appears as a whole in the form of operation, can directly form behaviors for the target service, can also be converted into coordinated operations, it is the main body to describe the collaborative operation.

3.2   Dynamic Web Service Behavior Adaptation Framework (DSBAF)

BAM can completely describe adaptation behavior, but need the corresponding infrastructure to complete the service adaptation operation. DSBAF model of Web services based on business document exchange, which dynamically loading and parsing the BAM, calling the source Web services, and adaptation convert into target virtual service. Its function structure as shown in Fig. 2:

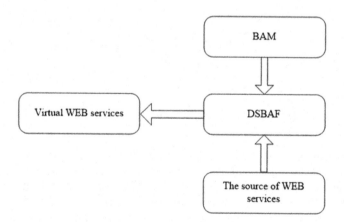

Fig. 2. DSBAF function structure

Web services based on XML, using SOAP protocol, is a kind of cross-platform interoperability specification. From the point of view of data exchange, the Web service is the software entities to realize the WSDL and SOAP standard business document exchange. SOAP message as a business document with business identification and business data set, can be dynamically generated and analyzed. SOAP communication is an exchange process that SOAP service call request message and return message as a result, it is an exchange process of SOAP standard business document, we can complete SOAP communication process through dynamical parsing and generating of SOAP business document, replace the binding of traditional Web service and function that communication process realize standard Web service calls. Web service release also can be regarded as an exchange process of WSDL document. DSBAF using Web services model of document exchange, documenting SOAP and WSDL, implementing Web services behavior adaptation by business documents mapping, its structure as shown in Fig. 3:

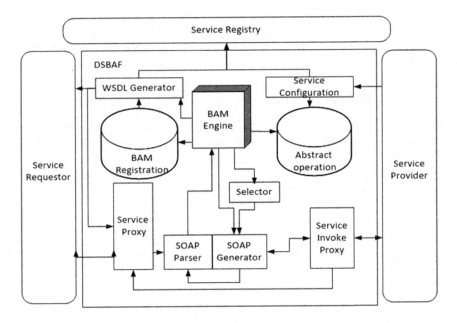

Fig. 3. Dynamic web service behavior adaptation framework

(1) BAM engine is the main part of the behavior adaptation model execution parsing, including a controller and multiple independent execution units. BAM model itself does not execute directly, it need to extract the behavior scene of BAM. The execution unit load and execute the intermediate code of BAM behavioral scene. Execution unit can dynamically load, Purge, suspend and resume the BAM behavioral scene intermediate code and behavior execution environment, at the same time, multiple execution units can form cluster, communicate with each other and cooperate through the messages, but Coupling

degree is low. This structure is very suitable for distributed execution environment. Perform controller provides the global environment, message soft bus and the control for execution and collaboration of execution unit, at the same time, provide the unity facade with the outer frame interaction for BAM engine.

(2) It formed the abstract operation information in the process of DSBAF parsing and compiling on BAM, which contains all the abstract operating information in the BAM, and the basic information of the corresponding external Web service set and runtime information. Abstract operation registration information is a structured data set (Table 1):

Table 1. Abstract operation registration information

ModelID		XDSM model identification, as the namespace of behavior scene;
AbstractOperation	Name	Abstract operation name;
	InputPin	The input of the abstract operation;
	OutputPin	The output of the abstract operation;
ServiceCount		The WEB service number of implementation abstract operation;
Service0	Name	Opration Name of the WEB services;
	URL	The URL address of WEB service;
	Protocol	The binding agreement of WEB service ;
	SOAP	SOAP binding information Corresponding to the WEB service;
	WSDL	WSDL service description corresponding to the WEB services ;
	InputMap	Document matching script information of service input;
	OutputMap	Document matching script information of service output;
	ResponseTime	The run-time information, the service average response time;
	Loaded	The run-time information, loading of service calling;
ServiceN	.....	With Message0, tied for description;

(3) DSBAF formed BAM registration information in compiling and Analysis process of BAM, it is the WS specification and Message specification of virtual service, scene matching Main Operation that action scene corresponding published in the BAM registration information and each Message formed a virtual Web services. The BAM registration information is a structured data set (Table 2):

Table 2. The BAM registration information

ModelID		The BAM model identification, as namespace of behavioral scene;
BSID		Behavioral scene unique identifier;
IsPublic		whether behavior scenarios publish identification;
MainOperation	Name	The main operation name of the action scene represented;
	InputPin	The input of the main operation tied;
	OutputPin	The output of the main operation tied;
MessageCount		The number which receives the message in the behavior scene;
Message0	MessageID	Message0 corresponding MessageID, for its unique identification;
	InputPin	Message0 input tied;
	OutputPin	Message0 output tied;
MessageN	.....	With Message0, tied for description;

(4) Service agent is the agent of Service Requestor and DSBAF interaction, which complete the SOAP protocol specification according to the Web services standards, receive Web Service requests (SOAP Service call request, WSDL request) and return the corresponding results (SOAP service return, SOAP service error return, WSDL service description), so the Service Requestor can use virtual Web services transparently and standardized.

(5) There are two aspects of functionality to the SOAP parser, On the one hand, calling request document on the basis of the SOAP service of BAM registration information parsing service agent receives, converted into action scenario and executed request message document, and sent to the BAM engine execution unit; On the other hand, calling the SOAP service results of agent receives based on abstract operation information parsing service returned documents and converted into abstract operation execution return message document, and which is sent to BAM engine execution units.

(6) There are two aspects functionality to the SOAP Generator, On the one hand, parsing BAM executed result message document of BAM engine unit returned basis on the BAM registration information, which convert into SOAP service results return documents, and transmitted to the service agent. On the other hand, abstract operation execution request message document on the basis of the abstract operation information analysis by Selector determined convert the SOAP service call request document, and sent to the service call agent.

(7) Service Invoke Proxy is the agent of DSBAF and Service Provider interactions according to the Web services standards to complete the SOAP protocol specification and protocol bindings, send Web Service call request and access to the

Web Service invocation corresponding results (SOAP Service results back, SOAP Service error return), so the DSBAF can transparently and standardized to invoke the Web service;

(8) WSDL Generator generates a WSDL service description document on the basis of BAM registration information, and sent to the service agent.

(9) Service Configuration is the set of Web services of the corresponding abstract operation configuration in BAM. Search Service Registry or directly specify the Service Provider, from the Service Provider obtain the WSDL and select the corresponding Operation, at the same time, define documents match the script of input and output for the Web Service Operation.

(10) Service Selector select the optimal invoke of the Web service calling according to correspondly the Web service collection Response Time and Loaded values in an abstract operation information.

4   Conclusion

Based on the problem that static Web service behavior adaptation method have difficult to deal with complex Web service behavior adaptation. This paper proposed a behavior adaptation model BAM of dynamic Web service behavior adaptation and adaptation framework DSBAF. The method by behavioral adaptation separate modeling, Adaptation framework dynamically load the model and the engine drive execution unit complete the Web service adaptation, can dynamically complete Web service adaptation. Furthermore, the use of behavioral adaptation model can build a virtual service on DSBAF at runtime, our Web services will be running in the external service environment. It provides a new train of thought to solve this complex Web service behavior adaptation. Future work will focus on the automatic adaptation method of dynamic Web service behavior adapter, if can obtain the desired results, will further promote of the development of SaaS and SOC technology, implementation and applications will carry out.

Acknowledgment. This work is funded by the Open Foundation of Key Laboratory of Software Engineering of Yunnan Province under Grant No. 2011SE13.

References

1. Armbrust, M., Fox, A., Griffith, R., et al.: A view of cloud computing. Commun. ACM (CACM) **53**(4), 50–58 (2010)
2. Gonzalez, L.M.V., Rodero-Merino, L., Caceres, J., et al.: A break in the clouds: towards a cloud definition. Comput. Commun. Rev. (CCR) **39**(1), 50–55 (2009)
3. Papazoglou, M.P.: Service—oriented computing: concepts, characteristics and directions. In: Proceedings of Fourth International Conference on Web Information Systems Engineering (WISE 2003), Roma, Italy, pp. 3–12 (2003)
4. Benatallah, B., Casati, F., Grigori, D., Nezhad, H.R., Toumani, F.: Developing adapters for web services integration. In: Pastor, Ó., Falcão e Cunha, J. (eds.) CAiSE 2005. LNCS, vol. 3520, pp. 415–429. Springer, Heidelberg (2005)

5. Zhang, Y., Chen, M., Mao, S., Hu, L., Leung, V.: CAP: crowd activity prediction based on big data analysis. IEEE Netw. **28**(4), 52–57 (2014)
6. Becker, S., Brogi, A., Gorton, I., Overhage, S., Romanovsky, A., Tivoli, M.: Towards an Engineering Approach to Component Adaptation. In: Reussner, R., Stafford, J.A., Ren, X.-M. (eds.) Architecting Systems with Trustworthy Components. LNCS, vol. 3938, pp. 193–215. Springer, Heidelberg (2006)
7. Brogi, A., Popescu, R.: Service adaptation through trace inspection. In: Proceedings of SOBPI 2005, pp. 44–58 (2005)
8. Brogi, A., Popescu, R.: Automated generation of BPEL adapters. In: Dan, A., Lamersdorf, W. (eds.) ICSOC 2006. LNCS, vol. 4294, pp. 27–39. Springer, Heidelberg (2006)
9. Massuthe, P., Wolf, K.: An Algorithm for Matching Non—determimstic Services with Operating Guidelines. Int. J. Bus. Process Integr. Manage. **2**(2), 81–90 (2007)
10. Massuthe, P., Reisig, W., Schmidt, K.: An operating guideline approach to the SOA. Annals Math. Comput. Teleinf. **1**, 35–43 (2005)
11. Lohmann, N., Massuthe, P., Wolf, K.: Operating guidelines for finite-state services. In: Kleijn, J., Yakovlev, A. (eds.) ICATPN 2007. LNCS, vol. 4546, pp. 321–341. Springer, Heidelberg (2007)
12. Gierds, C., Mooij, A.J., Wolf, K.: Specifying and Generating Behavioral Service Adaptor Based on Transformation Rules. Universitat Rostock, Germany (2008)
13. Nezhad, H.R.M., Benatallah, B., Martens, A., et al.: Semi-automated adaptation of service interactions. In: 16th World Wide Web Conference, pp. 993–1002. ACM Press (2007)
14. Sinha, R., Roop, P., Basu, S.: A Model Checking Approach to Protocol Conversion. Electron. Notes Theor. Comput. Sci. **203**(4), 81–94 (2008)

Cloud-Based Iterative RFID Tag Search Protocol Using Bloom Filters

Yuming Qian[1], Daqiang Zhang[1(✉)], Shengjie Zhao[2], Xiaopeng Fan[3],
and Ke Fan[1]

[1] School of Software Engineering, Tongji University, Shanghai, China
{lincolnmill08,dqzhang,kefan}@tongji.edu.cn
[2] The Key Lab of Embedded System and Service Computing,
Ministry of Education, Tongji University, Shanghai, China
shengjiezhao@tongji.edu.cn
[3] Shenzhen Institute of Advanced Technology, CAS, Shenzhen, China
xp.fan@siat.ac.cn

Abstract. RFID (Radio Frequency Identification) has achieved widespread success in supply chain management, object identification, and assets tracking. In these applications, we often need to search for a particular set of products in a large-scale collection of products. Existing schemes have been proposed, but they are limited by a couple of problems. Firstly, they fail to work under the situation when the cardinality of X is much larger than that of Y. Secondly, they implicitly assume the RFID readers are adequate powerful so that readers can handles a large number of query requests in a short time. To this end, we propose ITSP – Cloud-based Iterative Tag Search Protocol, which can locate the tags in a secure and efficient manner. To be secure, ITSP authenticates the communications between RFID readers and tags to in advance. To be efficient, ITSP reformats the single-round communication model to a multi-round communication one between readers and tags. Furthermore, ITSP employs a cloud-based service to rapidly conduct the searching process. Extensive experimental results show that the proposed scheme achieves high-levels of searching efficiency with the improvement at least 19 %.

Keywords: RFID · Cloud computing · Tag query · Iterative searching

1 Introduction

RFID (Radio Frequency Identification) is a wireless communication technology [1], which applies radio signals to identify specific targets without touching objects mechanically and optically. Usually, An RFID system consists of three parts: readers, tags, and antennae. The readers transmit encoded radio signal to interrogate the tags and gets stored information within tags. Readers have relatively powerful computation and storage capability [11]. Each tag has a unique ID according to the EPC global Class-1 Gen-2 standard [12]. It receives the reader message and responds with required information. RFID antenna receives and transmits the radio signal between tags and readers. Owing to its low cost, non-contact sensing, and miniaturization, RFID has been widely

© Institute for Computer Sciences, Social Informatics and Telecommunications Engineering 2015
V.C.M. Leung et al. (Eds.): CloudComp 2014, LNICST 142, pp. 145–154, 2015.
DOI: 10.1007/978-3-319-16050-4_14

adopted in inventory management [2], product tracking, intelligent transportation systems [3–5], animal identification [6] and healthcare systems [7, 8, 17].

In RFID applications, we may encounter the following scenario. A batch of new products are stacked in several warehouses that are physically remote. Sometimes, the manufacturer needs to detect inferior products by counting all tags attached to the products. Given the goal set of tags X, the problem is how to search them in the coverage area of all the readers, which have the set of the tags Y. The objective of the RFID search problem is to find the set of $X \cap Y$. Note that X may be totally exclusive to Y, i.e., $X \cap Y = \Phi$. For example, all of the products in some warehouse are qualified. On the other hand, X may be totally included by Y, i.e., $X \cap Y = X$. For example, all of the defective products are placed in some warehouse. Moreover, the RFID readers suffer from limited computation and computing capabilities. Each round detection, they will spend a second. Therefore, they cannot continuously check the large number of tags without break. Table 1 lists our notations used in this paper.

Table 1. Key notations used in the design of the proposed scheme

Symbols	Description
X	The set of the goal tags
Y	The set of the tags in the coverage zone
Y_C	The candidate set of the tags
$X \cap Y$	The intersection set of X and Y
$|\cdot|$	Cardinality of the set
$BF(\cdot)$	The bloom filter for a set
$A \cap BF(B)$	The subset of A that is filtered by the bloom filter for B
$h(\cdot)$	A uniform hash function
α	The transmission rate from a reader to a tag
β	The transmission rate from a tag to a reader
P_{req}	The false positive rate
K	The number of the hash functions
S	The random seed
t	The time for transmitting one bit

Many schemes have been proposed. However, they cannot deal with some problems. On the one hand, when the cardinality of X is larger than Y, some protocols cannot work. On the other hand, with the number of tags getting larger, the search efficiency drops due to the limited computing capabilities of readers. In this paper, we propose ITSP – Cloud-based Iterative Tag Search Protocol. In the given protocol, we reformats the single-round communication model to a multi-round communication one between readers and tags. Besides, we put the process of computing into the cloud which can make up the defects of readers in computing. To summarize, the contributions of this paper are two-fold. First, the protocol can still work well when $|X| > |Y|$ and we can choose the best search method according to the relationship of $|X|$ and $|Y|$ for the best efficiency. Secondly it uses the cloud-based service to get the efficient search performance.

The rest of the paper is organized as follows. Section 2 introduces the related works. Section 3 describes the details of the Cloud-based Iterative Tag Search Protocol. Section 4 evaluates the performance of our protocol. Section 5 draws the conclusion.

2   Related Works

Zheng and Li propose the Compact Approximator based Tag Searching [13] (CATS) protocol that improves the search efficiency dramatically. It is a two-phase protocol which considers all the readers as a whole. In the first phase, a bloom filter BF_1 is constructed with K_1 hash functions and the seed S_1. BF_1 and S_1 will be broadcast to all of the tags in the system. Once a tag receives BF_1, it checks whether it can be filtered by this bloom filter with parameter K_1 and S_1 or not. The tags that are not filtered will keep silent in the next phase and do not response to the reader any more. On the other hand, other tags will keep active as the candidate tags. In the second phase, the reader broadcasts parameter K_2 and S_2 as hash function and the seed respectively to the tags. The reader will build up a new bloom filter BF_2 according to the replies from those candidate tags. If the time slot is not empty, the corresponding element in the bloom filter will be assigned as '1', otherwise as '0'. According to BF_2, the target tags also are checked. The tags that keep active will be considered as the search results. Thus CATS can reduce the search delay by tolerating some false positive cases. However, it cannot work under the environment that the cardinality of X is much larger than that of Y [14]. Though the Iterative Tag Search Protocol (ITSP) protocol overcomes the disadvantage above, we can still decrease the search delay by adjusting the number of the filtering vector on the basis of the cardinalities of X and Y.

Both CATS and ITSP consider the readers as a whole, which results in the interferences among the readers in practice. Some existing works have been done to solve the interference problem. Waldrop et al. [9] proposed the colorwave algorithm that colors the readers in the system so that there is not any interference among the readers with the same color. Tang et al. [10] proposed the RASPberry that makes the system work in a stable way in the long term when the arrival rate of the tags are in the range of the readers.

The security issue in RFID search is also another focus in previous work. Based on the analysis work from Chun and Hwang [15], we found that the main reason for unsecurity in RFID search efficiency is the loss of strong authentication between readers and tags. If we have a sound mechanism for authentication, we can ensure the security during the RFID search.

3   ITSP: Cloud-Based Iterative Tag Search Protocol

In this section, we mainly talk about how to enhance the search efficiency based on the cardinality of X and Y and how to leverage the cloud-based service to improve the computing capacities of readers.

Figure 1 shows the architecture of RFID search in Cloud. First, we input the set of wanted tags into the readers. Then the readers request the cloud-based service for computing. After the cloud return the result, readers broadcast the computing results to the tags. Tags will response to the request from readers. The communication between readers and all tags may take several rounds and in each round, readers leverage the cloud service to do computation.

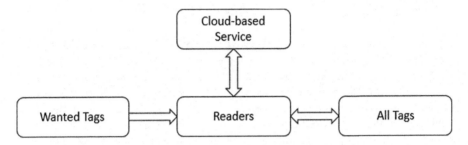

Fig. 1. The architecture of RFID Search on cloud-based service

3.1   Large-X-Query Algorithm

CATS cannot work when the cardinality of X is much larger than Y. The only one round interaction mainly results in the problem. Because in the communication process, CATS should meet both the false positive rate and the efficiency requirements. We increase the number of the interaction round to solve this problem based on the idea from ITSP [14].

We apply a partial bloom filter in Large-X-Query algorithm rather than a standard bloom filter. We define some variables. Let total number of the elements as m and the length of bloom filter as L. We define the hash function number as K. In the ith round, the candidate tags in X and Y are X_i and Y_i respectively. There are some other definitions, such as $W = X \cap Y$, $U_i = X_i - W$, $V_i = Y_i - W$. U_i and V_i represent the remaining tags that do not belong to the set X and Y respectively. $X_1 = X$, $Y_1 = Y$. In a partial bloom filter, the false positive rate obtains the minimum value 1/2 in each vector when $L/K = m \times \ln 2$ [16]. Thus, in each round, the reader transmits m_i vector to the tags and the tags transmit one vector to the reader. After one-round transmit, X and Y will change to:

$$Y_{i+1} = V_i \times (1/2)^{m_i} + W \tag{1}$$

$$X_{i+1} = U_i \times 1/2 + W = (X_i + W)/2 \tag{2}$$

The time of this round is:

$$f(m_i) = 1/\ln 2 \times m_i \times X_i \times t + 1/\ln 2 \times Y_{i+1} \times t \tag{3}$$

$$= t/\ln 2(m_i \times X_i + V_i/2^{m_i} + W) \tag{4}$$

When

$$m_i = \frac{\ln(\ln 2 \times V_i/X_i)}{\ln 2} \tag{5}$$

The transmission delay of each round obtains the minimum value. Because there is not any collision among vectors, the false positive rate is with no relation to the number of transmitted vector. The false positive rate of each round is always 1/2. If we assume there are b rounds of communication between the readers and the tags, the readers totally receive b vectors. To satisfy the false positive rate, b should meet the requirement $(1/2)^b < P_{req}$, i.e.,

$$b < -\log_2 P_{req} \tag{6}$$

Thus, total search time is:

$$T_{lxq} = \sum_{i=1}^{b} \left(m_i \times \frac{X_i}{\ln 2} + \frac{Y_i}{\ln 2} \right) \times t \tag{7}$$

In Large-X-Query, the reader transmits m_i vectors to the tags and the tags transmit one vector to the reader in each round (Fig. 2).

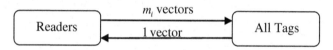

Fig. 2. The ith round in Large-X-Query algorithm

3.2   Large-Y-Query Algorithm

In Large-X-Query algorithm, the tags only transmit one vector to the reader. However, transmitting multiple vectors to the reader may improve the efficiency, especially when the cardinality of Y is much larger than that of X (Fig. 3).

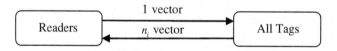

Fig. 3. The ith round in Large-Y-Query algorithm

The reader transmits one vector to the tags and the tags transmit n_i vectors to the reader. We name this algorithm as Large-Y-Query. After each round, X and Y will change to:

$$Y_{i+1} = V_i \times 1/2 + W = (Y_i + W)/2 \tag{8}$$

$$X_{i+1} = U_i \times (1/2)^{n_i} + W \tag{9}$$

The time of this round is:

$$f(n_i) = 1/\ln 2 \times X_i \times t + 1/\ln 2 \times n_i \times Y_{i+1} \times t \tag{10}$$

$$= t/\ln 2 (n_i \times Y_{i+1} + U_i/2^{n_i} + W) \tag{11}$$

When

$$n_i = \frac{\ln(\ln 2 \times U_i/Y_{i+1})}{\ln 2} \tag{12}$$

The time of this round can obtain the minimum value and total time is:

$$T_{lyq} = \sum_{i=1}^{b} \left(\frac{X_i}{\ln 2} + n_i \times \frac{Y_i}{\ln 2} \right) \times t \tag{13}$$

If there are b rounds of communication between the readers and the tags, the tags totally receive b vectors. To satisfy the false positive rate, b should meet the requirement $(1/2)^b < P_{req}$, i.e.,

$$b < -\log_2 P_{req} \tag{14}$$

3.3   Large-XY-Query Algorithm

We generalize the above algorithm to present Large-XY-Query. In each round the readers transmit m_i vectors to the tags and the tags transmit n_i vectors to the readers. After each round, X and Y will change to (Fig. 4):

$$X_{i+1} = U_i \times (1/2)^{n_i} + W \tag{15}$$

$$Y_{i+1} = V_i \times (1/2)^{m_i} + W \tag{16}$$

The time of this round is:

$$f(m_i, n_i) = t/\ln 2 \times (m_i \times X_i + n_i \times Y_{i+1}) \tag{17}$$

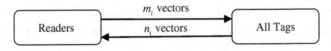

Fig. 4. The ith round in Large-XY-Query algorithm

This is an equation with two unknowns which change constantly so that we cannot obtain the optimal solution. Instead, we use the m_i and n_i in the two special conditions. Total time is obtained by the following equation:

$$T_{lxyq} = \sum_{i=1}^{b} \left(m_i \times \frac{X_i}{\ln 2} + n_i \times \frac{Y_i}{\ln 2} \right) \times t \tag{18}$$

The readers and the tags do not stop communicating until X_i or Y_i meets the following conditions.

$$\frac{|Y_i| - |W|}{|W|} < P_{req} \tag{19}$$

$$\frac{|X_i| - |W|}{|W|} < P_{req} \tag{20}$$

3.4 ITSP Algorithm

According to the experimental results in Sect. 4, we can get the final search protocol ITSP which can help us to choose the best algorithm based on the cardinality of X and Y.

Algorithm 1. ITSP algorithm

1: **if** $|W|/\min(|X|,|Y|) <= 0.45$ **then**
2:     **return** Large-XY-Query
3: **else if** $|X| > |Y|$ **then**
4:     **return** Large-X-Query
5: **else**
6:     **return** Large-Y-Query
7: **end if**

---

4 Evaluation

In this section we evaluate the performance of the proposed ITSP algorithm in our paper. We mainly focus on the search efficiency and compare it with other protocols. During the simulation process, we assume that there is no transmission loss between RFID tags and the reader. In each frame the reader initiates the communication by sending commands to the tags and waits for tag's response. The RFID reader is capable of detecting and distinguishing empty slots from nonempty slots. In the ITSP series algorithms, we mainly focus on the size of transmitting vectors while other operation in RFID search is negligible, such as estimating the size of Y and the cost of transmitting hash seeds. In our simulation, we set both the $R \Rightarrow T$ transmission rate and the $T \Rightarrow R$ transmission to be 100 kbps. Accordingly, $t = \frac{1\,bit}{100\,kps} = 10^{-5}\,\text{sec}$.

In our simulation, we will assume that $|W|$ and $|Y|$ is known. Because CATS protocol cannot work when $|X| > |Y|$ and we still need to take the variety of $|W|$ in account. We will mainly talk about four cases. Table 2 shows the parameters of the four cases. We set $P_{req} = 0.001$ among all of these four cases. Figures 5, 6, and 7 show the result of these cases respectively. From Fig. 5, we can observe that the performance of ITSP series algorithm is better than that of CATS in terms of search time. The larger the ratio is, the better ITSP series algorithms perform. For example, when $ratio = 0.9$, the Large-XY-Query, Large-X-Query, Large-Y-Query algorithm reduce the search time of CATS as much as 19.3 %, 22.6 % and 23.7 % respectively. As we decrease the ratio, the gap between CATS and ITSP series algorithms gradually shrinks. At the same time, we can find that Large-Y-Query is the best algorithm when $|X| > |Y|$. Since the cardinality of Y is larger than X, the tags transmitting n_i vectors will bring more valid information in order to decrease the search time. CATS perform poorly when $|X| > |Y|$, and even cannot work when $|X| \gg |Y|$. Figure 6 only analyzes the performance of ITSP series algorithms. In this case, ITSP series algorithms can work efficiently. We observe that Large-X-Query is the best algorithm in search efficiency. Because the cardinality of X is larger than Y, the readers transmitting m_i vectors will bring more valid information to tags.

Table 2. Parameter settings of four cases

Case	$|X|$	$|Y|$	$|W|$
1	$|Y| \times$ ratio	1000000	$|X|/2$
2	1000000	$|X| \times$ ratio	$|Y|/2$
3	500000	1000000	$|X| \times$ ratio
4	1000000	500000	$|Y| \times$ ratio

Next, we will focus the relationship between the search time and $|W|$. Based on this simulation, we will draw a conclusion that which is the best algorithm in ITSP series algorithms. Figure 7 shows that when $|W|/\min(|X|, |Y|) \leq 0.45$, Large-XY-Query is the best algorithm. While $|W|/\min(|X|, |Y|) > 0.45$, the best search algorithm was chosen depending on the relation of $|X|$ and $|Y|$.

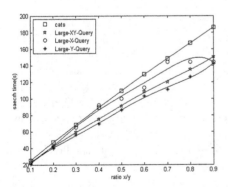

Fig. 5. The relation between search time and $|X|$

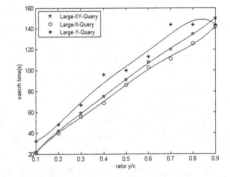

Fig. 6. The relation between search time and $|Y|$

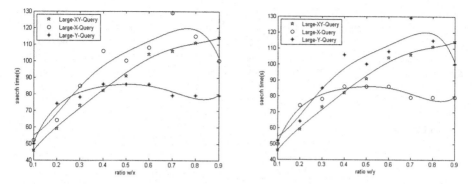

Fig. 7. The relation between search time and $|W|$

Another performance issue we want to investigate is relationship between the search time and P_{req}. Similarly, we will consider $|X| > |Y|$ and $|X| < |Y|$ these two cases. We use 3rd and 4th parameter settings in Table 2 and varying P_{req} from 10^{-1} to 10^{-5}. Figure 8 compares the search efficiency under different false positive rate circumstances. It is easy to find that the less false positive rate is, the longer search time is. Generally speaking, the gap between the search time required by the ITSP series algorithms and that by the CATS keeps getting larger with the decrease of P_{req}, particularly when P_{req} is small. Thus, ITSP series algorithm is more applicable for those application in which strict false positive rate is necessary. This also proves the validation of ITSP series algorithm in search efficiency.

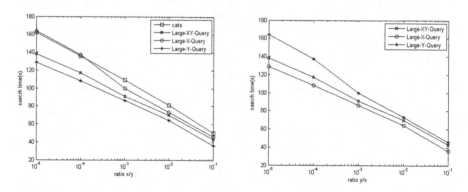

Fig. 8. The relation between search time and P_{req}

5   Conclusion

This paper have investigated the tag search problem in a large-scale RFID system and proposed ITSP – Cloud-based Iterative Tag Search Protocol. ITSP achieves high-levels of accuracy in a secure and efficient manner, no matter the cardinality of the wanted tags is bigger than all tags.

Acknowledgments. Dr. Zhang and Dr. Zhao are the corresponding author. This work was supported in part by the National Natural Science Foundation of China under Grant 61103185 and 61472283, the Fok YingTong Education Foundation of China under Grant 142006, the Research Funds for the Central Universities under Grant 2100219043, and the National Basic Research Program of China (973 Program) under Grant 2014CB340404.

References

1. Zhang, D., Zhou, J., Guo, M., Cao, J., Li, T.: TASA: tag-free activity sensing using RFID tag arrays. IEEE Trans. Parallel Distrib. Syst. **22**(4), 558–570 (2011)
2. Tan, C.C., Sheng, B., Li, Q.: Efficient techniques for monitoring missing RFID tags. IEEE Trans. Wirel. Commun. **9**(6), 1882–1889 (2010)
3. Chen, S., Zhang, M., Xiao, B.: Efficient information collection protocols for sensor-augmented RFID networks. In: INFOCOM 2011, pp. 3101–3109 (2011)
4. Lee, C.-H., Chung, C.-W.: Efficient storage scheme and query processing for supply chain management using RFID. In: SIGMOD Conference, pp. 291–302 (2008)
5. Qiao, Y., Chen, S., Li, T., Chen, S.: Energy-efficient polling protocols in RFID systems. In: MobiHoc 2011, p. 25 (2011)
6. Ni, L.M., Liu, Y., Lau, Y.C., Patil, A.P.: LANDMARC: indoor location sensing using active RFID. Wirel. Netw. **10**, 701–710 (2004)
7. Chang, J.-C., Wu, H.-L., Zhang, D.: On constant-time-identification and privacy-preserving RFID protocols: trade-off between time and memory. In: UIC/ATC 2013, pp. 613–618 (2013)
8. Li, Y., Ding, X.: Protecting RFID communications in supply chains. In: ASIACCS 2007, pp. 234–241 (2007)
9. Waldrop, J., Engels, D.W., Sarma, S.E.: Colorwave: an anticollision algorithm for the reader collision problem. In: ICC 2003, pp. 1206–1210 (2003)
10. Zhou, Z., Gupta, H., Das, S.R., Zhu, X.: Slotted scheduled tag access in multi-reader RFID systems. In: ICNP 2007, pp. 61–70 (2007)
11. Tang, S., Yuan, J., Li, X.-Y., Chen, G.: RASPberry: a stable reader activation scheduling protocol in multi-reader RFID systems. In: ICNP 2009, pp. 304–313 (2009)
12. Yoon, W., Vaidya, N.H.: RFID reader collision problem: performance analysis and medium access. Wirel. Commun. Mob. Comput. **12**(5), 420–430 (2012)
13. Zheng, Y., Li, M.: Fast tag searching protocol for large-scale RFID systems. IEEE/ACM Trans. Netw. **21**(3), 924–934 (2014)
14. Chen, M., Luo, W., Mo, Z., Fang, Y.: An efficient tag search protocol in large-scale RFID systems. In: IEEE INFOCOM, 2014, pp. 899–907 (2014)
15. Chun, J.Y., Hwang, J.Y., Lee, D.H.: Privacy-enhanced RFID Tag Search System (Chapter 9). In: Preradovic, S. (ed.) Advanced Radio Frequency Identification Design and Applications. InTech, Rijeka (2011). ISBN 978-953-307-168-8
16. Cha, J.-R., Kim, J.-H.: Dynamic framed slotted ALOHA algorithms using fast tag estimation method for RFID system. In: IEEE CCNC, 2006, pp. 768–772 (2006)
17. Chen, M., Gonzalez, S., Leung, V., et al.: A 2G-RFID-based e-healthcare system. IEEE Wireless Commun.**17**(1), 37–43 (2010)

Design and Optimizations of the MD5 Crypt Cracking Algorithm Based on CUDA

Renjie Chen, Yu Zhang, Jianzhong Zhang$^{(\boxtimes)}$, and Jingdong Xu

College of Computer and Control Engineering, Nankai University,
Tianjin, China
nkujie@mail.nankai.edu.cn,
{zhangyu1981,zhangjz,xujd}@nankai.edu.cn

Abstract. Message Digest 5 (MD5) is an algorithm to produce a MAC (message authentication code), which has been specified for use in Internet Protocol Security [1]. There exists a large computational complexity in cracking the MD5 hash; hence, implementations on common computing systems become less practical. CUDA (Compute Unified Device Architecture) is a parallel computing platform and programming model invented by NVIDIA. It enables dramatic increases in computing performance by harnessing the power of the graphics processing unit (GPU). This paper puts forward a CUDA-based algorithm and its comprehensive optimizations for cracking the MD5 hash. The experimental results have shown that the peek speed of checking passwords based on GPU reaches 987 Mkey/s, which is 5470 times of that in CPU. It presents an efficient implementation for cracking the MD5 passwords through GPU; meanwhile, these results have demonstrated the potential applicability of GPU in the field of cryptanalysis.

Keywords: MD5 · CUDA · Brute-force · GPU

1 Introduction

Since the MD5 collision attacking method cannot directly derive the plaintext from the MD5 hash value, this cracking method is unable to be applied to practice. The MD5 hash is a one-way cryptography, so decryption of the MD5 is a complex problem requiring great computing power. Therefore, implementations of the MD5 decryption on common computing systems are not practical. Recently, GPU has evolved into a highly parallel, multithreaded, manycore processor with tremendous computational horsepower and very high memory bandwidth [2]. Benefitting from the thriving computing power of the GPU, we can brute-force crack the MD5 by using GPU. Meanwhile, GPU with the capability of conducting general purpose computing is progressing very rapidly; therefore, GPU is more suitable for high-density parallel computing.

This paper first introduces the design of algorithm for cracking the MD5 based on CPU, and then it presents the design and optimizations for the MD5 cracking algorithm based on GPU. Finally this paper shows experimental results on GPU and CPU. Furthermore, we compare the performance of GPU with that based on CPU to analyze the experimental results.

© Institute for Computer Sciences, Social Informatics and Telecommunications Engineering 2015
V.C.M. Leung et al. (Eds.): CloudComp 2014, LNICST 142, pp. 155–164, 2015.
DOI: 10.1007/978-3-319-16050-4_15

2   Cryptanalysis of the MD5 Based on CPU

2.1   Definition and Problem Analysis

Let S denote the set of characters used for generating passwords. Let N denote the number of elements in the set S. Let K denote the maximum length of passwords. Let n denote the total number of passwords in the password space. Let T_P denote the cost time of parallel algorithm. Let T_s denote the cost time of serial algorithm. Let s denote the speed-up ratio i.e., T_s/T_P.

For example, we hypothesize the set of basic characters S is {0–9, a–z}, so the number of characters N = 36 characters. Simultaneously, we hypothesize the maximum length of password K = 6. For a password space with the charset S and the maximum length K, we have to calculate $n = \sum_{i=1}^{K} N^i$ passwords at most. Therefore, based on the above assumptions we must calculate $n = \sum_{i=1}^{6} 36^i$ passwords at most. The complexity of search space is $O(N^K)$.

The password space's structure is a complete k-ary tree. The value of root node is null, and the value range of each node except root node in the tree is S. Meanwhile, for each nonleaf node, it has N children nodes. The value of nth child node equals to the nth element of S. In order to brute-force crack the MD5, we have to traverse the complete k-ary tree till we find the correct password. Visiting a node in the tree is to calculate its MD5 hash and compare it with the given MD5 hash. When we visit a node in the tree, what is calculated MD5 hash is a string which is generated by concatenating its all ancestor nodes' values to this node's value. Because it is a complete k-ary tree traversal problem, we can draw lessons from the tree traversal methods.

2.2   Cracking Algorithm Based on Preorder Traversal

When we preorder traverse a tree, the first step is to visit the root, and then visit its children nodes from left to right. We can use the recursive traversal method to complete this operation. The key pseudo code is shown below:

Cracking algorithm based on preorder traversal

```
Procedure Preorder_tree(word)
Begin
    Calculate_Compare_MD5(word);
    If strlen(word) == K Then
        return;
    else
        For i:=0 To N
            word += S[i];
            Preorder_tree(word);
End
End Preorder_tree
```

2.3 Cracking Algorithm Based on Depth-First Traversal

According to the way of k-ary tree depth-first traversal, it is equivalent to brute-force crack passwords from length 1 to K. Due to the operation order of queue is FIFO, we can complete the depth-first traversal operation by the light of queue. We can pop the first node in the queue, and then push children nodes of this node into the queue from left to right. The key pseudo code is shown below:

Cracking algorithm based on depth-first traversal

```
Procedure Depth_first_traversal()
While(!queue.empty()) do
Begin
    Word := queue.front();
    Calculate_Compare_MD5(word);
    queue.pop();
    If strlen(word) < K Then
        For i:=0 To N
            queue.push(word + S[i]);
End
End Depth_first_traversal.
```

2.4 Preorder Traversal vs. Depth-First Traversal

The above analysis shows that the preorder traversal and the depth-first traversal have almost the same performance in addition to the different traversal order. However, when the preorder traversal algorithm is compared with the parallel algorithm, the parallel algorithm may have less workload giving rise to superliner speed-up ratio.

For example, we need to search for the correct password in a tree data structure showed in Fig. 1. Its solution node is marked with red. We assume that visiting a node needs t_c. If we use the preorder traversal algorithm, we must traverse all the 14 nodes in the tree. So it costs $14 t_c$ to search for solution. But if we use two parallel threads to search for solution; meanwhile, each thread searches for the solution in a sub tree, It only needs to search 9 nodes. Because two threads are concurrence, each thread only needs to search 4 nodes. The total time cost is $4t_c$ with addition of time cost of root node. Therefore, it costs $5\ t_c$ in total through the parallel algorithm. In this case, the speed-up ratio s = $14t_c/5t_c = 2.8 > 2$. But depth-first traversal algorithm doesn't cause such situation.

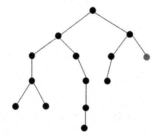

Fig. 1. Preorder traversal resulting in superliner speed-up ratio (Color figure online)

Above all, in order to obtain more objective experimental results, we should choose the depth-first traversal algorithm comparing with the parallel algorithm rather than the preorder traversal algorithm.

3 Cryptanalysis of the MD5 Based on GPU

3.1 Task Allocation and Mapping

As mentioned above, we assume that the input passwords have maximum length K; hence, the password space includes $n = \sum_{i=1}^{K} N^i$ passwords, which exponentially grows with the growth of K. In theory, n passwords can be checked to confirm whether each password is the correct password or not by calling n corresponding to GPU threads. However, the number of threads p is limited by hardware resources, and usually p is much smaller than n. Therefore, each thread needs to check (n/p) passwords.

If we just call a kernel, it will result in wasting threads. The reason is that it requires the distinct number of threads for the distinct K. For example, we assume that the set of basic characters S is {0–9, a–z}, the number of characters N = 36. In such case, if the maximum length of passwords K is 1, it only needs 36 threads at most to search for the correct password. If K = 2, it needs 1332 threads at most. It needs 47988 threads at most when K = 3. Hence, we should call K kernels to search for the correct password. Meanwhile, the mth (m ≤ K) kernel searches in password space which the length of passwords is m. Each kernel can choose the appropriate number of threads per block and the appropriate number of blocks per grid to improve performance. There is another advantage cracking the MD5 hash by this method. Due to be synchronous among kernels, if the mth(m ≤ K) kernel has found the correct password, the rest of kernels can just stop. So it can obtain more correct experimental time results.

We regard the password space as a positional numeral system with a radix, or base, of N. It uses N distinct symbols, such as the symbols 0–9 to represent values zero to nine, and a-z to represent values ten to thirty-five if the charset s is {0–9, a–z}. As an example, the string $(6z)_{36}$ can be converted to an equivalent decimal representation. It is equal to decimal number $251(36^1 * 6 + 36^0 * 35)$.

The mth kernel searches for the correct password in password space that length is m. Since the number of threads p in the kernel is limited by the hardware resources and p is usually much smaller than N^m, each thread in a kernel should check $N^m/(k_b \times k_t)$ values. The range value that a thread checks is calculated by knowing the total number of threads in the kernel, the maximum value in the password space and the index of the thread in the kernel. To do so, use these equations:

$$\text{From} = N^m/(k_b \times k_t) \times T_{id} \tag{1}$$

$$\text{To} = N^m/(k_b \times k_t) \times (T_{id} + 1) \tag{2}$$

Here, the From and To are decimal value, k_b is the number of blocks per kernel, k_t is the number of threads per block, T_{id} is the index of the thread in the kernel. The total number of threads is equal to the number of threads per block times the number of blocks.

However, although we have checked the majority values of the password space, $N^m\%(k_b \times k_t)$ Values are left which are not checked. So each thread needs to check one more value. To do so, check the value:

$$N^m - N^m\%(k_b \times k_t) + T_{id} \qquad (3)$$

In this calculation, the expression $N^m - N^m\%(k_b \times k_t)$ shows the maximum value that has been checked. Then, it is added to T_{id} to guarantee that all the values in the password space are checked.

3.2   Execution Algorithms

As described above we need to call K kernels to check all the n values. The mth ($m \leq K$) kernel searches in password space that the length of password is m. In a kernel, the decimal value between From and To should be converted to password strings. So we needs a function GenPasswd(value) to generate the passwords that a thread should check. It is defined as showed below (Assuming the length of the string the function generated is l and it is executed by the mth kernel):

Pseudo code of the function of generating passwords

```
Function Generating_passwd(value)
Begin
   GenPasswd(value)  = C_{m-l}C_{m-l+1} ... ... C_{m-1} by
      While(value  > 0)  do
            Location := value % N;
            Value = value / N;
            C_{--m}  := S[Location];
      C_0 = C_1 ... ... = C_{m-l-1} = "0";
End
End Generating_passwd
```

However, if l < m, we need to add m − l characters "0" to the head of the string. As an illustration, assuming that m = 4, we need to convert 298 to a password. The result of function GenPasswd(298) is "8a" whose length is 2. Because m = 4 > 2, we need to add 2 characters "0" to the head of the string "8a". So the final string generated is "008a".

The function GenPasswd(value) will generate a password. After that the hash function md5_vfy takes this password to generate the corresponding MD5 hash. This value of hash is compared to the original MD5 hash to decide whether the password is correct or not. If the value of hash is equal to the original MD5 hash, the global variable "isFind" will be set true. Then the remain kernels will abort. Pseudo code is showed below:

Pseudo code of the function of checking passwords

```
Function Checking_passwd(value)
Begin
    Passwd := GenPasswd(value);
    Md5_hash := md5_vfy(Passwd);
    If Md5_hash == original_hash Then
        isFind := true;
End
End Checking_passwd
```

4 GPU Implementation and Optimizations

4.1 Execution Configurations Optimization

The dimension and size of blocks per grid and the dimension and size of threads per block are both important factors [3]. The execution configuration which directly affects the execution time of a kernel grid is also intimately associated with the efficiency of the GPU implementation [4].

Higher occupancy does not always equate to better performance. A lower occupancy kernel will have more registers available per thread than a higher occupancy kernel, which may result in less register spilling to local memory. Local memory accesses have same high latency and low bandwidth as global memory accesses, resulting in performance degradation [3].

According to the CUDA_C_Best_Practices_Guide, between 128 and 256 threads per block is a better choice and a good initial range for experimentation with different block sizes. Furthermore, the number of threads per block, or block size should be a multiple of 32 threads, because this provides optimal computing efficiency and facilitates coalescing. When choosing the number of blocks per gird, or gird size we should take the number of multiprocessors into account. For there are 15 multiprocessors in the device, the number of blocks pre grid should be a multiple of 15 blocks so that all multiprocessors have consensus blocks to execute.

Figure 2 describes the cracking speed under different execution configurations executed by the kernel_4 when K = 4. The results show that for a given block sizes there are distinct performances in kernel_4. When the execution configuration is <<<240, 160>>>, the implementation reaches a peak speed, that is 920 MKey/s.

4.2 Memory Optimization

The memory accessing optimization has high priority in GPU programming. CUDA devices use several memory spaces, which have different characteristics that reflect their distinct usages in CUDA applications. Of these different memory spaces, global memory is the most plentiful. There are 400–600 clock cycles of memory latency in addition [2]. However, because shared memory is on-chip, it has much higher bandwidth and lower latency than local and global memory. There are five clock cycles of memory latency [2].

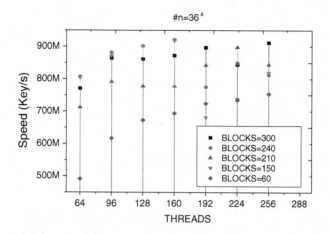

Fig. 2. Speed under different execution configurations

For the set of basic characters S and the MD5 hash value that we want to crack are shared by all threads per block; meanwhile, they are accessed frequently, they can be store in shared memory to improve performances [5].

4.3 Streams Optimization

CUDA Streams allow control over dependencies between grid launches: grids launched into the same stream execute in-order. Hence, streams can also be used to execute multiple kernels simultaneously to more fully take advantage of the device's multiprocessors. Because searching in password space that the length of passwords is m and searching in password space that length of passwords is n are independent, so the mth kernel(m ≤ K) and the nth(n ≤ K) kernel can execute concurrently. The following code showed below illustrates the basic technique. Kernel_m and kernel_n are executed in different, non-default streams, so a capable device can execute the kernels at the same time [6].

Pseudo code of using streams to optimize

```
Procedure Stream_Optimization
Begin
    cudaStreamCreate(&stream_m);
    cudaStreamCreate(&stream_n);
    kernel_m<<<gridsize, blocksize, 0, stream_m>>>();
    kernel_n<<<gridsize, blocksize, 0, stream_n>>>();
End
End Stream_Optimization
```

After choosing the most appropriate execution configuration parameters, we speedup the execution of the program by memory optimizations and streams optimizations.

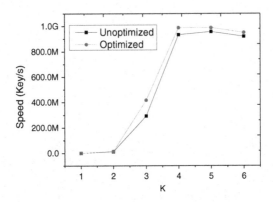

Fig. 3. The average speed of GPU before and after optimizations

To obtain more accurate results, we run the program 100 times to get the average running time of the program. Figure 3 shows the average speed of cracking MD5 implementations on GPU before and after memory optimizations and streams optimizations. We can see the average speed increases with the increment of the password space; furthermore, the performance after optimizations improves a lot. For example, When K = 4, the average speed of cracking increases to 980 MKey/s, an increase of 55 MKey/s.

5   Performance Analysis

This section compares the performances of the proposed implementations using CUDA with the implementations based on CPU. The tests were conducted using an Intel Core i7-2600, 3.40 HZ CPU, an NVIDIA GeForce 570 GTX and the set of lower characters and numeral characters S = {a–z, 0–9}. Table 1 compares the speed of generating and checking passwords on GPU with that on CPU.

Table 1. Time for cracking passwords on GPU and CPU

K	n	GPU	Speed (key/s)	CPU	Speed (key/s)	Speedup
1	36	0.02774 ms	1297764	0.5989 ms	60110	21.5
2	1132	0.1015 ms	14974536	10.8682 ms	104157	107
3	47988	0.1635 ms	417395842	0.2801 s	171324	1712
4	1727604	1.8523 ms	987517162	9.8897 s	174687	5339
5	62193780	65.0394 ms	987542383	5.93 min	174799	5470
6	2238976116	2.4371 s	949149832	3.55 h	175193	5243

As we can see in the Table 1, the speedup increases roughly with the increment of K. The speed of GPU can be 5470 times of that in CPU at most. It is even faster than that using 7GPUS [7]. Figure 4 shows that the speed of CPU is essentially flat

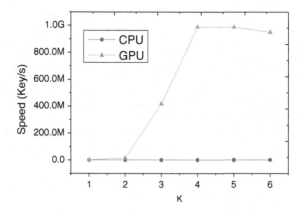

Fig. 4. Performance comparison

compared with GPU. When K is less than 5, the speed of GPU has significantly improvement with the increment of K.

In general, the performance of GPU has improved a lot compared with that based on CPU.

6   Conclusions

In this paper, we design MD5 hash cracking algorithm on CUDA platform, and optimize for performance improvement, finally achieve good performance. The strategies proposed in this paper are proved to be practical and efficient. Furthermore, it has reference value for implementations of other related hash cracking algorithm on GPU.

We can apply more techniques for improving the proposed algorithm. Currently, the function GenPasswd generates passwords through division and modulo operations. However, integer division and modulo operations are particularly costly [3], which will result in performance degradation. Moreover, if the number of elements of the base characters set increases and the maximum length of passwords increases, then the number of passwords in password space increases exponentially. So the algorithm proposed in this paper will become less practical.

In addition, we can add more GPUs to soup up computing. Furthermore, we can reduce the executing time through increasing the speed of generating MD5 keys.

Acknowledgements. This study is supported by the National Natural Science Foundation of China (Grant No. 61103214), the key projects for science and technology of Tianjin (Grant No. 13ZCZDGX01098) and the Doctoral Fund of Ministry of Education of China (Grant No. 20110031120030).

References

1. http://en.wikipedia.org/wiki/MD5
2. NVIDIA Corporation, NVIDIA CUDA Programming Guide V6.0

3. NVIDIA Corporation, NVIDIA CUDA C Best Practices Guide V6.0
4. Li, C., Wu, H.: Efficient implementation for MD5-RC4 encryption using GPU with CUDA. In: The 3rd International Conference on Anti-counterfeiting, Security, and Identification in Communication, August 2009
5. Wang, F., Yang, C., Wu, Q., Shi, Z.: Constant memory optimizations in MD5 crypt cracking algorithm on GPU-accelerated supercomputer using CUDA. In: 2012 7th International Conference on Computer Science & Education, pp. 638–642. IEEE (2012)
6. NVIDIA Corporation, NVIDIA CUDA Runtime API V6.0
7. Nguyen, D.H., Nguyen, T.T., Duong, T. N., et al.: Cryptanalysis of MD5 on GPU cluster. In: 2010 International Conference on Information Security & Artificial Intelligence (ISAI 2010). Chengdu, China, pp. 910–914. IEEE (2010)

A Model of Cloud Computing Federation Based on Complex Network Theory

Zhenli He[1]([✉]), Hua Zhou[1], Yin Zhang[2], Junhui Liu[1], and Lei Su[3]

[1] School of Software, Yunnan University, Kunming 650091, Yunnan, China
{hezhenli1987,HanksLau}@gmail.com, hzhou@ynu.edu.cn
[2] Embedded and Pervasive Computing Lab, School of Computer Science and
Technology, Huazhong University of Science and Technology,
1037 Luoyu Road, Wuhan 430074, China
yin.zhang.cn@ieee.org
[3] School of Information Engineering and Automation,
Kunming University of Science and Technology,
Kunming 650093, Yunnan, China
s28341@hotmail.com

Abstract. With the development of cloud computing technology, it is necessary to integrate multiple cloud computing service providers. Cloud computing federation is a kind of cloud model which integrates multiple cloud computing service providers, provides the cooperation between them and mutual operation mechanism, improves the service quality and implements the corresponding strategy. It has become one of hot research topics at present. The paper summarizes the demand at first and discusses the significance of cloud computing federation. Secondly, we introduce the related research in this field, pointing out the problems existed in the current study. Then, the paper puts forward a cloud computing federation model based on the theory of complex network, at the same time supporting vertical scaling and horizontal extension according to the study, what's more, the strategies of node join and leave are put forward. Finally, on the basis of above, the paper has carried out the qualitative analysis for the model.

Keywords: Cloud computing · Cloud computing federation · Complex network theory · modeling · Integrate

1 Introduction

The application of cloud computing technology allows the users to obtain the required software services, platform support or hardware resources (collectively referred to as computational resources) at any time according to their own needs, rather than to cost a huge of money to maintain a large number of hardware resources or develop the existed complex application service due to the occasional peak demand. Besides, it can not only increase the resource utilization ratio, but also enhance the earnings ratio, which has greatly promoted the development of information and technology industry [1].

© Institute for Computer Sciences, Social Informatics and Telecommunications Engineering 2015
V.C.M. Leung et al. (Eds.): CloudComp 2014, LNICST 142, pp. 165–174, 2015.
DOI: 10.1007/978-3-319-16050-4_16

However, the current cloud computing technology is still at the initial stage [2], with the development and application of cloud computing technology and it's further study, the demands of integrating multiple cloud computing service providers (can be referred to as supplier) to provide services to meet the interests of all parties appear, which are mainly manifested in the following aspects:

- Actually, the resources of an individual cloud computing service providers are limited. As for the individual supplier, they also face the problem that they have to continuously increase the hardware devices to satisfy their users' peak demand as the cloud computing users increase gradually. As a result, the individual supplier needs to use or rent other suppliers' idle resources to increase the availability of service as well as the resource extension ability.
- There is something wrong with providers' locking [3]. Users are locked in a fixed cloud service provider, so they will face with a monopoly provider, and it will cost a lot if they want to change the supplier.
- Users can not combine the services provided by multiple suppliers to achieve cost-optimized strategy according to their overall demand [4], under which users will have the requirement of grouping multiple suppliers with high quality and less money to implement the specific application or computing tasks.
- Another problem is the failure of the individual cloud service provider. In recent years, although a lot of suppliers have declared their service is reliable and can offer a steady stream of available services, the service disruption accident still exists [5,6].

To sum up, in order to meet the increasingly prominent needs, more and more scholars turn their attention to integrate different cloud computing service provider's computing resources, hoping to study and solve the requirements mentioned above. For such problems, there are many kinds of formulation, some call it Open Cloud Computing [7], and some call it Cloud Computing Market [8] from the aspect of economy, or call it InterCloud [9], Hybrid Cloud [10] or Cloud Fusion [11] and so on. However, I prefer to the term Cloud Computing Federation [12,13] proposed by some scholars, since this term accurately reflects the meaning of the multiple suppliers in the federation or providing interoperability among them and the key point of this technology (Fig. 1).

2   Correlational Research

In the existing research results, one of the most famous research is the research project funded by the EU FP7, called RESERVOIR model [14]. RESERVOIR model is mainly based on virtualization technology, integrating basic computing resources for specific virtualization layer, virtualization layer is composed of multiple suppliers, accurately, it is composed of hardware resources of multiple infrastructure suppliers, keeping service application running on the unified virtualization layer, so as to achieve the goal of cloud computing resources integration.

Buyya R, Ranjan R and others put forward Cloud federation model, which aims at practical [15]. In this model, setting up a conversion module (Cloud

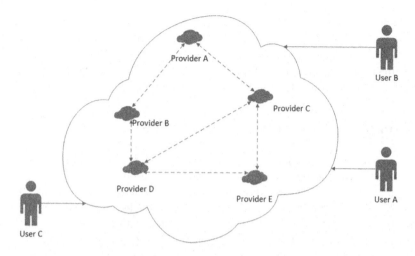

Fig. 1. Cloud computing federation.

Exchange) to achieve the goal of transformation and putting forward the idea that bank system is put into accessing the Cloud Computing Federation, which is used to guarantee the accuracy of relevant billing of users, agents or suppliers under federation status.

Kurze T, Klems M and others take out summary for all kinds of problems of cloud computing federation [12]. Cloud computing federation ways are summed up in two types by researchers: vertical extension and horizontal extension. Horizontal extension refers to the extension on a specific layer of the Cloud Computing architecture, such as IaaS layer while vertical extension refers to the extension across multiple layers.

3 The Problems Existing in the Existing Cloud Federation Model

Most of these research results are at an early stage, in addition, there are the following questions:

- Most of them extend on a layer of cloud computing structure, namely federation in the form of horizontal extension or cloud computing federation based on a certain specific level, such as infrastructure layer, etc. Did not comprehensively consider the overall architecture of the existing cloud computing or vertical extension way to take union problem.
- Some research results still expect to change the architecture of the existing cloud computing platform, then, the concept of open cloud computing is put forward, but the problem is not took into account where the existing large cloud computing service provider is willing to cooperate and make improvement or not.

- Though some research achievements consider the system structure of existing cloud computing, but don't consider the problem that some suppliers only provide a layer of computing resources (such as infrastructure namely a service IaaS), so we can not set up a coordinator at all levels to achieve the standardized interface for the federation problems.

4   Complex Network Theory Overview

In recent years, network has already caused the attention of many researchers, which work in related fields, complex network is the large-scale network, which has topological structure and dynamic behavior, it is a diagram made by the connected edges of the large number of nodes, where the nodes can be any basic unit of having specific power and the information connotation system, the edge represents the relationship between the basic units or interaction [16].

A specific network can abstract for the collection of points and edges:

$$G =< V, E > \tag{1}$$

where, V is the set of vertices, E is the set of edges, $N = |V|$ as the number of nodes, $M = |E|$ as the number of edges. The using node of each side in E shows as $< x, y >$, which illustrates the fact that there is a connection between node x and y. For any node $x \in N, y \in N$, if there is edge $< x, y >$, there must be corresponding edge $< y, x >$, the network is undirected network. If there is edge $< x, y >$, but there is none necessitating edge $< y, x >$, the network is directed network. For any edge, if there is a coefficient K, representing the weight of the edge and so on, the network is a weighted network. Several important measurement of features for complex networks:

- **Degree.** The degree of any node i in undirected network can be expressed as the all number of edges associated with the nodes, called $deg(i)$. In directed network, degree can divide into in-degree and out-degree, for any node j in the directed network, in-degree refers to the edge number of the node. Out-degree is the edge number by the node points to the other nodes.
- **Degree Distribution.** Degree distribution represents any node is chosen from the network, the degree just is the probability of K, called $P(K)$. In the actual application of the measure index, when it examines the network structure, usually adopting the method of cumulative distribution plotting for node degrees. The form of node degree cumulative distribution $P(K)$:

$$P(K) = \sum_{K' \geq K} p(K') \tag{2}$$

- **Average Path Length.** The distance between nodes i and j in network is defined as the number of the edges on the shortest path of two connected nodes, average path length is the average of the distance between any two nodes in the network.

- **Clustering Coefficient.** For any node i of the undirected network, if its degree $deg(i) = k_i$, the node i has k_i neighbor nodes altogether. For the neighbor nodes, they may also have certainly edge connection, the maximum number of the edges is $k_i(k_i - 1)/2$, then the clustering coefficient of node i is defined as the ratio of the actual links number E_i between neighbor nodes and maximum connection edge number $k_i(k_i - 1)/2$, referred to as C_i:

$$C_i = \frac{2E_i}{k_i(k_i - 1)} \tag{3}$$

5 The Cloud Federation Model Based on Complex Network Theory

The environment of cloud computing federation belongs to a complex environment, which has many suppliers and many computing resources, belonging to a certain extent of complex system, complex network theory is one of the effective methods of exploring complex systems in this paper. Cloud computing federation model mainly describes cooperation between suppliers and interoperable cloud model. If the computing resource of each supplier are abstracted as a point, the cooperation and interoperability of the charge computing resources among suppliers are abstracted for edge, some cost are abstracted for weight, then, the cloud computing federation environment can be abstracted as a network.

5.1 Model Particle Size Selection

What kind of particle size for the modeling of cloud computing federation environment is very important. Selecting suppliers as node for modeling is not appropriate, because a supplier has multiple data centers, which distributes in many regions around the world, so selecting suppliers as particle size makes the important information missing and the efficiency of the allocation of resources low. Using a single virtual machine for modeling is also not reasonable, because this causes model scale large due to particle size is too small, causing a large number of network load, which are not conducive to model research and also not practical. Therefore, using the suppliers' multiple data centers as a node is very appropriate, which can avoid the fact that model size is too large, what is more, it can also avoid the loss of some important information.

5.2 Model of the Cloud Computing Federation

Define a cloud computing federation model $CF =< DC, E >$, where DC the set of data center is, E is the relationship among the data centers and the relationship have the directivity, so the network is a directed network. In addition, a data center can't point to their own side, this is because the indoor relationship of a data center does not need to be shown in cloud computing federation model, this is not a issue to consider in cloud federation environment. Precisely, therefore, the network is a directed weighted network of having no ring structure.

Define a data center $DC_i = <R_i, DC_i'>$, where R_i is a list of local resources belong to data center, DC_i' is other data center list of having points-to relation, that is, the collection of the data center pointing to other data center, there is $DC_i' \subset DC$.

Define an edge $E_j = <W_j, T_j, D_j^+, D_j^->$, which W_j represents the interaction price of the edge, T_j represents the resource type of this edge, D_j^+ represents out-degree of the node that the edge points, D_j^- represents in-degree of the node that the edge points.

The fact can be seen from the Fig. 2 that each data center via interaction constitutes directed weighted networks of a no ring structure, the nodes in the network by certain rules (such as resource query rule, load balancing rule, trust model, etc.) interact to form a autonomous structure, where there is no central node, based on this model, we will be able to discuss the system overall emergent property and discuss a series of strategies under the model.

Cloud computing federation environment is a dynamic environment, data centers can join or leave the network structure at any time and use the complex network theory to support the DC to join or leave policy. Cloud federation environment is an overlay network based on Internet, so the edge is not fixed and dynamic, which can be added or deleted.

A. Join Strategy of Data Center

When a new data center join federation environment, first of all, it should be associated with the surrounding data centers, which needs to broadcast news, but too much forwarding will cause "flood" of the message, in addition, for its own sake, the more "potential" data center node association will gain more benefits, because this means that you are more likely to have to find relevant computing resources by the data center. Therefore, we will introduce clustering

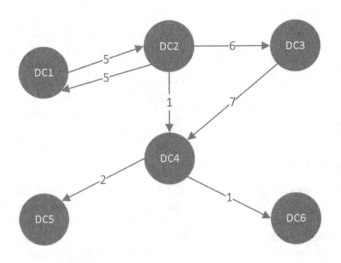

Fig. 2. Model figure of the cloud computing federation.

coefficient to complex networks theory, because a high clustering coefficient node always have the possibility of finding more resources, they relatively has more "potential". We extend the clustering coefficient.

Definition 1

1. i represents any data center of data center set DC, $DC_i =< R_i, DC_i' >$.
2. There is a collection $E' \subset E$, any one of the edges of E' points to a data center association in the DC_i'.
3. The definition $D_i = |E'|$ represents out-degree of DC_i.
4. If there is an edge $E_j =< W_j, T_j, D_j^+, D_j^- >$, from node i pointing to node j, D_j^+ represents the out-degree of node j. The importance of node j to node i is as follows:

$$C_{ij} = \frac{2D_j^+}{D_i(D_i - 1)} \tag{4}$$

According to the formula (4), it can be seen that the importance of node j to node i represents the ratio of the number of edge that node j points to nodes and the maximum number of edge of neighbor nodes of node i. The greater importance of nodes, the more valuable. But when the formula (4) initially join in the data center, it cannot be calculated, it is due to the fact that out-degree of a new node is 0, so here is another definition:

Definition 2

1. Defining the constant L_i represents that a query gets the number of nodes around, when a new data center initially joins.
2. The importance C_{ij} can be improved for:

$$C_{ij} = \frac{2D_j^+}{L_i(L_i - 1)} \tag{5}$$

When a data center i joins, the collection DC_i' is an empty set, so a query gets a collection of nodes around when DC_i' initially joins. So the strategy of the data center joins can be expressed as the following steps:

1. Conduct a search and find other data centers around the data center, form a set DC_i'.
2. In order to avoid hot nodes (that is, most of the data center select to connect it), define an upper limit D_{max}, if finding in-degree D_j^- of the node exists $D_j^- \geq D_{max}$, exclude the node not to connect.
3. For each the element of DC_i', calculate the importance C_{ij} aimed at this node.
4. Sorting the results of the importance, selecting the results of the former C to establish a connection.

B. Leave Strategy of Data Center

When a data center due to various reasons (fault or need overall migration) needs to leave the cloud federation environment, they can stop accepting any computing tasks, and directly offline. Therefore, its related data center needs to detect the exception and disconnect with the data center. When the data center i leaves cloud federation environment, the strategy of the surrounding data center can be expressed as the following steps:

1. The connection test was carried out on the data center i, if exceeding the time limit T_{max}, there is no longer to try, selecting to contact the other data centers.
2. When the failure time is more than F_{max}, it can be concluded that the data center has been offline, deleting the edges associated with the node, and no longer trying.

6   The Qualitative Analysis of the Model

The cloud computing federation model considering the problems mentioned above can support vertical and horizontal extension, which has the dynamic and autonomy, so as to support further research (such as resources query strategy, load balancing strategy, trust models).

Figure 3 is a hierarchical structure representation of Fig. 2, from the Fig. 3, it can be seen that data center 1, 2 belong to the SaaS computing resources, data center 3, 4 belong to the PaaS computing resources, data center 5, 6 belong to IaaS computing resources. The link between data center 1, 2 and data center 3, 4 represents horizontal extension while the rest of the edges represent the vertical extension.

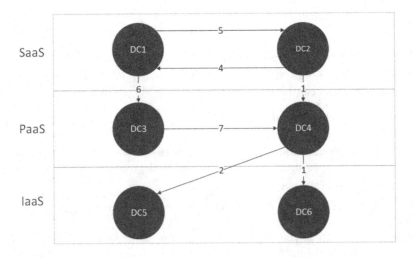

Fig. 3. Level structure figure of cloud computing federation model.

Observing the relationship between data center 1 and 2, the different of the weight represents the different pricing between each supplier, therefore, the model can support the difference between each supplier.

The model only needs suppliers to realize a coordinator on their data centers, which can be easily combined with existing cloud computing technology, the suppliers only need to open its data center to whom willing to federation without having to open all of its resources, which more embodies the suppliers' intention.

7   Conclusion

First of all, the paper discusses the importance of cloud computing federation, secondly, it analyses the existing model of cloud computing federation and puts forward the deficiencies. Aiming at these deficiencies, this paper presents a cloud computing federation model based on complex network theory so as to address these deficiencies. At the same time, the paper has carried out the qualitative analysis for the model and puts forward the strategies of node join and leave. Quantitative analysis and the corresponding experimental results are not presented in the paper. Although the laboratory has developed a corresponding model platform, it is not perfect. Therefore, it will be discussed in the future study. Qualitative analysis results show that it has a large number of valuable future research based on the model.

Acknowledgements. This work was supported by the National Natural Science Foundation of China (No.61365010). This work was also supported in part by China National Natural Science Foundation under Grants 61300224, the International Science and Technology Collaboration Program (2014DFT10070) funded by China Ministry of Science and Technology (MOST), Hubei Provincial Key Project under grant 2013CFA051.

References

1. Chen, M., et al.: Big Data: Related Technologies, Challenges and Future Prospects. SpringerBriefs in Computer. Springer, Heidelberg (2014)
2. Dillon, T., Wu, C., Chang, E.: Cloud computing: issues and challenges. In: 2010 24th IEEE International Conference on Advanced Information Networking and Applications (AINA), pp. 27–33. IEEE (2010)
3. Cowan, R.: Tortoises and hares: choice among technologies of unknown merit. Econ. J. **101**, 801–814 (1991)
4. Buyya, R., et al.: Economic models for resource management and scheduling in grid computing. Concurrency Comput. Pract. Experience **14**(13–15), 1507–1542 (2002)
5. Summary of the Amazon EC2 and Amazon RDS Service Disruption. http://aws.amazon.com/message/65648
6. Post-mortem for February 24th, 2010 outage. https://groups.google.com/group/google-appengine/browse_thread/thread/a7640a2743922dcf?pli=1

7. Metsch, T.: Open Cloud Computing Interface-Use cases and requirements for a Cloud API. Open Grid Forum (2009)
8. Sultan, N.: Cloud computing for education: a new dawn? Int. J. Inf. Manage. **30**(2), 109–116 (2010)
9. Grozev, N., Buyya, R.: Inter-cloud architectures and application brokering: taxonomy and survey. Softw. Pract. Experience **44**(3), 369–390 (2012)
10. Mell, P., Grance, T.: The NIST definition of cloud computing. National Institute of Standards and Technology **53**(6), 50 (2009)
11. Sakashita, Y., et al.: Cloud fusion concept. FUJITSU Sci. Tech. J. **48**(2), 143–150 (2012)
12. Kurze, T., et al.: Cloud federation. In: The Second International Conference on Cloud Computing. GRIDs, and Virtualization (2011)
13. Goiri, I., Guitart, J., Torres, J.: Characterizing cloud federation for enhancing providers' profit. In: 2010 IEEE 3rd International Conference on Cloud Computing (CLOUD), IEEE (2010)
14. Rochwerger, B., et al.: The reservoir model and architecture for open federated cloud computing. IBM J. Res. Dev. **53**(4), 1–4 (2009)
15. Buyya, R., Ranjan, R., Calheiros, R.N.: Intercloud: utility-oriented federation of cloud computing environments for scaling of application services. In: Hsu, C.-H., Yang, L.T., Park, J.H., Yeo, S.-S. (eds.) ICA3PP 2010, Part I. LNCS, vol. 6081, pp. 13–31. Springer, Heidelberg (2010)
16. Wang, X.F., Li, X., Chen, G.R.: Complex Network Theory and Application. Tsinghua University licensing agency, Beijing (2006)

The Implementation of IKEV2 for IPSec

Xiaojin Yang[(✉)] and Jianhua Liu

Department of Information Engineering,
Guilin University of Aerospace Technology, Guilin, China
{yxj,ljh}@guat.edu.cn

Abstract. According to the characteristic of IKEv2 key exchange mechanism, this paper is designed and realized the frame construction and the module constitution of IKEv2. Establishing the transform relations between the exchange states and the news operation, this research had determined the message handling step and the key exchange flow. It also produced the detailed elaboration to each function module concrete realization.

Keywords: IPSec · IKEV2 · Load · Message handling

1 Introduction

Aiming at the safe problem of network data transmission, IETF (Internet Engineering Task Force) in 1998 November announced the Internet security protocol standard: IPSec, it can be "seamless" for the IP (IPv4 and IPv6) into security characteristics. It has some specific forms of protection: data origin authentication, non-integrity verification of linked data, confidentiality of data content, anti replay protection and limited data flow confidentiality. The IPSec protocol is used for protect communication can achieve end to end; the IPSec component is configured on the router and firewall equipment, it can easily construct safety which is extended VPN.

IPSec is the foundation of security alliance (SA). It is an agreement between two communicating entities established by negotiation. SA can be set by user manual configuration mode, dynamic can also be used for key exchange method. The former is simple, but because of the static configuration method it leads to the lack of security. The latter can be used between two communicating entities, building a safe passage through the network consultation verification. Consensus of the IPSec SA proposal is the protection of the security channel, configuration to make SA more flexible and safe. It is because of this advantage, key exchange becomes more and more important in the field of communication security. IKE IPSec is the default key exchange protocol (Internet Key Exchange).

IKE is a hybrid protocol, its complexity inevitably brings some security and performance of the defect. IETF has been in the unreasonable part of existing versions of IKE positive for amendments. The IPSec working group introduced a draft agreement – IKEv2 IKE latest edition in 2004 September, 2–17 is the version number. IKEv2 based on sharing strategy consultation method of the original protocol, the first protocol was optimized and improved overall cost, to make it better performance, higher safety and

© Institute for Computer Sciences, Social Informatics and Telecommunications Engineering 2015
V.C.M. Leung et al. (Eds.): CloudComp 2014, LNICST 142, pp. 175–180, 2015.
DOI: 10.1007/978-3-319-16050-4_17

lower system. Replace the IKE as a new generation of key exchange protocol standard has gradually become the consensus of the industry in IKEv2.

2   The Idea of the IKEv2 Protocol

In order to fully consider and support IKEv2, the periodic key updates and identity re certification, implementation of key generation is safe and effective and the mechanism of exchange. It requires to complete the functions: through the exchange of four news – IKE_SA_INIT switching and IKE_AUTH switching to realize the original IKE protocol in stage 1 and stage 2 functions, namely the establishment of IKE SA and IPSec SA. It completes definition of various loads in the agreement; the necessary control of the SA life cycle and other attributes, to ensure the safety, it must be promptly removed due to negotiate a new SA. The abnormal condition of certain is timely processing (such as message retransmission timeouts).

In this paper, by modifying the existing IKE source Linux to achieve IKEv2, it involves three aspects of Linux system: IKE source code, IKEv2 protocol mechanism and a comprehensive analysis, which is implementation of IKEv2 problems. Linux existing IKE implementations is lack of clear structure, different switching type, and the lack of a clear definition of message processing. By using existing IKE implementation, the user wants to initiate dynamic negotiation, the configuration file writing tedious, complicated operation command parameters. IKEv2 implementation simplifies user configuration; IKEv2 encryption and authentication mechanism and key generating method is quite different from IKE, need to be redefined. IKE SA is both sides through consultations. IKEv2 agreement no longer negotiate SA life cycle, life cycle of SA responsible parties. Due to SA events, communication both sides must make appropriate treatment; the existing of IKE implementation, it generates the IPSec SA proposal when the program runs to stage 2, and in IKEv2, the initial exchange third messages must send IPSec SA load, therefore need to generate the IPSec SA proposal.

In view of the problem above, in order to achieve functional goals of IKEv2, it adopts the following methods: interactive demand of IKEv2 key exchange process important link, the user spaces and kernels space and to provide the user with the IKEv2 configuration interface simple these aspects into consideration. It designs the overall framework of IKEv2 protocol, according to the function is divided into different modules. It no longer sets the exchange type more confusing, the initial exchange as the implementation of key agreement procedure body. Message processing is functioned by using the original IKE to using for the naming method at the beginning of the set. Encryption authentication module is used for IKEv2 encryption and integrity verification, authentication and key generation. In order to achieve these functions the appropriate location and exchange processes in the initial, it defines the IPSec SA proposal generating function of IKEv2 initiation. It defines a new IPSec SA initialization function for the receiver. In accordance with the procedure of IKEv2 communication between the two sides, it negotiations on IPSec SA. According to the requirements of the standard definition of SA is the due processing function. Setting the configuration management module is used to generate IPSec SA and SA this kind of need due to the kernel SAD, SPD interactive function.

3   The Structure and Module of IKEv2

IKEv2 is to achieve the main function is divided into five modules: the session monitoring module, control and conversion module, configuration management module, message processing module, encryption and authentication module. The dotted line outside the region is the core part of. Database key algorithm library provided by OpenSSL. The administrator can through the user interface configuration of security strategy and the security attributes, and monitoring start negotiation session. The IKEv2's user interface using Java language extensible development platform based on Eclipse writing. The kernel of SPD, SAD and configuration management module interface using the PF_KEY key management interface. The structure diagram as shown in Fig. 1.

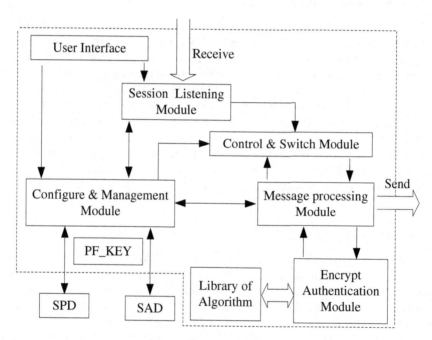

Fig. 1. The structure diagram

The conversational monitor module is responsible for initiating negotiations on a network session information as well as the kernel of demand information monitoring receiver. When the core of a dynamic negotiation needs, the communication began to sponsor identity launch key exchange. When it received the network of the side negotiation request, the communication is in response to the identity of the key exchange requests for comment. No matter what kind of situation is caused by the key exchange, it will be delivered to the control and conversion module to determine the state of the. Exchanging state of different type and different order determines the load message. The message processing module is the core part of IKEv2, which is responsible for message sending and receiving process. In the initial exchange after the two message processing, message processing module also needs and encryption authentication module. Extract the corresponding algorithms from the algorithm library, it communicates entity to verify the identity of encryption and decryption and integrity verification. When the IKEv2 negotiation process is completed, the configuration management module is added to SAD kernel and treatment due to SA. When IPSec SA expires, the configuration management module receives the PF_KEY message to the SA kernel, delete expired. If the initiator receives the IPSec SA message is transferred to expire, control and conversion module, to start negotiations.

4   Realization of Key Modules '

4.1   Session Listening Module

IKEv2 mainly needs to monitor treatment of two kinds of information: from the kernel configuration information and from other ISAKMP information consultation. Submitting session monitoring module is responsible for these two types of information, analysis and monitoring, receiving the next function module. First, it establishes a socket for two types of information to monitor: ISAKMP socket and pfkey socket. Then listening process, when the message is received it becomes the news source. Only if the socket received information belongs to the consultation session information ISAKMP, which is called the ISAKMP handles (isakmp_handle) processing the message, after delivery to the IKEv2 control and conversion module. When the pfkey configurations information sent to the kernel, it calls the pfkey handle (pfkey_handle) treatment the news, delivered to the configuration management module is finished processing.

4.2   Control and Switch Module

Controlling and conversion module is responsible for IKEv2 negotiation before initialization, message receiving and sending messages, exchange interface and message processing function conversion between. Consultation before initialization includes the creation of a ph1handle structure and to set the initial state, and according to the initial state of SIT_START, through an array of sit exchange to find and enter the message processing module of the corresponding function ident_i1send or ident_r1recv. Cohesive message receiving and message transmission is completed by the switch_main function, when receiving treatment after return, the message looks up exchange state change corresponds to a message processing flow. The state transition arrays are used to establish the corresponding relationship between the switching state and message processing functions provided in this module.

4.3   Message Processing Module

Message processing includes the message processing and message receiving and processing. Message processing refers to according to the protocol requirements and assembly of all types of loads, and the loads are the loads chain general loading head. If it needs to encrypt or loading verification and validation data encryption module inter-action, in accordance with the algorithm specification key operations that are necessary. Then loads encrypted payload header. Finally, it loads the IKEv2 message header, sending the message from the UDP500 port. There are four main message processing functions: two genera two species initiator, responder. The message receiving and processing is the inverse operation message processing. First off the message header, the load removing message, make corresponding processing according to the load type. If the message header "under a load" domain that is encrypted with the required load, encryption and authentication module interaction, to decrypt and verify the integrity of encrypted payload, isolated from various types of loads from the decrypted data, further processing. If you have a AUTH load message by encrypting, authentication module to verify its. There are four main message receiving and processing function: two genera two species initiator, responder. Process is shown in Fig. 2 message processing.

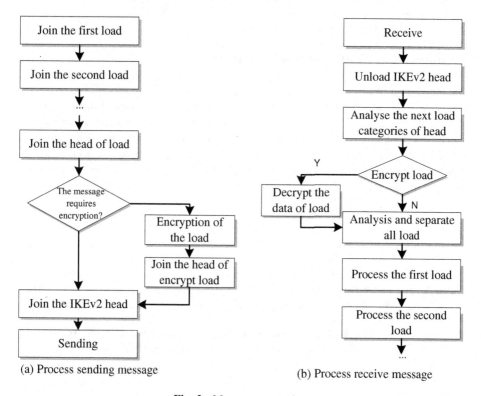

(a) Process sending message

(b) Process receive message

Fig. 2. Message processing

4.4   Encryption and Authentication Module

Encryption and authentication module mainly has three parts: the function key material generation, message encryption and integrity verification, the communication party identity information verification. Through the oakley_skey seed, oakley_skeyseed_dae, oakley_skeyseed_auth three functions are generated key used for encryption and decryption of SKEYSEED strips. The establishment of sub SA exchanges key material, used for key materials AUTH load authentication information. Encryption and decryption and integrity verification applies all the messages in the third, four messages and initial exchange. IKEv2 protocol encryption payloads format within the specified time to clear the way to the initial vector IV before the encrypted data region, this paper realized to account for this IV is easy to leak, and according to the requirements in the agreement. It can be pseudorandomly generated or with a final ciphertext block of a message as a IV. Therefore the encrypted payload format for IKEv2 was improved – set IV is not in the structure of encryption load domain, while the last ciphertext block before a messaging approach to derivative IV.

To validate the data domain AUTH loads placed in the signature or when using pre shared key MAC. In response, the signature bytes including the second messages (in sending second messages, save it as r_buf), and additional Ni, PRF (SK_pr, IDr') value. For starters, the signature bytes including the first message (in sending the first message, save it as i_buf), and additional Nr, PRF (SK_pi, IDi') value.

5   Innovation Points Are Summarized

The innovation of this paper is based on the principle of IKEv2 protocol. Based on the important link, the key exchange process user space and kernel space information and to provide the user with IKEv2 configuration interface simple these requirements, framework, functional module design of IKEv2 protocol. According to the initiator and the responder roles determine the program flow of key agreement which is using the state transition array to convert the exchange state and processing function, control message processing etc.

References

1. Ari Huttunen, UDP Encapsulation of IPsec Packets. http://www.faqs.org/rfcs/rfc3948.htm
2. Petersen, R.: Linux Technology Guinness, vol. 1. Mechanical industry press, Brussels (2002)
3. Davis, C.R.: IPsec: VPN Security Implementation, vol. 1. Tsinghua University Press, Beijing (2002)
4. Yonghe, L.: IP Based End to End Security Model of Communication Network Analysis and Design, vol. P1, pp. 3–10. Micro computer information, Beijing (2005)

CLOUDCOMP Workshop

Research and Design of Power Companies Unified Communications System

Hanshi Zhao[✉], Jinglong Wu, Pan Deng, and Ming Cai

Laboratory of Parallel Software and Computational Science,
Institute of Software Chinese Academy of Sciences, Beijing, China
zhs_0407@163.com, 455675491@qq.com
{dengpan, caiming}@iscas.ac.cn

Abstract. The unified communications system have a great advantage in coordination office and information management. The system can combine different communications networks and share information through a variety of protocols. This paper briefly described the development and composition of unified communications system, studied its typical applications in electronic power company, designed its overall structure and introduced each layer of the system. Through the descriptions, explained the unified communications system can improve the management efficiency.

Keywords: Unified communications system · Electronic power company · Overall structure · Platform architecture

1 Background

Communication industry, IT (Information Technology) and the Internet have achieved rapid developments in recent years. People have become increasingly dependent on their cell phones, computers and the Internet. In work and life people communicate with each other by telephone, voice mail, e-mail, fax, video, audio conferencing, IM (Instant Messaging) software and so on. This gives people's work and live great convenience. However, these systems exist independently and use inconsistent interfaces currently. So users have an urgent need for a platform which consolidates existing means of communication. Users can use it easily and quickly in different networks, communication methods and communication environment of different devices. The platform should have a unified user interface, with all the features which users need. The Unified Communications System came into being, which is the inevitable result of developments in communications industry, IT industry and Internet industry [1].

Unified Communications products include unified communications clients, enterprises in network presence, and instant messaging, unified messaging, IP telephony, multimedia conferencing, contact center applications, communications infrastructure and management tools and so on. Unified messaging is an important part. Unified Communications System does not combine the features of each part simply, but provides an intelligent structure, helps enterprises (this article on the background of the power companies) to integrate their communications and business processes more closely, and through the most suitable media to ensure that the information can be transferred to the recipient quickly.

© Institute for Computer Sciences, Social Informatics and Telecommunications Engineering 2015
V.C.M. Leung et al. (Eds.): CloudComp 2014, LNICST 142, pp. 183–188, 2015.
DOI: 10.1007/978-3-319-16050-4_18

Unified Communications System can build a highly efficient and stable unified communications platform, achieve a variety of systems based on message passing, establish a unified power company address book and application directory, solve the problems in the process of internal coordination office fundamentally, improve power company in personnel management and the fluency of communication, increase core competitiveness in the increasingly complex market environment, adapt the development strategy of "centralized management, centralized system, fusion system, specification for unified", strengthen the exchange of information within and outside of the power companies, improve the efficiency of coordination office and overall information management of the whole power company.

2   Introduction to Unified Communications System

Unified Communications System uses standard protocols such as SIP (Session Initiation Protocol), RTP (Real-time Transport Protocol), T.38 (Procedures for Real-Time Group 3 Facsimile Communication Over IP Networks) to communicate with IP phone or voice gateway, uses SMTP (Simple Mail Transfer Protocol) or POP3 (Post Office Protocol 3) to communicate with mail server, uses SMS (Short Message Service) gateway to connect to the mobile network of operators, provides users with all types of messages' (including voice mail, fax, mail, e-mail) unified receive, management, storage, extraction, message reminder, and other services to simplify operations and improve work efficiency [2].

Unified Communication System combines different communications networks and news media by different protocols, integrate various types of messages (such as voice mail, faxes, short messages, instant messages, e-mail, online meetings, and so on) into a unified entrance and interface to manager, transform, distribute, and store [3]. Provides a unified mailbox for each user to ensure users can send and receive messages through this mailbox by types of terminal equipment and media (such as fax machines, telephones, computers, and so on) at any given time or place to get information in a timely manner, improve the efficiency of communication.

3   Typical Application of Unified Communication System in Electric Power Companies

3.1   SMS

Users can send short message to communicate with online users point to point, send multiple messages to offline users or transform messages (when user is not on line) into short messages to send to others; Power companies can send a notification in the system in broadcasting model. Users can set the notification service to make the unified message system sends short messages to mobile phones immediately when the status of the unified mailbox changes, remind the user has new messages need to handle in the first time.

3.2   Make IP Calls

Users can call each other through a communication client. If user is busy can transfer into voice mail.

3.3   Voicemail

When the called phone is busy or unanswered calls, the phone will be automatically transferred to voice mail of the calling user, and play comparable prompt. Caller leaves a message according to prompt, called user get the message at a convenient time [4]. In the past, users must use telephones to listen or handle the messages, when they do not have the phones, they are unable to get the messages. The appearance of unified messaging provides more ways to get the messages.

3.4   Send Mail

E - Mail can not only use the telephone network, but also can be transmitted by any other communication networks. When using the telephone network, can also transmit information during the off-peak, it has special value for the business mail. Electronic systems controlled by the central computers and small computers for limited users can be regarded as a computer conferencing system. E - Mail gradually passing information over the network in store - forward way, not as directly as the phone, but the cost is low.

3.5   Video Conference

General video conference system scheme includes MCU (multi-points controller), conference room terminal, PC desktop terminal, PSTN (Public Switched Telephone Network) Gateway, Gatekeeper and so on. Different terminals are connected to MCU for centralizing exchange, form a video conferencing network. With the advent of cloud computing technology, cloud computing video conference mode appears in the video conferencing systems areas, cloud computing of video conference system supports multiple server dynamic cluster deployment and provides high-performance servers, greatly enhanced the conference on stability, security, availability. In recent years, as cloud computing video conferencing can significantly improve the efficiency of communication, reduce communication costs continuously, bring the internal management level upgrades, is greeted by many users, has been widely used in government, military, education, transport, transportation, finance, operators, enterprises and other fields [5–7]. No doubt, after the video conference using cloud computing, has more attraction in convenience, fast and easy-to-use nature, will motivate video - conferencing application to the new climax. Cloud computing video conference is a perfect combination of video conference and cloud computing, brings the most convenient remote meeting experience.

Based on there have been many separate messages, email, voice and video conferencing systems at present, so unified communications systems can open interfaces to each other with the power companies' system for integration.

4   Design of Collective Structure

As power company currently uses a video conferencing system and a relatively sound client platform which can send messages, make phone calls, send faxes, email, launch a video - conferencing. In the unified communications system designed for the power company, make them open port each other to achieve communication collaboration.

Unified communications system for power company is a system which integrated instant messaging, telephone, voice-mail, video conferencing, messaging, and other major communications, provides users a feature - rich, easy-to-use communications environment. The whole platform is based on the data center, uniform identity authentication, e-mail and video conferencing systems and other public support platforms. Data center provides user data for platform; uniform identity authentication system provides user authentication, identity services, and information service of the organization for platform; e-mail system provides message sending and receiving service for platform. Unified communications system video conference system provides protection to video conferencing between two users in point-to-point and even system initiates a conferencing make users to participate. Unified communications platform uses hierarchical design ideas, platform, application, and channel are designed and implemented hierarchically. Open access interface design contents individual systems to insert; standard message access protocol contents all types of SMS gateway, email, voice and video to access seamlessly. Unified communications platform also need to set up sophisticated platform management center, working system and management system to ensure the sustainable development of the unified communications platform [8–10].

The general structure of unified communications platform uses hierarchical design ideas to achieve a clear structure by layering and modular, reduce couplings between different modules, have flexibility to expand and extend functions when the requirements change (Fig. 1).

(1) Terminal for users to access:
    Achieve the unified user interface. Users can use communications services provided by the platform through the unified communications system client, including instant messaging, text messaging, email, call, and so on.

    Users can send meeting notices to the personnel in the office network easily and initiated the meeting by unified communications video conference system, users also can join the meeting voluntarily.

    The interfaces of unified communications system client and video conference system are opening each other to achieve the systems call each other. Achieving comprehensiveness of the features and uniqueness of the way to access to terminal.

(2) Platform interface layer:
    Through the interface layer, platform can not only abutted joints to the applications of the unified communications platform, various Internet products and third-party business applications directly. But also can integrate a variety of other products and business system plugins, or value-added functions modules developed by third party developers, systems integrators.

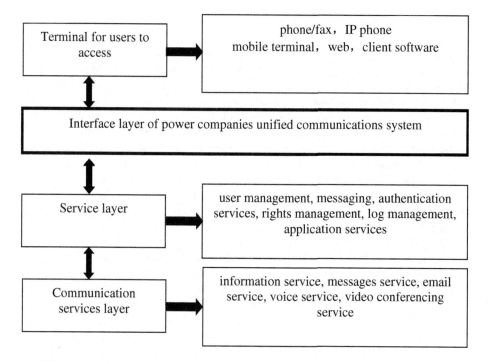

Fig. 1. The overall architecture of power companies unified communications system.

Achieve the unified user management through the portal of power company and Novell Directory user data to complete the user access to various functions which terminal provides. Based on the openness of platform interface layer, it is more convenient to other applications and plugins to join.

(3) Service layer:

Platform service layer offers a range of unified communication platform shared infrastructure services module for upper - class communications and business applications call. Platform service components include: user management, messaging, authentication services, rights management, log management, application services, and so on.

(4) Communication services layer:

Communication services layer accesses a variety of information channels, offers information, messages, text messages, voice and video conferencing services. Communication services offer more ways for communication, such as Instant messaging, SMS, email integration, video conferencing; make communication faster, send messages to remind instantly, no matter messages get or not. Make ways to communicate better, using intelligent communication structures, without checking contacts strenuously.

5 Conclusions

Unified communication platform can combine different communications networks and media through a variety of different protocols. The platform also combines various types of messages, such as messaging, voice, fax, SMS, e-mail, video conferencing, consolidates a unified interface system to ensure users access to information in a timely manner and improve the efficiency of communication. As the communication platform of power company, unified communications system will become a very important part of the power company's unified communications program. Modern communication systems are growing to networked, integrated and intelligent. Advantages of unified communications systems integration are exchanging links, share resources, speed. This is also in the line with requirements of science and technology development, help to improve the management efficiency of the power companies, business capacity and competitiveness of enterprises.

Acknowledgments. The work was supported by the National Natural Science Foundation of China (no.61100066).

References

1. Pang, M, Huang, L.: Design and implementation of the same messaging system, 9–15 (2013)
2. Wang, J.: Research and Policy Analysis of Chinese Unified Communications. BUPT, Beijing (2009)
3. Jia, C., Zhao, Y., Cheng, Y.: Research and design of the unified communications platform of Zhejiang university. Exp. Technol. Manage **09**, TN915 (2009)
4. Saint-Andre, P.: Extensible messaging and presence protocol (XMPP) core. RFC 3920 (2004)
5. Chiang, T.-C., Douglas, J.: IN services for converged telephony. IEEE Com. **38**, 108–115 (2010)
6. Deng, P., Zhang, J.W., Rong, X.H., Chen, F.: A model of large-scale device collaboration system based on PI calculus for green communication. Telecommun. Syst. **8**(52), 1313–1326 (2013)
7. Deng, P., Zhang, J.W., Rong, X.H., Chen, F.: Modeling the large-scale device control system based on PI-calculus. Adv. Sci. Lett. **4**, 2374–2379 (2011)
8. Rong, X.H., Deng, P., Chen, F.: A large-scale device collaboration resource selection method with multi-QoS constraint supported. Adv. Mater. Res. **143**, 894–898 (2011)
9. Rong, X.H., Chen, F., Deng, P., Ma, S.L.: A large-scale device collaboration mechanism. J. Comput. Res. Dev. **9**, 1589–1596 (2011)
10. Chen, F., Rong, X.H., Deng, P., Ma, S.L.: A survey of device collaboration technology and system software. Acta Electronica Sinica **39**, 440–447 (2011)

The Application of Inspection Robot in Substation Inspection

Yang Song[✉], Pan Deng, Ming Cai, and Feng Chen

Lab of Parallel Software and Computational Science, Institute of Software
Chinese Academy of Sciences, Beijing, China
09301022@bjtu.edu.cn, {dengpan, caiming, chenfeng}
@iscas.ac.cn

Abstract. According to the development of electric power and the expanded range of substation equipment, which caused workload of the equipment inspection increasing, a program which using inspection robot to help the sub-station inspection mission has been proposed in this paper. The inspection robot system and software design have been researched to provide a modernization, information and intelligent method of substation inspection.

Keywords: Substation inspection · Inspection robot · Intelligent inspection

1 Introduction

With the development of power grid and improvement of substation voltage grade, the work area of substation has been expanded constantly and the operational condition has become more complicated, which cause that the inspection range and the work load become heavy. The usual mankind inspection and other methods simply rely on inspectors' sense and experience which is hard for them to find out the problems accurately, may cause many hidden dangers for the equipment and power grid. Sub-station equipment inspection is a basic work to effectively ensure the safe operation of the substation equipment and enhance the reliability of power supply, which is mainly divided into the routine inspection and special inspection. Routine inspection is request at least two times a day; Special inspection is request of the hot weather, heavy load operation, strong wind, fog, snow, hail, thunderstorm. The main existing inspection ways are include artificial patrol, manual and handheld PDA records, each patrol time is at least two hours. There are a lot of substations which geographical conditions is very bad in China, such as high altitude, extreme heat, cold, wind, dust, rain, etc. So manual work in outdoors for a long time is very difficult to finish equipment inspection work. And there are many problems for manual inspection, such as high intensity of labor, low efficiency, high management cost and decentralized detection quality. Inspection robots can aid inspectors to inspect equipment to avoid hidden dangers.

Inspection robots assist to complete visible light and infrared inspection in high-voltage substation equipment through autonomous system or remote operation. In connection with the loss of image monitor system and the weakness of temperature check in the head of electric equipment from home and abroad, Inspection robots use infrared cameras to monitor accurate temperature now which results in that the inspectors could get equipment temperature information.

© Institute for Computer Sciences, Social Informatics and Telecommunications Engineering 2015
V.C.M. Leung et al. (Eds.): CloudComp 2014, LNICST 142, pp. 189–196, 2015.
DOI: 10.1007/978-3-319-16050-4_19

2   Research on Inspection Robot Application

The inspection robot provides mobile carrier platforms for substation equipment to collect non-electrical signal, then professionals can build different monitoring systems or devices on this platform. Many inspection robot applications are used, such as remote on-line infrared system, acquisition of visible light image and processing system, detection and diagnosis system for remote image, sound collecting and processing system and warming system to detect moving object.

2.1   Remote On-line Infrared System

This system uses online infrared thermal imaging device acquisition equipment to acquire infrared image, the processes the infrared image to display, storage, and query and generate report. Before the system is in motion, system need to preset equipment's' temperature threshold, through the automatic judgment on the threshold, it can give voice and text alarm to the base station equipment main control computer when some equipment is beyond the alarm value.

This system can determine the internal temperature gradient in some key equipment. It can generate the temperature curve about some key equipment at a certain moment, or generate the temperature curve for one key equipment in a certain period of time.

2.2   Remote Image Detection and Diagnosis System

The system use robots to recognize the visible light image, then the image data is passed to the base station, system can analysis and diagnosis the image data in the base station.

The main process includes, first of all, preprocess the acquisition of image, identify the power equipment which is monitored, then analyze between this image and the last collecting image by a series of related operations, finally identify whether the equipment is in the normal state.

2.3   The Sound Collection and Processing System

The system is mainly to detect transformer system noise and diagnosis analysis, using the robot noise data, through wireless network back to the base station. Then using related comprehensive testing model, to test and analyze the noise data from the base station system, it can conclude that the working state of the transformer, if abnormal, go to further analysis of the exception type.

2.4   Moving Objects Detecting and Alarming System

This system is mainly to monitor the suspicious target in the substation environment, then track the suspicious target, get his video and alarm for the staff. Professionals can analyze the target video, extract the athletic areas, suspicious target type, and remind supervisors to pay more attention to these situations.

3 Research on Inspection Robot System

Substation inspection robot system is divided into two system layers, one is base station, and the other is mobile station.

The system layer of base station is mainly composed of wireless bridges and monitoring computers. It is mainly used to display visible and infrared images dynamically, collect and store the visible and infrared images automatically, then analysis and process them. It is also used to display the real-time position and movement of the robot, display the power status of the robot, then analysis and alert exception. It is also used to query historical data which is collected in the scene by the robot, then compare and analyze it. It can provide the appropriate commands for the robot operation and environmental information.

The system layer of mobile station is mainly composed of power systems, navigation systems, detection systems, control systems, communication systems and motion systems. It is primarily responsible for the acquisition and processing of navigation and positioning information, it can complete inspection tasks automatically according to the predefined tours, it also can position at preset points automatically, collect visible and infrared images, and then upload them to the base station. After the robot completes the inspection tasks, it can charge automatically. When the robot encounter an obstacle during operation, it can alert to the base station. The main component is robot body and charging case. The operation modes of the robot are visible detecting, infrared detection, and all detection of three. The system layer of base station can control of the operation modes. Visible detection is mainly for daylight hours, infrared detector is mainly for night time, and all detection is mainly for visible and infrared detection of the actual testing needs. By setting the operation mode, not only reduce power consumption effectively, increase the using of robot time, but also protect the infrared cameras and other equipment under strong light, then extend the life of the equipment.

Inspection robot system architecture is shown in Fig. 1, the use of inspection robot for wireless communication devices, base station and mobile station system, to accomplish inspection data command remote and base station by remote control. On this basis, the ability to easily access dedicated optical fiber communication network can be done in power system to exchange data with the dispatch Center.

Research of inspection robot system works as follows. In inspection robot monitoring main station by running personnel issued visits task or by base station system automatically to issue inspection task, to started inspection robot for work; inspection robot uses local planning mobile to visits task in the of docked points, and in docked points parking; they are sent arrived docked points of information to base station system, according to configuration file in the docked points of information issued advance set of visits command, and inspection robot uses mobile cloud on inspection equipment for precise positioning for equipment of visible and infrared imaging detection; Inspection robots in time save and upload the visible and infrared images of

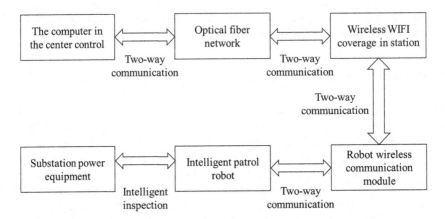

Fig. 1. The overall structure of the inspection robot system Photographs.

the device. If the temperature exceeds a predetermined maximum temperature detection device robot alerts the operator. Robotic testing has been completed, base station for inspection robot issue instructions to inspect the docking points.

The inspection robot system uses infrared cameras and visible light cameras measured Imaging signal, uses the robot wireless network devices via fiber channel transmissions to the control room monitor computers on your network to finish implementing in a two-way channel for intelligent control of inspection robot. Combining optical image, image registration, image fusion algorithms, temperature information obtained from infrared images can be displayed in the visible image. Solving the problem at high temperature and pressure under harsh ambient conditions temperature detection, anti-robbing, anti-theft and alarming problem, so what you see is measured.

4   Software Design on Inspection Robot System

System software functionality can be divided into four modules: human-computer interaction interface, control module, monitoring module, information management module. System specific software functionality as shown in Fig. 2. Taking into account the various functions of the system, structure and later ease of scalability requirements and development environments, the system is modular in software development using object-oriented programming methods.

(1) Human-computer interaction interface: the top system is the core user interface management, an operator press button to operate instructions.
(2) Control module: respectively using the decoder head from top to bottom and move around, and the visible light (infrared) CCD aperture adjustment, scenes telescopic adjustments, etc. Achieve control over the front of CCD and functions transferred control of the robot. The software interface for the operation, due to that it is the top layer, called down-level functional modules to implement.

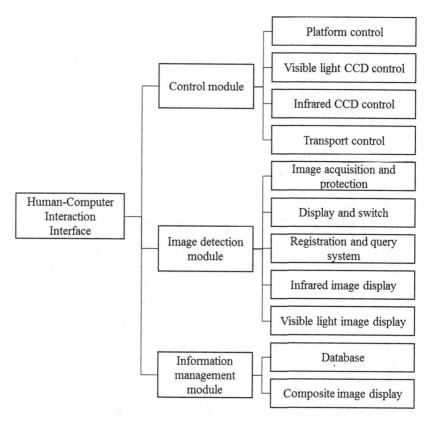

Fig. 2. The overall design of system software.

(3) Video monitor module: monitor independently for infrared thermal image and optical image, including image acquisition, preservation, infrared thermal image display, visible and infrared image and optical images matching the image display, processing, synthetic image is displayed after the match and switch of the display window. Also it can check image saved in image databases at any time.

(4) Information management modules: client login, manage users, queries. Complete system features such as parameter settings, system configurations, and agent services, and provide common emission rate of queries, and so on.

Considering the image on-line monitoring for electrical equipment in substation needs, ease of scalability requirements and development environments, system software distribution client program and a server-side program to achieve a centralized control station and substation network communications between, it provides powerful features such as controls, display, storage, and provides other computers on the network with visible light, infrared imaging and synthetic images. By accessing the server, managers can get the remote monitor image and can be remote controlled robot with pan/tilt movements and complete synthesis features such as intelligent.

5 Design on Base Station Control System

The base station control system mainly consist of the supervisory computer system, switch and the corresponding wireless communication equipment. The master monitoring station system is based on the Windows system, design and development by java object-oriented programming language, it can provide friendly operation interface and complete monitoring functions for users. It also can provide command and corresponding information for robot motion planning, store and analyze the equipment data acquisition, then provide diagnosis from experts. Its main functions include:

(1) Remote control of the robot. It is used the keyboard or mouse to control some of the robot's actions. Such as robot running and the movements of platform, camera focusing, the operations of thermal infrared imager, acquisition of the visible light and infrared data, then realize the remote inspection robot.

(2) Automatic inspection. Operators can create, store and delete inspection task automatically. When operators create or delete patrol tasks in the man-machine interface, operators can manually set automatic execution time. When automatic inspection tasks is executed, system need to send the docked points of this task and the task information to the mobile robot. The robot can perform many assignments, such as movements of platform, automatic camera focusing, automatic operations of infrared thermal imager, acquisition of automatic operation visible light and infrared data and self-charging.

(3) Real-time data monitoring. The visible light cameras and infrared thermal imager can be displayed by real-time video, with the remote control and automatic inspection function, implement the background of inspection by operators and real-time data storage. In order to obtain better control, there is a need to connect monitor system with inspection robot together, it can make the inspection robot accept the monitoring end's instructions, and can deal with real-time information which is collected at the scene to monitor system. Monitoring system is running in the monitoring terminal, responsible for the tele operation control of inspection robot. As the top of the inspection system, monitoring system is the only interface between operators and inspection robot. The quality of its design will directly affect the whole system function.

Monitoring system is used to record inspection robot running conditions and data automatically, and used for artificial monitoring, remote control, query and management of inspection data. The monitoring system software platform is composed of man-machine interface, power management and image database. In addition to complete the basic switch and mobile operation for the robot and the equipment, it also need to pro-vide more advanced and humanization functions, including to control the robot operation mode, alarm of ab-normal information and self-treatment, and manage software operators. Instrument or equipment which is needed to inspect regular in the substation, can firstly save the position information and the platform information what can make robot to carry out normal shot as calibration list. It will the need to save the inspection time to the operation parameter list, then triggered by a timer. When arriving at the inspection time, it can control the robot to complete the automatic inspection task. The automatic inspection involves and operates various equipment, so the state machine model is used to coordinate and control the modules, then inspect smoothly. The monitoring software is also equipped with the instrument recognition function, it can identify instrument photos what is taken by the HD camera automatically, when beyond the normal range instrument calibration, it will alarm to operators about the abnormal data, then can remind the operator attention. Similarly, robot equipped with infrared camera can detect abnormal temperature equipment, if it is found that exceeded the normal operating temperature of the device, will also carry out alarming. Due to the daily inspection produces a huge amount of data, so it needs to check the data which is stored in the database, then is convenient for the follow-up management. Therefore, software has the ability to connect to databases, and can store, modify and delete the data. The need for management of the data can be divided into five main parts, including the user login information, user information, image information, the calibration information, and operation parameters information. Then it need to establish a corresponding table for storage and be man-aged in database. In addition, human interface software also need to provide a convenient user operation.

(4) Showing state information of the robot. It provide to the internal real-time state information about the robot, which can reflect the running status of the robot, so it is convenience to control and inspect the robot, using the electronic map can display the real-time location of robot.

(5) Data storage and analysis. Some data needs to be saved to the database, such as the robot the operational needs of the electronic map information, task management information, system information and real-time database information, at the same time, it can create the robot running logs and inspection records, it is very useful for Historical queries and analysis. So it can provide analysis functions to test data.

(6) The Analysis of historical temperature of the equipment. It can analyze the variation trend of the historical temperature about the equipment, compare temperature among the similar types of equipment, contrast the friendship between load and temperature about the equipment, provide decision support for equipment maintenance and condition assessment, implement the analysis and diagnosis of substation equipment running status.

(7) MIS system interface. Associated with the production of MIS system, MIS system will provide patrol data sharing.

6 Conclusions

Inspection robot system in this paper is described in General, mainly related to the detailed description of hardware and software systems. The power industry is the prerequisite and guarantee of people's daily life and industrial production. With rapid economic development and the improvement of people's living standard, China has increased investment in the power system to enhance technical and managerial levels to ensure safe operation of the power system. Inspection robot for substation equipment put up in unmanned substation and strengthening safety background. Inspection robot monitors devices in the substation, and timely delivery of execution video images to the main control room to support staff to handle exceptions within a substation. However, the substation's unmanned patrol there exist certain problems, such as rapid response capabilities to reduce accidents, inclement weather or timely monitoring substation devices, causing the normal operation of substation a hazard. So inspection robots technology need to be constantly improved and perfective.

Acknowledgments. The work was supported by the National Natural Science Foundation of China (no.61100066).

References

1. Smith, T.F., Waterman, M.S.: Identification of common molecular subsequences. J. Mol. Biol. **147**, 195–197 (1981)
2. Xie, X.Z.: Research on navigation and positioning of robot for substation equipment inspection (in Chinese). SWUST, Mianyang Sichuan (2008)
3. Wang, J.F., Jia, X.X., Fang, J.: Substation inspection robot encoder inertial trackless navigation (in Chinese). Water Conservancy Electr. Power Mach. **35**(8), 11–14 (2013)
4. Wu, G.P., Li, C., Ma, Y.L., Guo, K.X.: High voltage grid inspection robot research and application review (in Chinese). In: The Collection of the National Power Transmission and Transformation Equipment State Maintenance Technology Exchange Conference (2009)
5. Zhang, X., Wu, S.L., Wang, S.A.: Research on key technology of outdoor mobile robot autonomous navigation based on information fusion (in Chinese). In: The Sixth National Conference on Fluid Power Transmission and Control (2010)
6. Wei, J.Y., Wang, J.D., Zhou, F.Y.: Structure design and kinematics analysis of mew inspection robot (in Chinese). Coal Mine mach. **6**, 45–46 (2005)
7. Huq, R., Lacheray, H., Fulford, C., et al.: QBOT: an educational mobile robot controlled in MATLAB Simulink environment. In: Proceedings of Canadian Conference on Electrical and Computer Engineering. St. John'S, NL, Canada (2009)

The Application of RFID
and Two-Dimensional Bar Code
in Substation Inspection

DeYi Zou$^{(\boxtimes)}$, Ming Cai, Feng Chen, Pan Deng, and Huahua Ning

Lab of Parallel Software and Computational Science,
Institute of Software Chinese Academy of Sciences, Beijing, China
{deyi, caiming, chenfeng, dengpan, huahua}@iscas.ac.cn

Abstract. According to the disadvantages of traditional methods of substation inspection, a new substation inspection system using radio frequency identification and two-dimensional code technology has been developed in this paper. The goals and advantages of substation inspection system which based on radio frequency identification and two-dimensional code technology have been researched. It's proved that the system willing improve the efficiency and scientific of electricity inspection management.

Keywords: Substation inspection · Radio frequency identification · RFID · Two-dimensional bar code

1 Introduction

In the power industry, for power equipment, especially the substation, doing regular and well placed patrol inspection is necessary. It is the important guarantee for safe and stable operation for power system. Substation inspection can find the defects and faults of power equipment in time and nip in the bud [1]. In modern power industry, power supply circuit is various, and more long transmission lines come into being, many voltage grades and wide geographical distribution. These factors have brought many difficulties to the line inspection and management.

Traditional antiquated working styles in power equipment inspection tour, hand-made paper records are generally used. There are many loopholes in substation inspection and management, such as record loss, low efficiency, long working period, inspection in place not easy to monitor and so on. Therefore sometimes electric department cannot timely and accurately grasp the condition of the equipment of power supply system.

The advanced radio frequency identification (RFID) technology and two-dimensional bar code, together with the function of radio frequency identification and two-dimensional bar code scanning mobile terminal substation inspection equipment can solve the problems existing in the substation inspection [2].

© Institute for Computer Sciences, Social Informatics and Telecommunications Engineering 2015
V.C.M. Leung et al. (Eds.): CloudComp 2014, LNICST 142, pp. 197–203, 2015.
DOI: 10.1007/978-3-319-16050-4_20

2   The Introduction of Radio Frequency Identification and Two-Dimensional Bar Code

RFID (Radio Frequency Identification, RFID) is a rapidly developing automatic identification technology in electronics, which uses radio frequency signal through space coupling (alternating magnetic field or electromagnetic field) to make non-contacting information transmission possible, access to relevant data labels, achieving the goal of automatic Identification [3, 4].

Radio frequency identification (RFID) system is general composed of RFID tags, antenna, and RFID read-write unit. RFID tag is composed of coupling components and circuit, and the energy for emission waves and internal processor running all from card reader of electromagnetic waves. After passive tags receive the electromagnetic wave signal from the reader, part of the electromagnetic energy will be converted into energy for their own work, and then antenna transmits signal between tag and reader. RFID card read unit is the equipment to read the electronic tag information, and it can non-contact read and identify the data preserved in the electronic tags, and it also can automatically identify the object.

Two-dimensional bar code is relative to the case of one dimensional code. Based on a particular geometry, a 2D (two-dimensional) bar code is a graphical image that stores information both horizontally as one-dimensional bar codes do and vertically. In the aspect of the code instrumentation, it is a clever use of the concept of "0" and "1" bit stream, which form the basis of computer internal logic, using a number of geometric shapes which corresponding to the binary to express numerical information to represent text automatically recognized by image input device or photoelectric scanning equipment in order to realize the automatic processing of information. It has some commonness of bar code technology: each code system has its particular character set; each character has a certain width; each has a certain calibration function, etc. At the same time it also has the automatic recognition function to different lines and processing graphics rotation changes, etc.

Two-dimensional bar code is a code format, which is more advanced than one-dimensional code bar. Compared with the one-dimensional bar code, two dimensional bar codes can show information in horizontal and vertical two bearing at the same time, making up for the flaws of the one-dimensional bar code. First of all, the two dimensional bar code can show a lot of information within the small area, without any dependence on database; Secondly, two dimensional bar code can represent Chinese characters, images and other information, expanding the application field of the bar code. Thirdly, two-dimensional bar code has error correction function, improving the anti-interference ability of the bar code. So the application field of two-dimensional bar code is much wider.

In the process of substation inspection, two-dimensional bar code technology and radio frequency identification can greatly improve the efficiency of inspection and ensure the inspection to complete with good quality on time. It is very significant to ensure the security of the power.

3   The Applications of Radio Frequency Identification and Two-Dimensional Bar Code Technology in the Substation Inspection

All the time, in the substation inspection task management, it always needs inspection personnel to investigate and record the acquisition of power equipment usage, inspection and maintenance information. In the substation inspection data acquisition, problems like how to ensure the inspection work completed efficiency, how to obtain accurate information about the effective inspection and how to ensure that inspection personnel not absence to complete inspection tasks draw more and more attention. With the development of science and technology and the accelerating pace of modernization construction, technical assistance are provided to solve this problem. Using radio frequency identification and two-dimensional bar code scanning technology standard informatization, we can realize the optimization of substation inspection system, in order to realize daily inspection standard informatization, data record specification informatization, work performance informatization and the ability of querying the accident responsibility and so on. This can greatly improve the ability of the electric power industry safety inspection.

3.1   The Target Research RFID Radio Frequency Identification Technology and Two-Dimensional Bar Code Applied in the Construction of the Substation Inspection

Data control center management system mainly includes data management workstation, data server, etc. Data control center management system can receive, sorted store, query the inspection data sent from mobile terminals and generate related reports. Of these devices can be abnormal statistics or into the information generated in the equipment maintenance management system defects. The data management system also has the function of database maintenance, can be carried out inspection site, inspection items, inspection cycle, the custom inspection line, etc. It is also responsible to establish the communication for the management system with upper management information system (MIS), to realize information sharing [6].

When inspection personnel do inspection operations, they can carry a handheld mobile terminal as inspection equipment. The mobile terminal should conform to the requirements of the three levels of prevention, and wireless Internet access, 3G Internet access and voice call, with functions of GPS navigation and positioning, and must have the function of the RFID radio frequency identification and two-dimensional bar code scanning. Using it automatically or manually to send interval information about the current location and direction of the MIS of inspection personnel to data control center every time If there appears the circumstances that power equipment doesn't normally operate, it will send fault types, equipment code and combined with the current handset terminal of RFID information or two-dimensional bar code data information to the data monitoring center. Receivers of data monitoring center receive related information, and then store them. At the same time, the checking data center system will check the information in the receiver system and identification after receiving, showing when and where the fault happened accurately, and the types of equipment failure, the inspection staff at that time. These data information is automatically deposited in the database server, can be launched on the Internet. Setting up on the substation RFID tags, a global unique identifier, to ensure that the inspection personnel in order to make the RFID identification number can only live for himself (herself). So it can guarantee for inspection staff in place in time. Through setting two-dimensional bar code identification on the different equipment in substations, by scanning two-dimensional bar code, inspection personnel can get the device information conveniently, such as model, manufacturer, and the operation needing to check, and conveniently uploading to the data center after finding the fault. Data center can identify according to the two-dimensional bar code, and match equipment of the database. By combining the RFID and the two-dimensional bar code, the arrival rate of routing inspection can be guaranteed. At the same time, power inspection personnel can strengthen management and formulate measures to ensure the safe operation of the power equipment by checking, summarizing, analyzing and forecasting the data in the database.

3.2   The Value of RFID Radio Frequency Identification Technology and Two-Dimensional Bar Code Applied to Substation Inspection

There are many advantages for RFID radio frequency identification and two-dimensional bar code technology applied in the substation inspection. Such as:

Using RFID substation is helpful for planning and monitoring inspection line. Substation equipment using two-dimensional bar code can be convenient for inspection and maintenance. The two methods can also be used to effectively supervise whether the inspection personnel in place.

With the help of a mobile terminal software and hardware and data center statistics database query function, the convenient application program can be developed according to the inspection task and checking process. It will record automatically inspection tag, simplify record defects or reading content, improve the efficiency of the normative and execution of inspection work.

Comparing with the traditional way (manual record or bar code), RFID radio frequency identification and the two-dimensional bar code technology applied in electric power inspection has higher security, and also provides for the total assets life cycle management of power equipment, and various equipment and personnel management of consistency and linkage of technology base.

3.3   System Design of RFID Radio Frequency Identification and Two-Dimensional Code Technology Applied in Substation Inspection

In general, electric inspection carries out according to the route designated by inspection task. Each task contains some inspection routes and each inspection route contains some inspection orientations and each orientation contains some equipment need to check. Inspection personnel need to check the working condition of equipment and lines according to certain process and record the defects and meter reading. The advantages of RFID radio frequency identification and two-dimensional code technology is suitable for power transmission line inspection, all routes, range and the device identifier. For the equipment which only need to record the meter reading, we can use relatively simple, inexpensive two-dimensional code label. For the equipment which need more complex inspection, the RFID label can be used to record the status information of the equipment for each inspection.

Schematic of carrying out two-dimensional code recognition and RFID recognition through handheld terminal as follow:

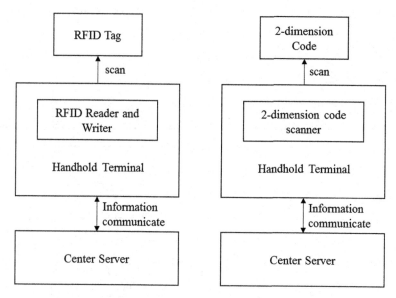

Fig. 1. The diagram of handheld terminal identification function.

After the inspection, we can download the current inspection task to the handheld terminal through making the center control server and handheld terminal be online. When the inspection personnel with the handheld terminal arrived to the scene, according to the inspection task route, using handheld terminal to locate and identify inspection equipment, displaying the inspection card relative and two-dimensional code and electronic label can supervise weather the inspection personnel's inspection is in place. Therefore it can be ensured that the inspection to be completed to meet the requirements of quality and quantity (Fig. 1).

Traditionally, when the substation inspection completed, inspection personnel are required to record the inspection result to the center control monitoring server by hand. But the handheld terminal can communicate with the center control monitoring server automatically and complete the data checking task.

Implementation of inspection task as follow:

The offline operation text will be created after the inspection task has been completed by the person in charge on the center control server. After the task text is downloaded to the terminal, the inspection personnel with handhold terminal will go to the scene, according to inspection route in the inspection task to inspect the equipment, scan the two-dimensional code and RFID tag. In this way, we can not only ensure that every equipment can be inspected, but also can gain the status information of the equipment conveniently and quickly. After the inspection completed, we can upload the inspection result. The center control server will compare the inspection result to the Remote monitoring data, if they are consistent, and then prove the inspection is unmistakable (Fig. 2).

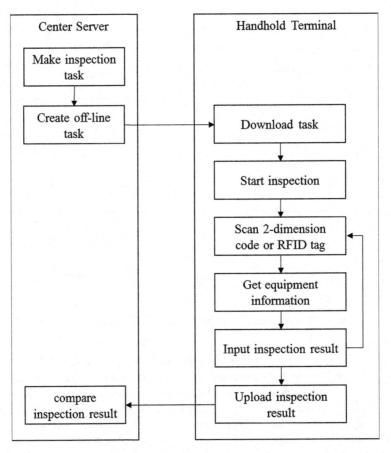

Fig. 2. Implementation of inspection task.

4   Conclusions

With the rapid development of China's market economy, the power supply require-ments of economic development becomes more and more important. Safe operation of power transmission equipment is related to the guarantee of power supply of reliable and economic production. So it is proposed that RFID radio frequency identification and the two-dimensional bar code technology applied in the exploration of electric power inspection can be used to realize the real-time monitoring and implementation of the transmission line state. Focusing on the actual, this paper introduces the equipment patrol management system, the role of the two-dimensional bar code and RFID technology in the system. The use of this technology can make the process of substation inspection and inspection process more intelligent and more specification, and can effectively improve the working accuracy, increase the exchange of information, speed up the flow of information to do effective supervision on inspection personnel, so as to improve the work efficiency of equipment inspection personnel. This application has a high practical value.

Acknowledgments. The work was supported by the National Natural Science Foundation of China (no.61100066).

References

1. Deng, P., Zhang, J.W., Rong, X.H., Chen, F.: A model of largescale Device Collaboration system based on PICalculus for green communication. Telecommun. Syst. **52**, 1313–1326 (2013)
2. Deng, P., Zhang, J.W., Rong, X.H., Chen, F.: Modeling the largescale device control system based on PI-calculus. Adv. Sci. Lett. **4**, 2374–2379 (2011)
3. Zhang, J.W., Deng, P., Wan, J.F., Yan, B.Y., Rong, X.H., Chen, F.: A novel multimedia device ability matching technique for ubiquitous computing environments. EURASIP J. Wirel. Commun. Netw. **2013**, 1–12 (2013)
4. Rong, X.H., Deng, P., Chen, F.: A largescale device collaboration resource selection method with MultiQoS constraint supported. Adv. Mater. Res. **143**, 894–898 (2011)
5. Rong, X.H., Chen, F., Deng, P., Ma, S.L.: A largescale device collaboration mechanism. J. Comput. Res. Dev. **9**, 1589–1596 (2011)
6. Chen, F., Rong, X.H., Deng, P., Ma, S.L.: A survey of device collaboration technology and system software. Acta Electronica Sinica **39**, 440–447 (2011)

Web Service Information Mining and Correlation Calculation Method Study

Huahua Ning[⊠], Feng Chen, Pan Deng, Yao Zhao, Wei Yuan,
Chaofan Bi, and Biying Yan

Institute of Software Chinese Academy of Sciences, South Fourth Street,
Zhong Guan Cun, Beijing 100190, People's Republic of China
{huahua,chenfeng,dengpan,yuanwei2011,
biying}@iscas.ac.cn,chaofb@qq.com,zhaoyao@bupt.edu.cn

Abstract. With the development of Internet technology, more and more web services are published on the Internet. How to efficiently and accurately obtain the specific services for users become more important. Based on this, web service vertical search engine emerged. This vertical search engine can improve the service retrieval efficiency compared with the traditional search engine. However there are still several deficiencies: required services are difficult to be filtered from the limited information that the users can refer; Moreover, sort principle of the search results are not transparent to users, they cannot reorder the search results according to their needs. This paper aims to solve this problem. Through mining service information, multi-dimensional information can be referred; through correlation calculation, users can search personalized information according to their needs, which enhances the power of web services retrieve and improves user experience of the search engine system.

Keywords: Web service · Information mining · Correlation

1 Introduction

Along with rapid increase of web services, those websites that provide a list of services such as XMethod [1], WebServiceList [2], webxml and seekda emerged. However, they are not able to meet the requirement of service search and selection. Because these sites are built based on UDDI, in which QoS support is not provided. QoS is an important indicator of many fields, for example, large-scale device collaboration system [3–7], network, web service selection, multimedia device ability matching [8] and so on. For web services, QoS is the kernal characteristic of services. To improve such situation, a number of specialized vertical search engine like SD2S [9], Merobase [10] as well as service discovery search engine supporting QoS emerged. However, they are currently prototype systems and technically not mature. To sum up, there are several deficiencies. First, service information presented is not comprehensive, which only includes the service name, service WSDL link and service providers. It is difficult for users to filter out the required services through these simple information. Second, the search results are presented in the form of a sorted list. However, the users neither know the relationship between these search results and keyword nor the sorting principle. In addition, they cannot search personalized information based on their needs.

© Institute for Computer Sciences, Social Informatics and Telecommunications Engineering 2015
V.C.M. Leung et al. (Eds.): CloudComp 2014, LNICST 142, pp. 204–215, 2015.
DOI: 10.1007/978-3-319-16050-4_21

In addition, the current situation that the non-functional properties of web services such as QoS information, context information like geographic information were not considered, service information mining and correlation calculation are in need. Through mining service information, multi-dimensional information can be referred to the users; through correlation calculation, the users can search personalized information according to their needs. Finally, web services retrieve is enhanced and the user experience of search engine system is improved as well.

2   Study of Key Problem

This article aims at doing service information mining and correlation calculation based on existing service search engine. The users simply input keyword and send request to search engine system. Then a list of search results can be returned. This article studies the following aspects: (1) service information mining based on simple information like service name, WSDL link, service provider. (2) Service correlation calculation. A method is put forward to calculate the correlation based on multiple filter conditions. We conduct research on similarity calculation like between simple words, between compound words and between simple word and compound word.

2.1   Service Information Mining

In this paper, we mainly mining information such as domains information in WSDL document, service QoS information and service geographic information. The data collection process are introduced below.

(1) Service WSDL domain information
Service WSDL contains 5 domains those are service, binding, message, type and porttype domain. WSDL4J toolkit is used to parse these domains.
(2) Service QoS information
Service QoS information contains 13 indicators. They are RTT, Performance, Reliability, Availability, Security and so on. Among them, RTT is the most basic and important aspect. Therefore, in the study of this paper, RTT is used as raw data. 27 nodes are deployed on the planet-lab for real-time measurement and RTT information is measured by each node. However, what we really want is RTT information that users perceive. Based on this, a similar calculation method is proposed. RTT information measured by node which is nearest to user's current location is considered as RTT information that user perceives and returned to user as shown in Fig. 1.
As seen in Fig. 1, 10 measurement nodes $N1 \sim N10$ are located at different places. Among them, N7 is the nearest one to the user's current location. Therefore, RTT measured by N7 is taken as the real RTT data that perceived by the user.
(3) Service geographic information
Service geographic information are latitude and longitude of the service provider. In this article, service geographic information is collected by IP address of the

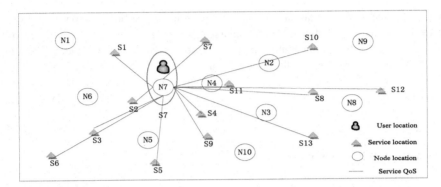

Fig. 1. Relationship among user, service and measurement nodes.

service provider GeoIP database [11] which provided by MaxMind is used to query the latitude and longitude information.

(4) Service tag information

Tag extraction is one difficulty encountered during the implementation. In this paper, classic TF-IDF algorithm [12] is used to calculate the weight of each word.

(5) Service description information

Service description only exists in the document type WSDL document, the RPC type WSDL document does not have description information. In this paper, we use WSDL4 J to parse WSDL document and get description information.

2.2   Service Correlation Calculation

Service correlation calculation needs to be done after obtaining the search results and before the presentation. The users can filter efficiently by using different filter conditions, correlation calculation and reordering. These filter conditions contain functional information which includes each domain information in WSDL and non-functional information which includes QoS that user perceives, service tags, service description information and physical distance between the user and service. To calculate the correlation between keyword and search results, correlation calculation methods for three kinds of information are defined as follows.

$$Sim_{intergrate} = k \times Sim_{func} + (1 - k) \times Sim_{non-func} \tag{1}$$

$$Sim_{func} = \sum_{i=1}^{m} \left(k_i \times Sim_{func(i)} \right) \tag{2}$$

$$Sim_{non-func} = \sum_{j=1}^{n} \left(k_j \times Sim_{non-func(j)} \right) \tag{3}$$

The Eq. (1) is the integrated correlation which contains functional and non-functional correlation between the input keyword and search results. For the search results, functional elements and non-functional elements are equally important, so k value is set to 0.5. Equations (2) and (3) are correlation calculation method based on function information and correlation calculation method based on non-functional information. k_i is the weight of i-th domain information, k_j is the weight of j-th non-functional information. Since service information is divided into numerical information and text-based information according to their appearance. Therefore, the core issue is numerical information correlation calculation and text-based information correlation calculation. Following are the two ways to conduct correlation calculation.

2.2.1 Numerical Information Correlation Calculation

In mathematics, absolute value of two numbers is used to represent the distance between these two numbers. The greater the absolute value of two numbers is, the farther away the two numbers are, the lower the correlation is and conversely the higher. Based on this idea, a Linear Similarity Calculation Method (LSCM) is proposed. Following is an example.

Given a keyword, there are 10 search results, their QoS values are list below (Table 1).

Table 1. Service - QoS information table

Sname	S1	S2	S3	S4	S5	S6	S7	S8	S9	S10
QoS	4	7	4	2	4	1	4	2	10	7

From the users' perspective, they hope to get better services. So, during the implementation, the smaller the QoS value, the greater the correlation is. The LSCM is as follows.

Step1: Sort the QoS value of $S1 \sim S10$ and merge the same value as below (Table 2).

Table 2. Sorted results according to the QoS value

Sname	S6	S4,S8	S1,S3,S5,S7	S2,S10	S9
QoS	1	2	4	7	10

Step2: Assign specific values to the sorted QoS sequence. We set the last one's similarity to 0, and set the first one to 1. Therefore the linear relationship between similarity and QoS is: $= -\frac{1}{9}x + \frac{10}{9}$. Then other services' similarity are as follows (Table 3).

Table 3. Similarity calculation results based on the QoS

Sname	S1	S2	S3	S4	S5	S6	S7	S8	S9	S10
QoS	4	7	4	2	4	1	4	2	10	7
Sim	5/9	1/3	5/9	8/9	5/9	1	5/9	8/9	0	1/3

Based on the above calculation, the similarity of physical distance, service star etc. can be calculated.

According to the above method, numerical LSCM can be defined as following:

$$y_i = \frac{x_2 - x_i}{x_2 - x_1} (x_1 < x_2) \tag{4}$$

$$y_i = \frac{x_i - x_2}{x_1 - x_2} (x_1 > x_2) \tag{5}$$

Where x_1 is the first value, x_2 is the value ranked last, x_i is the i-th value, y_i is the similarity which needs to be calculated.

2.2.2   Text-Based Information Correlation Calculation

For text-based information, WordNet [13] which is a lexical semantic network based on the relationship and JWS(Java WordNet Similarity) are adopted. Details of the algorithm is described in the paper of Lin [14].

In the service search results, the relevant text of services are not only simple words but also compound words. For example, the search results of keyword "weather" are like "weatherService", "usWeather" and "globalWeather". Since the compound word is beyond the scope of WordNet, and the service name is defined by developers, the traditional method of correlation calculation does not apply. Therefore, how to calculate the correlation between two compound words or between a compound word and a simple word is a problem. In this section, how to conduct correlation calculation method with compound words involved is discussed.

(1) Similarity between a simple word and a compound word

For compound words, first split it and several simple words can be got. Then calculate the similarity through calculating the similarity between simple words based on the algorithm put forward by Lin [14]. Here gives an example. W_a is a simple word and W_b is a compound word. Suppose that W_b can be split into two simple words W_{b1} and W_{b2}, and similarity between W_a and W_{b1} is S_{ab1}, similarity between W_a and W_{b2} is S_{ab2}. A calculation method between the simple word A and the compound word B is defined:

$$S_{a,b} = k_1 \times S_{a,b1} + k_2 \times S_{a,b2} \tag{6}$$

Where k_1 and k_2 are the similarity between simple words in proportion to the similarity between the simple word and the compound word. $k_1 + k_2 = 1$. Assuming k_1 is 0.1 and k_2 is 0.9, this indicates that the similarity between W_a and W_b is more inclined to W_b. To characterize this tendency, we give the following definition:

$$k_1 = \frac{S_{a,b1}}{S_{a,b1} + S_{a,b2}}, k_2 = \frac{S_{a,b2}}{S_{a,b1} + S_{a,b2}} \tag{7}$$

Thus the similarity between W_a and W_b is:

$$S_{a,b} = \frac{S_{a,b1}^2 + S_{a,b2}^2}{S_{a,b1} + S_{a,b2}} \tag{8}$$

More generally, when the compound word is split into m simple words, the similarity formula is expanded to:

$$S_{a,b} = \frac{S_{a,b1}^2 + S_{a,b2}^2 + \cdots + S_{a,bm}^2}{S_{a,b1} + S_{a,b2} + \cdots + S_{a,bm}} \tag{9}$$

(2) Similarity between compound words

According to the above similarity calculation method, a similarity calculation method between compound words is proposed, that is CWSCM (Compound Words Similarity Calculation Method). Assume that A and B are both compound words. A can be split into m simple words, B can be split into n simple words. The similarity between A and B can be calculated through following steps.

Step1: Calculate the similarity between each simple word W_{ai} and compound word W_b according to the previous calculation method as follows (Fig. 2).

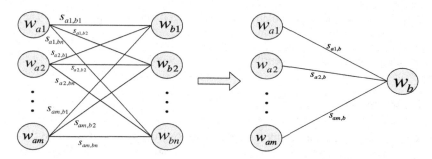

Fig. 2. The similarity calculation process between simple word W_{ai} and compound word W_b

Step2: Results of step1 can be seen as the similarity between the whole word W_b and W_a's all simple words. Since the simple words by split has already played a role in first step, so in this step, the whole word B is taken as a simple word, again using the method before, the similarity calculation between compound words A and B is converted into calculating the similarity between simple word B and compound word A. The method is:

$$S_{a,b} = \frac{S_{a1,b}^2 + S_{a2,b}^2 + \cdots + S_{am,b}^2}{S_{a1,b} + S_{a2,b} + \cdots + S_{am,b}} \tag{9}$$

Where, $S_{ai,b} = \frac{S_{ai,b1}^2 + S_{ai,b2}^2 + \cdots + S_{ai,bn}^2}{S_{ai,b1} + S_{ai,b2} + \cdots + S_{ai,bn}}$.

Through the above steps, the similarity between the compound words A and B can be got. During the calculation, the similarity between the simple word W_{ai} and the compound word B is calculated first, then W_b is seen as a simple word, and then calculate the similarity between the simple word B and the compound word A. Similarly, the similarity between each simple word W_{bj} and the compound word W_a is calculated first. The process is shown below. Where $S_{a,bj} = \frac{S^2_{a1,bj}+S^2_{a2,bj}+\cdots+S^2_{am,bj}}{S_{a1,bj}+S_{a2,bj}+\cdots+S_{am,bj}}$. In step 2, A is seen as a simple word, and calculate the similarity between A and the compound word W_b as follows (Fig. 3).

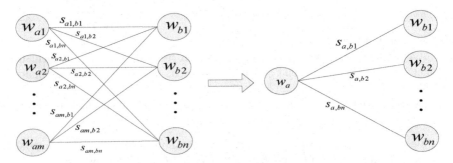

Fig. 3. The similarity calculation process between simple word W_{bj} and compound word W_a

Based on the above two calculation methods, two different results are got. They are $S_{a,b} = \frac{S^2_{a1,b}+S^2_{a2,b}+\cdots+S^2_{am,b}}{S_{a1,b}+S_{a2,b}+\cdots+S_{am,b}}$ and $S_{a,b} = \frac{S^2_{a,b1}+S^2_{a,b2}+\cdots+S^2_{a,bn}}{S_{a,b1}+S_{a,b2}+\cdots+S_{a,bn}}$. Finally, the maximum value is taken as the ultimate similarity between the combination words.

3   Experiment

For simple words, there are many recognized datasets that can be used to do the test, such as Miller and Charles data set [15]. And there are many standards and ways to validate. However, for compound words, there is no recognized accurately datasets. Therefore, in this research, experimental data used to verify the accuracy of the method needs to be designed. The experiment steps are organized as follows.

Step1: Two data sets are selected from our own service library, they are Set_{map} and Set_{random}. Set_{map} contains 12 services that are associated with word "map", and Set_{random} contains 12 services that are selected randomly.

Step2: Assuming that given a compound word "mapService", the similarity between it and the words in Set_{map} and Set_{random} is respectively calculated applying the above method CWSCM. See appendix for the specific calculation results.

Step3: Compare similarity of two groups.

According to the above CWSCM, the following scatterplot is made. Where blue points and red points respectively represent the similarity between the given word "mapService" and Set_{map}, "mapService" and Set_{random}.

As seen from the chart, the similarity between "mapService" and Set_{map} is greater than the similarity between "mapService" and Set_{random}. This is because according to the CWSCM proposed above, in Set_{map}, the compound words mostly contain the simple word "map" or "service", they are highly related to the given compound word "mapService". On the contrary, in Set_{random}, the simple words split are random and the words have low correlation with the word "mapService" (Fig. 4).

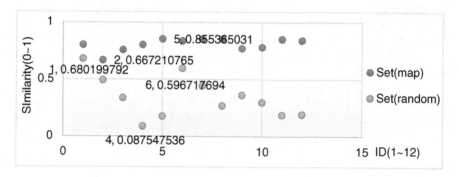

Fig. 4. Scatterplot of similarity between the two datasets and "mapService"

Five points are chosen for analysis. Where A(5) is the similarity between "map-Service" and the fifth data in Set_{map} named "MapAjaxService". Since both words contain the two simple words "map" and "service", the similarity value weighs more in similarity calculation. Therefore the final similarity value is greater. B(1) is the similarity between "mapService" and the first data in Set_{random} named "UserProfileService". Since both words contain the word "service", the similarity value has a certain contribution to the weight of similarity calculation. Therefore the final similarity value is greater than others. B(6) is the similarity between "mapService" and sixth data in Set_{random} named "CommunityWebServiceSoap", since the simple word contains "service", so the similarity value has a certain contribution to the weight of similarity calculation. Therefore the final similarity value is greater than others as well. B(4) is the similarity between "mapService" and the fourth data in Set_{random} named "XmlRout-erSoap", since the similarity between this word and "mapService" is low, which gives a certain effect on the similarity between the word and "mapService". Eventually it makes the similarity between compound word and "mapService" small.

4   Conclusion

Since there are several deficiencies in traditional service vertical search engine. First, service information presented is not comprehensive. Second, users neither know the relationship between search results and keyword nor the sorting principle. In addition, they cannot search personalized information based on their needs. We conduct research on the following.

In summary, work of this paper focuses on two parts. First is the Service information mining. Five kinds of information are mined. They are WSDL domain information, QoS information, geographic information, tag information and description information. Therefore, multi-dimensional information can be referred to the users. Second is the study of the correlation calculation method. Two correlation calculation methods are proposed. They are LSCM and CWSCM, respectively solve the similarity calculation problem based on numerical and text information. Therefore, users can search personalized information according to their needs, which enhances the power of web services retrieve and improves user experience of the search engine system.

The correlation calculation method is the secondary processing of the search results, which will affect the retrieval performance, how to balance the needs of real-time retrieval and user demand for secondary processing of search results also has the further research value.

Acknowledgements. The work was supported by the National Natural Science Foundation of China (No. 61100066).

Appendix

See Tables 4 and 5.

Table 4. Similarity between "mapService" and service in Set_{map}

ID	Map related	sourceURL	Field in WSDL	Similarity
1	GenerateMapService	http://www.viamichelin.com/ws/services/GenerateMap?wsdl	Service Name	0.803479653
2	GetBestMap DefinitionService	http://www.viamichelin.com/ws/services/GetBestMapDefinition?wsdl	Service Name	0.667210765
3	MapHelper	http://www.jasons.com/Services/MapHelper.asmx?WSDL	Service Name	0.758101797
4	MapManagementService	http://www.viamichelin.com/ws/services/MapManagement?wsdl	Service Name	0.80405465
5	MapAjaxService	http://maps.tourismus-landkreis-kelheim.de/MapAjaxService.asmx?WSDL	Service Name	0.855365031
6	mapData	http://safarimappers.com/webservice/maphelper5.asmx?WSDL	Service Name	0.838492372
7	MyMapService	http://www.objectmap.nl/WebService/MyMapService.asmx?WSDL	Service Name	0.855365031

(Continued)

Table 4. (*Continued*)

ID	Map related	sourceURL	Field in WSDL	Similarity
8	BarrioMapService	http://mdl.chicos.edu.ar/Services/MapLocation/BarrioMapService.asmx?WSDL	Service Name	0.855365031
9	MapLocationService	http://mdl.chicos.edu.ar/Services/MapLocation/MapLocationService.asmx?WSDL	Service Name	0.772081011
10	MapTileService	http://mdl.chicos.edu.ar/Services/MapTile/MapTileService.asmx?WSDL	Service Name	0.784102515
11	CoberturaMapService	http://www.monitoreowifi.aui.edu.ar/Services/Objects/CoberturaMapService.asmx?WSDL	Service Name	0.855365031
12	MapRequest	http://www.gatewayhorizons.com/VEdemo/services/MapRequest.asmx?WSDL	Service Name	0.84326418

Table 5. Similarity between "mapService" and service in Set_{random}

ID	Map related	sourceURL	Field in WSDL	Similarity
1	UserProfileService	http://www.ldb.lt/TDB/Plunge/Apie/_vti_bin/UserProfileService.asmx?WSDL	Service Name	0.680199792
2	priceChecker	http://www.villarenters.com/villarenterswebservice/priceChecker.asmx?wsdl	Service Name	0.493072886
3	MessageAccess	https://db-msg1.travelclick.net/DataBridgeMessaging/MessageAccess.asmx?WSDL	Service Name	0.33912412
4	XmlRouterSoap	http://jewishcharlotte.org/XmlRouter/XmlRouter.asmx?WSDL	PortType Name	0.087547536
5	ConvertorSoap	http://www.softwaremaker.net/webservices/swm/Convertor/Convertor.asmx?wsdl	PortType Name	0.177075212
6	CommunityWebServiceSoap	http://www.kievchurch.org.ua/CommunityWebService.asmx?WSDL	PortType Name	0.596717694
7	getSmallImage	http://webservice.webxml.com.cn/webservices/ChinaStockSmallImageWS.asmx?wsdl	Operation Name	0.444477918

(*Continued*)

Table 5. (*Continued*)

ID	Map related	sourceURL	Field in WSDL	Similarity
8	GetCommonManager	http://www.grandchallenges.org/_vti_bin/UserProfileService.asmx?wsdl	Operation Name	0.269462401
9	loadSelection	http://www.memo.fr/Partenaires/MWGroupeService.asmx?WSDL	Operation Name	0.362415594
10	GetRateSoapOut	http://www.jajah.com/api/MemberServices.asmx?WSDL	Message Name	0.298699795
11	LoginSoapOut	http://golffacility.com/api/crmteetimeapi.asmx?WSDL	Message Name	0.190550403
12	convertResponse	http://www.viamichelin.com/ws/services/XYToPixels?wsdl	Message Name	0.194741805

References

1. http://www.xmethods.net. Accessed 20 May 2014
2. http://remotemethods.com/. Accessed 20 May 2014
3. Rong, X.H., Deng, P., Chen, F.: A large-scale device collaboration resource selection method with multi-QoS constraint supported. Adv. Mater. Res. **143**, 894–898 (2011)
4. Deng, P., Zhang, J.W., Rong, X.H., Chen, F.: A model of large-scale device collaboration system based on PI-Calculus for green communication. Telecommun. Syst. **52**, 1313–1326 (2013)
5. Deng, P., Zhang, J.W., Rong, X.H., Chen, F.: Modeling the large-scale device control system based on PI-calculus. Adv. Sci. Lett. **4**, 2374–2379 (2011)
6. Rong, X.H., Chen, F., Deng, P., Ma, S.L.: A large-scale device collaboration mechanism. J. Comput. Res. Dev. **9**, 1589–1596 (2011)
7. Chen, F., Rong, X.H., Deng, P., Ma, S.L.: A survey of device collaboration technology and system software. Acta Electronica Sinica **39**, 440–447 (2011)
8. Zhang, J.W., Deng, P., Wan, J.F., Yan, B.Y., Rong, X.H., Chen, F.: A novel multimedia device ability matching technique for ubiquitous computing environments. EURASIP J. Wirel. Commun. Netw. **2013**, 1–12 (2013)
9. Willmott, S., Ronsdorf, H., Krempels, K.H.: Publish and search versus registries for semantic web service discovery. In: Proceedings of 2005 IEEE/WIC/ACM International Conference on IEEE , pp. 491–494 (2005)
10. Atkinson, C., Bostan, P., Hummel, O., et al.: A practical approach to web service discovery and retrieval. In: ICWS, pp. 241–248 (2007)
11. http://www.maxmind.com/en/geolocation. Accessed 22 June 2014
12. http://zh.wikipedia.org/wiki/TF-IDF. Accessed 28 June 2014
13. http://WorldNet.princeton.edu. Accessed 28 June 2014

14. Dekang, L.: An information-theoretic definition of similarity. In: Proceedings of the Fifteenth International Conference on Machine Learning, San Francisco, vol. 98, pp. 296–304 (1998)
15. Miller, G.A., Charles, W.G.: Contextual correlates of semantic similarity. Lang. Cogn. Process. **6**(1), 1–28 (1991)

A New Distributed Strategy to Schedule Computing Resource

Qi Wang[1]([⊠]), Pan Deng[2], Qinghong Yang[1], Wei Yuan[2],
Yaolong Nie[2], Chaofan Bi[2], and Han-Chieh Chao[3,4]

[1] Department of Software, Beihang University, No. 35 Northern Shining Tower,
10th Floor, 1003, Xueyuan Road, Haidian District, Beijing 100191, China
daniel_qi@outlook.com, ycrainbow@163.com
[2] Institute of Software, Chinese Academy of Sciences, 4# South Fourth Street,
Zhong Guan Cun, Beijing 100190, People's Republic of China
{dengpan,yuanwei2011,yaolong}@iscas.ac.cn,
chaofb@qq.com
[3] Institute of Computer Science and Information and Department of Electronic
Engineering, National Ilan University, I-Lan, Hualien, Taiwan
hcc@niu.edu.tw
[4] Department of Electrical Engineering, National Dong Hwa University,
Hualien, Taiwan

Abstract. Distributed scheduling strategy for computing resource (DSSCR) talks about a wide range of knowledge, such as distributed parallel computing, resource scheduling, heartbeat monitoring and data security. When people deal with a large number of concurrent computing tasks, designing a reasonable, efficient, safe scheduling system becomes important, it needs not only to execute safely, reduce the pressure on the server, but also improve the efficiency of task execution and correct results return. So the focus of this paper is to propose a DCRSS to solve the above problems. Nine categories of test cases are designed to assess its efficiency. There are 355 tests are executed, the success rate is over 90 %, saving 60 % time.

Keywords: Distributed scheduling · Computing resource · Parallel computing · Video analysis task

1 Introduction

It is common to execute computing tasks in distributed system. However, due to the traditional technology architecture design, as with the increasing of the amount of data and the number of parallel, the current distributed computing systems are in face of a lot of problems and defects, such as low computing execution efficiency, low reuse rate of historical data, and low efficiency of massive concurrent tasks execution. How to quickly and reasonably deal with massive data, the constraints of time and space, and optimize computing resource scheduling algorithms to provide users safe, efficient service mission is the goal of this study.

One of key features of distributed computing is large-scale device collaboration, it is another important research goal of this paper [1]. How to create an efficient distribution structure model to control the existing physical resources is very important [2, 8].

© Institute for Computer Sciences, Social Informatics and Telecommunications Engineering 2015
V.C.M. Leung et al. (Eds.): CloudComp 2014, LNICST 142, pp. 216–224, 2015.
DOI: 10.1007/978-3-319-16050-4_22

The paper aims to design a new solution in distributed computing resource scheduling areas, where they can play important roles.

At first, this paper introduces the background and analyze disadvantage of original solution. Then a new distributed strategy to schedule computing resource is put forward. At last, there is a result to assess the efficiency of the new solution.

2 Background

This study derives from the data and computing center of a certain city's high-definition video surveillance platform. The goal is to establish a standard, safe and efficient computing center open for the third party development organizations.

This platform are designed to deal with a lot of intelligent applications with large-scale video analysis, face recognition, secondary analysis, detection and retrieval of video images, which requires massive computing power. Therefore, a set of efficient, intelligent DCRSS is in need.

2.1 The Original Scheduling Strategy Solution

The city is divided into 14 regions, each of which is equipped with its own independent computer machinery room, each room runs the traffic surveillance videos of the corresponding jurisdiction. All services and tasks of processing and analysis are based on these videos. There are 15 computer machinery rooms including a center one in total. All computer machinery rooms are connected by high-speed fiber networks. Due to the inconsistencies of the network environment between regions, only some of the regions can enjoy high-speed video sharing between each other. The computing resources network topology of this city is shown in Fig. 1 below:

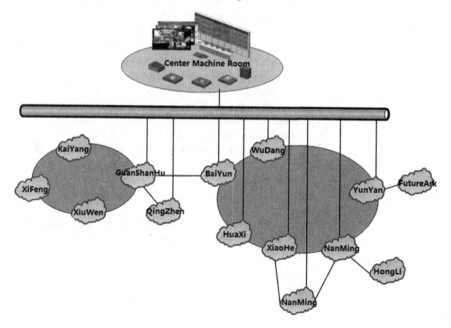

Fig. 1. The computing resources network topology of the city

The places of the bottom of the Fig. 2 represents each partition computer machinery rooms, the black lines are the network connection between the nodes.

The foundation system provides users with the services of face searching, the vehicle searching, videos shrinking and some others. Nowadays, video analysis technology is common [3]. Upper users select video search periods, monitoring points, function types and other conditions. Then issue the tasks to dispatch system. According to the scheduling algorithm, the computing center finds the machine room corresponding to the video for analysis and processing. It returns the results when the calculation is completed.

2.2   The Disadvantages of Original Scheduling System

See Table 1.

Table 1. Disadvantages of the original system.

Disadvantage	Explanation
Single step	If the upper tasks are to be treated with different functions of a video, people have to deal with it twice or more, but after researching authors found that the existing video-task is divided into two steps. First step is the formation of video analytic features documents (the intermediate data processing), and the second step is to conduct further analysis based on the video analytic features documents. The original system does not make rational use of the intermediate data generated by the first step, which reduces the efficiency of secondary tasks
Underutilized resources	After research authors found that the use of high-speed fiber-optic connections between some computer machinery rooms can achieve real-time, high-speed video sharing. When loading pressure of one computer machinery room is too large, the original system does not reasonably assign this task to another room for processing, which results in some of the rooms with too much pressures while others with idle resources there
Task caching lack	The original system provides external computing resources based on the actual existence of the physical resources of the computer machinery room. However, it does not realize the task caching mechanism. Therefore, if the target machinery room does not store the videos, the system will refuse to accept the task request from upper interface. So the lack of the ability to achieve a large amount of concurrent task requests is a serious disadvantage
Low reusability of historical results	When the system completes a 10-min. video analysis task, and the next task is the subtask of this task, the original system cannot use the historical results. On the contrary, if it executes again, it may cause the waste of resources and low reusability, which reduces the overall efficiency

3 Solution

3.1 Architecture Design

Each machine room is defined as a secondary node management area, and determine a server or a virtual machine as a secondary node. Other computing resources is defined as computing nodes, managed uniformly by the secondary node. In addition, the center room plays a central node role, managing all secondary nodes. Thus a three-tier mode is developed. The status of each running compute nodes is shielded from the central node. So all the information transmission between the central node and the computing nodes needs the second nodes to help.

The specific hierarchy is shown in Fig. 2 below:

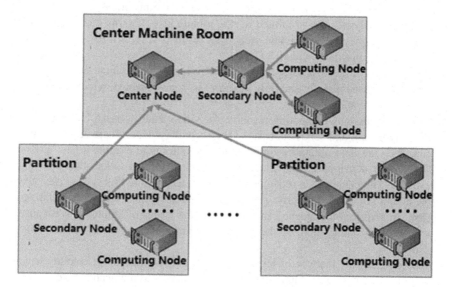

Fig. 2. Three-tier system design Structure

Since the role of the central node play the task to do the scheduling, all need is to establish a mechanism to monitor the heartbeat and resource between each node with the subordinate management node.

3.2 Process Design

1. To increase the reusability of the historical task and improve the efficiency of secondary tasks, this solution is constrained for asynchronous execution computing tasks at first. Because all video analysis tasks are based on the intermediate data (video feature file). Some tasks need to be done under different conditions may be characterized by the same video file. So the original system may do much repetitive

work. After testing, it is found that the time of the first step about generating video analysis features file takes more than 80 % of the execution time. So the reuse of video analysis features file should make the computing tasks more efficiently. Therefore, when performing computing tasks, each of them must be checked whether each task has the features file in order to meet their computing needs.

2. When the central node receive the upper computing tasks, the system will split the task into many minute-particle video tasks. There are three reasons for this assignment. First, One minute of video processing has small pressure on computing nodes, and time of the execution is relatively short. If the time period of the task is set too long, the entire task results may turn into junk data if abnormal situation happens; Second, one minute is short, each subtask can be executed quickly by the computing node, can transfer the resources for other tasks to prevent the task queue from being overloaded; Third, in order to increase the historical task of reuse rate, the video analysis tasks is limited to one minute size. It turns out that the multi-plexing efficiency of one-minute video task result is several times higher than the result of the ten-minute video.

   Therefore, all tasks will be split into a collection of one minute tasks. Historical results are reused directly and only the new tasks are executed, which improves the overall operational efficiency.

3. The system assigns computing resource for video analysis tasks based on scheduling algorithm, and sends subtasks to the secondary node. There are two types of subtasks. One is to obtain historical results, another is to execute a new task.

4. The system develops a tasks caching mechanism for the tasks obtained without resource. The center node sets a tasks queue to ensure that this system can receive any number of computing tasks and prevent the limit of task request from the upper users. In addition, this queue can also handle the issues of failures that because of network traffic congestion. So the tasks caching mechanism can help to prevent loss of mission.

5. According to the analysis of regional distribution of computing resources, when assigning computing resource, the system sends tasks to the nearest machine room secondary node where stores the videos required by the task. If the nearest secondary node is not idle, then the task is resent to another secondary node which is in the same schedule group including the nearest node. Because computing resources can be effectively shared in the same schedule group. The task will never be sent to other computing nodes of other schedule groups.

6. When computing resource is insufficient in one secondary node, the system can dynamically assign the task to other secondary nodes in the same scheduling group. If the whole schedule group is lack of resources, there are two solutions. The first is to send the task to the center computing node to execute, another is to push the task into the caching queue to wait for idle resource. Resource selection and large scale diverse Collaboration are two goals of this papers, there are many methods are worth learning nowadays [4–6].

Task execution flow chart is shown in Fig. 3 below:

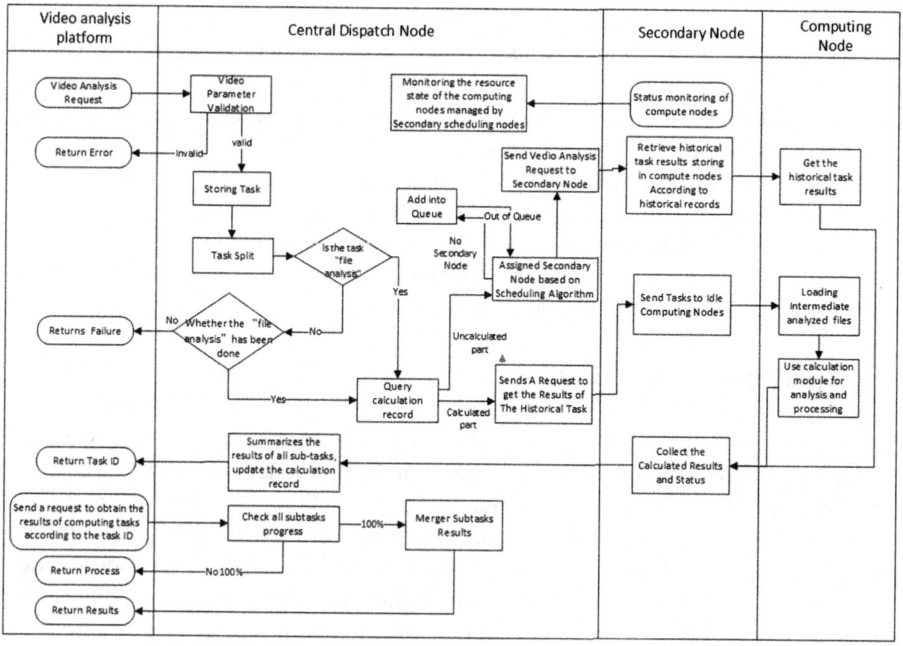

Fig. 3. Task execution flow chart

3.3   Scheduling Algorithm

One Key feature of schedule algorithm is to use rationally and efficiently the resource in this system. There are many different methods to solve this problem. The article made reference to the advantage of a lot of other solutions [7, 9].

A. Static Scheduling:

The central dispatch node will search for the specific secondary node which stores the corresponding video resources. If the node has enough idle computing resources, then the central dispatch node will assign the task to this secondary node, and then search for the idle computing node according to the location of the video resources and assign the analysis task to this computing node.

B. Dynamic Scheduling:

1. If the secondary node corresponding to the video has no idle resources, then the central dispatch node will assign this subtask to other secondary nodes which has idle resources within the same scheduling group (select secondary node with the maximum number of idle resources).

2. If all the secondary nodes under the same scheduling group have no idle resources, the central dispatch node will add this subtask to the queue of the central node.

3. If a secondary node comes across with a system crash, the central dispatch node will query the task list which is kept in the database and get all the processing tasks. If there are subtasks assigned to the lost secondary node, the central

dispatch node will transfer all the subtasks to the center machinery room to execute (including the completed and uncompleted subtasks, considering the result of the completed subtasks is stored in the secondary node, and the central dispatch node needs to load task results from the sub-machinery room when gathering results. Even if the task processing has been completed, but the results still could not be calculated), if the central dispatch node does not have available resources, the tasks will be added to the task queue.

4. If the computing node under the secondary node comes across with a system crash, the scheduling solutions is similar to the above item 3.

5. If the central dispatch node comes across with a system crash, after the system returns to normal, it will load the tasks executing which should have been executed in the queue if there is no crash.

4   Experiments and Results

Considering the above solutions, relevant testing experiments are designed. A central dispatch node, four secondary nodes, seven computing nodes under each secondary node are designed. There are two scheduling groups, and the four secondary nodes are defined as Region 1–4. Theoretically, the testing system supports 4 * 7 = 28 channel paralleling execution of video processing tasks. No. 1, No. 2 and No. 3 secondary nodes form a scheduling group, No. 2 and No. 4 secondary nodes form the second scheduling group (the same secondary node can exist in two different scheduling groups at the same time, this is decided by the geographical factors and network bandwidth).

Nine categories of test are designed and there are 355 test cases in total.
The test case design table is as follows (Table 2):

Table 2. Test Case Design Table

Id	Test-case category	Expected result	Test node
1	Dynamic scheduling	Issue full load video analysis tasks to secondary node	1
2	Reuse of historic tasks	Does not execute the historic tasks the second time	1
3	Asynchronous execution(1)	Verify front constraints	2
4	Asynchronous execution(2)	Conduct video analysis based on the video feature files	1
5	Computing results sharing between the same scheduling group	Issue the task to other secondary nodes under the same scheduling group when there's no computing resources available	2, 4
6	No free resources in the scheduling group	Issue the task to the waiting queue in the central dispatch node	2, 4
7	Crash of the secondary node	Lost tasks are sent to the central dispatch node	1
8	Crash of computing node	Tasks in the computing node are sent to the other computing node	4
9	Persistence validation of the task queue	Stores the uncompleted and unissued tasks in the queue	3

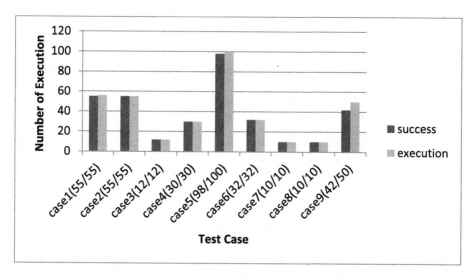

Fig. 4. Test results

Test results analysis is as follows (Fig. 4):
The new solution supports four kinds of task types, sharing the same intermediate data. The new strategy reduces duplicate operations at least three times, shorten the time to 40 % of the original one. Nine categories of test cases are designed to assess its efficiency. There are 355 tests are executed, the success rate is over 90 %, saving 60 % time.

5   Conclusion

DCRSS designed in this paper can greatly improve the efficiency of the upper computing tasks execution, shorten the processing time of repetitive tasks execution, rationally control the existing computing resources, improve utilization and prevent the resources waste. In addition, it can achieve real-time monitoring and integration of all the servers.

This three-tier architecture can hierarchically manage the distributed computing resources to achieve a reasonable and controllable resource management strategy, split the functions of the computing center into pieces and assign to each node to control the resources and reduce risks. This solution can solve a large amount of concurrent real-time computing tasks to reduce the user's constraints as well.

DCRSS involves multifaceted knowledge, such as parallel computing, data security, data storage, scheduling. And the strategy is limited by several specific network conditions such as network bandwidth, server computing power, the amount of data and the geographic constraints. Now there are many organizations and academics earn some achievements in this field. The solution aims to make some contribution to this field. Of course, the strategy is still not perfect in solving a large amount of concurrent real-time processing. Further improvement is needed.

Acknowledgement. The work was supported by the National Natural Science Foundation of China (No. 61100066).

References

1. Deng, P., Zhang, J.W., Rong, X.H., Chen, F.: A model of large-scale device collaboration system based on PI-calculus for green communication. Telecommun. Syst. **52**, 1313–1326 (2013)
2. Deng, P., Zhang, J.W., Rong, X.H., Chen, F.: Modeling the large scale device control system based on PI-calculus. Adv. Sci. Lett. **4**, 2374–2379 (2011)
3. Zhang, J.W., Deng, P., Wan, J.F., Yan, B.Y., Rong, X.H., Chen, F.: A novel multimedia device ability matching technique for ubiquitous computing environments. EURASIP J. Wireless Commun. Netw. **2013**, 1–12 (2013)
4. Rong, X.H., Deng, P., Chen, F.: A large-scale device collaboration resource selection method with multi-Qos constraint supported. Adv. Mater. Res. **143**, 894–898 (2011)
5. Rong, X.H., Chen, F., Deng, P., Ma, S.L.: A large scale device collaboration mechanism. J. Comput. Res. Dev. **9**, 1589–1596 (2011)
6. Chen, F., Rong, X.H., Deng, P., Ma, S.L.: A survey of device collaboration technology and system software. Acta Electronica Sinica **39**, 440–447 (2011)
7. Mezmaz, M., Melab, N., Kessaci, Y., et al.: A bi-objective hybrid metaheuristic for energy-aware scheduling for cloud computing system. J. Parallel Distrib. Comput. (JPDC) **71**(11), 1497–1508 (2011)
8. You, X-d., Xu, X-h., Wan, J., el al.: RAS-M: resource allocation strategy based on market mechanism in cloud computing. In: Fourth ChinaGrid Annual Conference, pp. 256–263 (2009)
9. Lee, Y.C., Zomaya, A.Y.: Energy efficient utilization of resources in cloud computing system. J. Supercomput. **53**, 1–13 (2010)

An Algorithm to Detect the Automobiles Using the Copied Vehicle License

Chaofan Bi[(⊠)], Wei Yuan, Biying Yan, Pan Deng, and Feng Chen

Institute of Software Chinese Academy of Sciences, #4 South Fourth Street,
Zhong Guan Cun, Haidian District, Beijing 100190, China
chaofb@qq.com,
{yuanwei2011,biying,dengpan,chenfeng}@iscas.ac.cn

Abstract. Due to fast development of technology and enhanced global connection, the number of vehicle running on the road in China increases with an amazing speed, while related illegal behavior appears and increases as well. One of them is copied vehicle license (CVL), in which the driver uses a fake license to avoid relevant punishment, to save annual tax and to commit crimes. To better maintain healthy traffic operation environment, a spatial distance based method is put forward in this paper to detect possible vehicles with CVL. With big data mining skill and parallel technology, the work can be done automatically by the computer with a good speed and accuracy. The results turn out to be clear and can be used directly by the police department, which improves the processing efficiency in this field. Both the government and public drivers benefit from this.

Keywords: Big data mining · Copied vehicle license · Spatial distance · Traffic operation

1 Introduction

Nowadays, as technology develops and global connection increases, residents' life quality has been improved a lot. This situation is more obvious in China especially after the country joined the World Trade Organization (WTO) in year 2001 [6]. As China opens its market, advanced manufacturing knowledge starts to flow into, which brings lots of commercial opportunities. Lots of industrial fields benefit from the policy, one of them is transportation. Being an essential part of transportation, automobile enjoys the best period of development. For example, Guiyang, an 8,034 sq. kms. city in China which locates in Guizhou Province, owns about 800,000 automobiles with only 4,451,700 citizens [7]. It means at least one person in six owns a vehicle. As an effective transportation tool, automobile satisfies passengers' travel demand and saves them bunch of time. However, problems like congestion, pollution, noise, safety begin to turn on public attention as the situation becomes more serious. In order to reduce the impact, some cities put forward new punishment policies. To avoid new punishment, another problem appears, some drivers choose to use the fake vehicle licenses. Usually there are three reasons result in such bad behavior [3]. First, the drivers who use the fake licenses can escape from relevant accident punishment. Second, they do not have

© Institute for Computer Sciences, Social Informatics and Telecommunications Engineering 2015
V.C.M. Leung et al. (Eds.): CloudComp 2014, LNICST 142, pp. 225–231, 2015.
DOI: 10.1007/978-3-319-16050-4_23

to pay the annual tax. This helps them save money. Third, with a fake license, they have more freedom to commit crimes. This situation affects the healthy traffic operation environment which should be stopped.

In front of such situation, this paper points out an algorithm to detect the suspicious licenses based on big data mining skill which takes speed instead of time as the threshold. The results can be used by the police department to better regulate the traffic operation.

The paper is organized like this. Second section discusses related work done by others before. Then the data used in doing the research is introduced. The way to refine dataset and improve data quality are discussed as well. Followed section talks about the methodology from which the final results come. The results are shown and discussed in the fourth section which is followed by the whole paper summary in the end.

2   Literature Review

In year 2007, Yinli Jin and Jianping Wang [3] pointed out an algorithm to detect CVL by using speed and distance matrixes to screen the traffic data. This method can result in good identification results. However, since real speed and distance information are not available at most time, this method is not able to process big data effectively. In another word, it is not a universal method. In year 2009, Xiaochun Lu et al. [4] put forward an idea to detect the vehicles with copied licenses. A time threshold from one site to another is the kernel part of the method. The paper focuses on introducing the algorithm. No test results can be seen from it. There is no way to evaluate whether it is reliable or not.

3   Data

In this section, two steps about data preprocessing work are discussed below. It is a necessary part to promise reasonable results. First step is called dataset refining, which talks about how to reduce the data size in order to expedite processing speed. Second step is called data quality control, which is essential to promise unbiased results. Details are discussed below.

3.1   Dataset Refining

The data used in this paper comes from a city's Transportation Management Bureau. The device used to collect the data adopts advanced photoelectric, image processing and mode identification technology. For each vehicle passes by any device, a picture of it is captured and all related data such as vehicle license, vehicle logo, vehicle type is extracted automatically. Once a vehicle pass the device, a group of data is recorded and kept in the database. Each day, 20,000,000 new data groups are transported into the database and each data group has 21 attributes.

As the size of each day data can get to 20 GB, in order to expedite processing speed, all those unnecessary data such as vehicle logo, vehicle color should be eliminated in the first step. The final dataset consists of 6 columns, which includes vehicle license, time, location, location ID, location latitude and location longitude as shown in Table 1 below.

Table 1. Dataset attributes

Vehicle license	Location	Time	Location ID	Latitude	Longitude
......	......	......	......	......	......
......	......	......	......	......	......
......	......	......	......	......	......

Table 1 shows the columns of the dataset. Vehicle license is the license of the detected vehicle. Location is the place where the picture is taken. Time is the time when the picture is taken. Location ID is the ID of the location. Accessary information, latitude and longitude are tied to each location.

3.2 Data Quality Control

After refining the dataset that is going to be used, the second step is about to improve data quality. This is a big and important part. Because bad data can lead to biased results and biased results come across wrong conclusion. As the result of this paper is to help policeman to identify those licenses that might be copied, wrong identification results definitely waste the time and disturb regular management.

There are two typical types of bad data. One are those with meaningless vehicle license. Another are those with incomplete information. For this two kinds of data, they are just deleted from the dataset to make sure each data group has all six attributes. After this, the whole dataset is sorted first by the vehicle license, then by the time. All the work is done by using a computer language-Python (https://www.python.org/) which is especially designed for processing data.

4   Methodology

Usually when people talk about CVL, what people could think about first is two different vehicles with the same license appear at different places at the same time. However, it is rare to see this situation happens. Another way to test whether a license is copied is to see whether it can make the distance given the exact time difference. For example, vehicle A appears at L1 at the time T1, vehicle B appears at L2 at the time T2, A and B are carrying the same license. What needed to be test is whether A can get to L2 from L1 within the period of T2-T1. If it can, then it is Ok, otherwise, the license might be copied. The idea is the same as the one proposed by Xiaochun Lu [4] However, in this paper, travel speed is selected as the threshold instead of the time. As the whole dataset has been sorted. So all the data groups of the same vehicle license should be listed together. From top to bottom, for each pair of data groups, calculate the time difference. As the time information is given, just do the subtraction directly as shown below.

$$\Delta t = t_i - t_{i-1} \tag{1}$$

In the Eq. (1), t_i denotes the captured time of the second data group, t_{i-1} denotes the time of the former one. i (i > 1) denotes the index of the data group under the same vehicle license (once it gets a new license, i changes back to 1), Δt denotes the time difference.

For the distance between the two locations, it can be known by using location latitude and longitude information as shown below.

$$C = \sin(MLat_i) * \sin(MLat_{i-1}) * \cos(MLon_i - MLon_{i-1}) + \cos(MLat_i) \\ * \cos(MLat_{i-1}) \tag{2}$$

$$Distance = R * Arccos(C) * Pi/180 \tag{3}$$

In the Eq. (2), $MLat_i$ denotes the changed latitude of the second data group (if the location locates on the north part of the Earth, $MLat_i = 90 -$ Latitude. Otherwise, $MLat_i = 90 +$ Latitude. The same rule is applied to $MLat_{i-1}$), $MLat_{i-1}$ denotes the changed latitude of the former one, $MLon_i$ denotes the changed longitude of the second data group (if it is located on the east part of the Earth, $MLon_i$ is the positive value, otherwise it is negative), $MLon_{i-1}$ denotes the changed longitude of the former one, R is the radius of the Earth which is 6371.004 km [5].

The distance calculated from the equation above is different from the real path. Actually, it is the shortest one between the two points on the Earth. Once distance and time difference become available, speed can be calculated. Then some speed threshold should be set in order to do the screening. As for the city where all the data are collected, the speed cannot get higher than 100 km/h from the survey feedback. So 100 is selected to be the speed threshold. If the speed is higher than 100, the vehicle license from which pair of data groups is suspicious. To further increase the accuracy of the results [8, 9], another step is needed. For each license, count the time of being suspicious. After all the data groups under the same license have been checked, the license should be considered copied only if it has been considered suspicious for more than 3 times [10]. The test results are shown in the next section.

5 Results

After implementing the methodology above, two result tables are acquired. First one gives the results about how many times a license has been considered suspicious as shown below.

Table 2 shows the number of each license considered suspicious. Because of some privacy issue, some information needs to be kept as secrets. Authors do not have the right to publish the vehicle licenses and locations. However, this does not affect how we explain the results. In each row, five attributes can be seen. First one is the vehicle

Table 2. Times of being suspicious for each license

Vehicle license	Time 1	Location 1	Time 2	Location 2
×××1266	2014/1/1 9:28	×桥路交叉口	2014/1/1 9:29	×××高架桥
×××1266	2014/1/1 9:29	×××高架桥	2014/1/1 9:29	××路交叉口
×××1266	2014/1/1 17:17	×××口断面	2014/1/1 17:18	×西路交叉口
×××1266	2014/1/1 17:18	×西路交叉口	2014/1/1 17:18	×西路口断面
×××1266	2014/1/1 17:18	×西路口断面	2014/1/1 17:20	××路交叉口
×××1269	2014/1/1 18:55	××路交叉口	2014/1/1 18:56	×××高架桥
......	......	......	......	......
......	......	......	......	......
......	......	......	......	......

license of interest. Second one is the time for the vehicle to arrive at location 1. Third is the address of the location 1. And then is the time for the vehicle to arrive at location 2, followed by the address of it. Actually, through the methodology, it is impossible for the same vehicle to get to Location 2 from Location 1 within the period of Time2–Time1. So this license is considered being copied once. As scrolling down the table, it can be noticed that license × × ×1266 is considered suspicious for 5 times, which satisfy the requirement (more than 3 times). So license × × ×1266 is selected by the final dataset.

The second dataset is also the final dataset as talked above. This dataset lists all the CVLs as shown below.

Table 3 lists all the possible CVLs based on the data collected on some specific day. 52,919 vehicle licenses are identified to be copied from 800,000 in total. Previous authors have concluded that the number of vehicle with copied licenses can get amount to 10 % in China [3]. So 52,919 from 800,000 is a reasonable quantity. The results can be used by the policemen directly to penalize such bad behavior instead of sitting in the office and waiting for some victim to report. Such bad behavior should be reduced since the policemen are able to take positive action, which could result in a better traffic operation environment.

Table 3. Copied vehicle licenses

Copied vehicle license
× × ×1266
× × ×1272
× × ×1305
× × ×1340
× × ×1345
× × ×1346
× × ×1381
......
......
......

6   Conclusion

Due to fast development of technology and enhanced global connection, the number of vehicle running on the road in China increases with an amazing speed, while related illegal behavior appears and increases as well. Nowadays, most illegal cases are noticed and prevented by the policemen who patrol outside. This is an old way with low efficiency. In order to improve traffic behavior monitoring speed and build up a healthy traffic operation environment, data mining skill based on big data is needed.

CVL is one of the illegal cases that become popular in recent years. A spatial distance based method is pointed out in this paper to deal with this problem. By using this way, monitoring process can be done by the computer automatically with good speed and accuracy instead of low efficiency on site human patrol [11]. The results turn out to be clear and can be used by the police department directly. This is good for the police to better regulate the healthy traffic operation.

However, in order to avoid the punishment, some "smart" driver tend to buy an exactly the same vehicle with a copied license [12, 13]. In this way, no one can see any difference just from the outside appearance, unless the ID of the engine is checked. This also gives a challenge to validate whether the algorithm is reliable or not by using the pictures captured by the devices. How to better validate is the number one future work.

Acknowledgement.   The work was supported by the National Natural Science Foundation of China (No. 61100066).

References

1. Qi, G., Pan, G., Li, S., Zhang, D.: When intelligent transportation meets taxi trajectory mining. China Comput. Fed. 9(8), 30–37 (2013)
2. http://baike.baidu.com/view/758812.htm?fr=aladdin. Accessed 30 July 2014
3. Jin, Y., Wang, J.: Investigation about how to govern vehicles with copied vehicle licenses based on traffic flow collection. China Water Transp. 7(9), 173–176 (2007)
4. Xiaochun, L., Zhou, X., Jiang, X., Pan, W., Wang, F.: Fake plate detection system based on grid monitoring. J. Comput. Appl. 29(10), 2847–2848 (2009)
5. http://baike.baidu.com/view/758812.htm?fr=aladdin. Accessed 02 Aug 2014
6. http://zhidao.baidu.com/link?url=q6dp93II0BvN50hwX49fJQ6uRUz7IqsH_t2shm298U1ZVS6zhzGMBrV8j-52_rOahvUfGJIcVonPgoxuH_iORq. Accessed 02 Aug 2014
7. http://baike.baidu.com/subview/9862/8427740.htm#sub8427740. Accessed 02 Aug 2014
8. Deng, P., Zhang, J.W., Rong, X.H., Chen, F.: A model of large-scale device collaboration system based on PI-calculus for green communication. Telecommun. Syst. 52, 1313–1326 (2013)
9. Deng, P., Zhang, J.W., Rong, X.H., Chen, F.: Modeling the large scale device control system based on PI-calculus. Adv. Sci. Lett. 4, 2374–2379 (2011)
10. Zhang, J.W., Deng, P., Wan, J.F., Yan, B.Y., Rong, X.H., Chen, F.: A novel multimedia device ability matching technique for ubiquitous computing environments. EURASIP J. Wirel. Commun. Netw. 2013, 1–12 (2013)

11. Rong, X.H., Deng, P., Chen, F.: A large-scale device collaboration resource selection method with multi-Qos constraint supported. Adv. Mater. Res. **143**, 894–898 (2011)
12. Rong, X.H., Chen, F., Deng, P., Ma, S.L.: A large scale device collaboration mechanism. J. Comput. Res. Dev. **9**, 1589–1596 (2011)
13. Chen, F., Rong, X.H., Deng, P., Ma, S.L.: A survey of device collaboration technology and system software. Acta Electronica Sin. **39**, 440–447 (2011)

Research and Utilization on RFID Label in Substation Inspection

Ziwei Hu[✉], Yang Wang, Xin Li, and Dongmei Liu

China Electric Power Research Institute, Beijing, China
{huziwei,yangw}@epri.sgcc.com.cn,
longfengshaonian@126.com, dongmeiliu@sgcc.com.cn

Abstract. By using RFID technology of the network, device label can storage the basic information and necessary information about devices. And system manager can use the IPv6 network protocol to achieve unified management of these labels. Through these methods, it realizes standardized management of the equipment information. The RFID technology and IPv6 design have been researched to provide a modernization, information and intelligent method of substation inspection.

Keywords: Substation inspection · RFID · IPv6

1 Introduction

It is a headache problem for many traditional substation or power factory enterprises to manage the equipment inspection and fixed assets. Because most enterprises still rely on using the original paper records manpower to deal with most of complex and cumbersome work, such as the equipment check, maintenance, repair, self- examination and scrap management work and so on [1]. Besides workers must be very familiar with the preventive maintenance project, it will lead to the large difficulty for education, training and work handover. The early equipment management was unable to automatically summarize and analyze the important data, such as electric equipment temperature each hour, voltage change, oil is sufficient and so on. It led to the emergence of jump power or other non-expected loss in production, and derived various industrial safety problems. These data copying, relying on manual data collection by paper way, may become a mere formality, become routine work, lead to greatly reduce the accuracy of the device data, such management behavior has no reference value. Moreover, because the range of equipment inspection is too wide and excessive, the inspectors may not arrive at the designated location, if the inspectors did not fill out the information accurately, industrial safety risk coefficient will increase, so manager must make sure the equipment inspection manage strictly [2].

Therefore, electronic inspection system was born out of necessity. Electronic inspection system is a kind of device for monitoring patrol, inspection process. Handheld devices and inspection label is this system mainly involved in the equipment. Inspection label is used to bind the machine equipment, some information of the device will be stored on the label, such as the device name, device enable time, equipment maintenance records and so on. Handheld devices obtains information from the

© Institute for Computer Sciences, Social Informatics and Telecommunications Engineering 2015
V.C.M. Leung et al. (Eds.): CloudComp 2014, LNICST 142, pp. 232–239, 2015.
DOI: 10.1007/978-3-319-16050-4_24

inspection labels through thrift (Radio Frequency Identification) or NFC (Near Field Communication) technology, and communicating with the center server completes the inspection task [3]. Workers can manage enterprise equipment inspection by using this electronic inspection system, Apart from achieving the paperless acquisition, if system can make each inspection label unique, it can ensure the inspection workers arriving at exact place, data collection can also be more accurate, and the collected information can be used as credible analyze material, and can also be used as inspection planning and intelligent dispatching. At the same time, workers can use the handheld devices electronic, such as mobile phone, tablet computer and so on, data upload and operation is also very simple, inspection workers can operate directly, for example recording the repair of equipment, real-time usage, equipment operating parameters, and can be combined with the background database for more extensive management.

2 Research on Application of RFID in Station Inspection

RFID (Radio Frequency Identification) is a kind of wireless communication technology, can identify specific target, read and write data by wireless signal, there is no need to establish a mechanical or optical contact between recognition system and specific target [4].

The radio signal is transferred into the radio frequency field, and transmit data out from the attached label on the items, then identify and track of the goods automatically. Some labels can get energy from the electromagnetic which is emitted from recognizer, when they are at recognition time, so it does not need batteries. Some labels also have their own power, and can emit radio waves (tune into radio frequency electromagnetic field) [5]. The label contains electronic storage information, can be identified within several meters. Unlike barcodes, RFID labels do not need in the recognizer sight, can also be embedded inside tracked objects.

Many industries use radio frequency identification technology. The label is attached in a car which is in production, it is convenient for factory to trace this car at the production line. And the warehouse can track the drug where it is. RFID labels can be attached to the livestock and pets, it is convenient to positive recognize livestock and pets (positive recognize means prevent number of animals using the same identity). RFID of identification card can enable employees to enter the locked building part, a radio frequency transponder on the car can also be used to collect toll roads and parking fee.

In the process of substation inspection, the use of RFID played a crucial role, the use of RFID in the station inspection is shown in Fig. 1.

The inspection workers arrive at the designated place and begin the inspection work, first of all, the workers use the short distance radio frequency technology of RFID to get the inspection equipment list by the mobile terminal [6]. After the completion of getting, workers call management system to provide inspection equipment for matching which needs to be inspected in this inspection, if the equipment is lost or label damaged, workers can discover and report timely. System generates reasonable inspection route according to the important degree and the distance of the inspection equipment, the workers carry out effective inspection work according to the route. The workers can use mobile RFID reader in the process of inspection, when they arrive each device, it can read the RFID label attached to equipment, gets a series of basic information about the device [7]. Then equipment inspection, after inspection, the mobile terminal upload the inspection results to the management background.

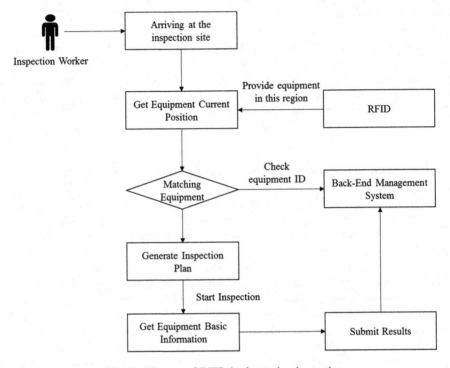

Fig. 1. The use of RFID in the station inspection.

3 Advantage About RFID in Substation Inspection

RFID is an easy to control, simple and practical application technology, and it is particularly suitable for automation and control. It can work in a variety of harsh substation environments freely: short-range radio frequency products are not afraid of grease, dust pollution, high temperatures, high winds, fog, snow, hail, thunderstorms and other harsh environments, it can replace bar codes, such as equipment's location records used in the stations inspection. In terms of stations inspection radio frequency identification system mainly has the following aspects of the system advantages:

Quick and easy to read: read data without light, even though the outer packaging to carry out, identify a greater distance effectively, while using the built-in battery of active labels, effective distance up to 30 m.

Fast identification: once label entered the field, reader can read the information in real time, and can handle multiple labels, achieve mass recognition; it can penetrate the snow, fog, ice, paint, dirt and other harsh substation environment to read the label, and read fast, in most cases less than 100 ms [8].

High Data capacity: the maximum data capacity of two-dimensional barcode (PDF417) just can store the most 2725 figures, if letters are involved, the amount of storage will be less. RFID label can be expanded to dozens of K according to the user's needs. RFID can store the basic information about inspection devices, such as type of equipment, model and serial number, GPS, and so on.

Label data can be changed dynamically: workers can use program to write data to the label, then RFID label is given to a function of the interactive portable data file. And RFID is less than barcodes in writing time; once some basic device information be changed, such as location information, RFID data can be modified immediately.

Better security: not only RFID can be embedded or attached on different shape and type of product, and can provide password protection to read and write label data, which has a higher security [9]. Outside speakers will not be stolen the device information with such station protection, and even modify device information. Then improving the security of the entire power substation.

Dynamic real-time communication: label communicate with reader 50–100 times per second, so when the label appears in the range of effective identification, which RFID is attached to, system can track and monitor their location dynamically. When the inspection workers arrive at the designated location in the substation, they can identify device location effectively, and see effective inspection equipment's line through mobile devices. As well as emergency situations arise, workers can reach the equipment area quickly.

4　Research on Application of IPv6 in Substation Inspection

The ways of existing label marks are too simple. In the case of MifareClassic label by using RFID/NFC technology, the use of the label itself mostly distinguished from other labels only by product identification. In other words, when devices use label, workers is not concerned with "what label is", but pay more attention to the content of label, which the label key information is missing precisely, then it is difficult to manage the labels effectively [10]. So workers need to mark the labels by means of a method, using IPV6 can provide a good solution for this technology. IPv6 (Internet Protocol version 6) is the latest version of the Internet protocol, as network layer protocol for the packet-switched network, designed to solve the problem of ipv4's dwindling address pool. IPv6 address is 128 bits length, 16 bit as a group, can provide about 340 trillion trillion trillion (i.e. 2^{128}) IP addresses under the binary system. IPv6 address has a huge pool, is ideally suited for a variety of network which has a huge number of tiny devices. By means of the huge capacity of IPv6, if workers use IPv6 to mark for labels, then inspection labels can be managed easily, so that inspection work can be carried out more efficiently and accurately.

According to the existing inspection label mode, the purpose of this paper is to use IPv6 addressing mode, system binds the virtual IPv6 address with specific inspection label, so that the inspection label is incorporated into the network of inspection system, communicate in all the network, make the inspection label manage effectively, and enhance the accuracy and effectiveness of the inspection work [11].

Workers use IPv6 technology as marked way for inspection labels, it can solve unmanageable problem, such as how to manage existing inspection labels. To solve the above problems, This paper presents a method for label to mark itself, its content is that inspection labels are addressed by the use of IPv6, the virtual IPv6 address binds with specific inspection labels, So that inspection label is incorporated into the network of inspection system, then manage the inspection label effectively.

To achieve the above objectives, technical scheme adopted in this paper is: One inspection system apply for a piece of IPv6 address pool, then it will be divided into sections and addressed address according to geographic distribution of enterprise equipment and department [12]. Then workers mark the label, attached on the equipment, according to the classification of IPv6 address, so the network address label on the device can reflect which department or where it belongs to. Then labels can be brought into the scope of network management system and achieve full network communication. Including the following steps:

(1) Apply for IPv6 address block;
(2) Develop IPv6 address assignment scheme according to the distribution of business equipment;
(3) IPv6 written to the label;
(4) Distribution of the actual address records to the label database;
(5) Label be managed according to the IPv6 address.

Technical innovation:

(1) Use IPv6 to respond to the huge number of labels that may arise.
(2) Incorporated into the scope of network management, strengthened the labels' management, and obtain a more accurate device feedback.

Through the way of the whole network communication, strengthen the inspection system, so that scheme is developed more accurately.

5 Application of IPv6 in Substation Inspection

Network topology graph (Fig. 2) shows the way to build a possible electronic inspection network. The inspection label use IPv6 addresses as identification, the inspection label has also become a device in the network. Taking 1 K MifareClassic type of label as an example, the label has 16 partitions, each partition has 4 blocks, and each block can store 16 byte data. Because the binary length of IPv6 address is 128 bits, so it is just right to store the IPv6 address in a block for label. Based on the IPv6 addressing mode, described in RFC 3513, Assuming that the electronic inspection network can manage 4000000000 labels, so the company applies for 32 bit address pool which starting address is 2000:1234:5678:9ABC: DEFF: FFFF:: a/96, and power facilities in the area is allocated 28 bit address area which starting address is 2000:1234:5678:9ABC: DEFF: FFFF: 1000:: a/100. Assuming the area has A, B two town. For all the substation in A Town, they will be allocated 20 bit address area which starting address is 2000:1234:5678:9ABC:DEFF:FFFF:1010::/108, for a substation in A Town, and they will be allocated 16 bit address area which starting address is

2000:1234:5678:9ABC:DEFF:FFFF:1011::/112. Then manager will have about 65000 IPv6 addresses to mark the substation inspection labels. For all the substation in B Town, they will be allocated 20 bit address area which starting address is 2000:1234:5678:9ABC:DEFF:FFFF:1020::/108, for a substation in B Town, and they will be allocated 16 bit address area which starting address is 2000:1234:5678:9ABC: DEFF:FFFF:1021::/112. Then manager will also have about 65000 IPv6 addresses to mark the substation inspection labels. It can be saw, prefix of IPv6 address is allocated according to the geographical location naturally t, and it is different from the subnet of IPv4 address, the use of IPv6 address is more intuitive, and it has a larger address pool. Based in huge address pool, address allocation of each device can have much room, and can have significant section. For example, for the main transformer equipment, the last bit of IP address were 000 for first three bits, For 220 KV interval equipment, the last bit of IP address were 001 for first three bits, so IPv6 address information in the labels can reflect location and subordinate about the label.

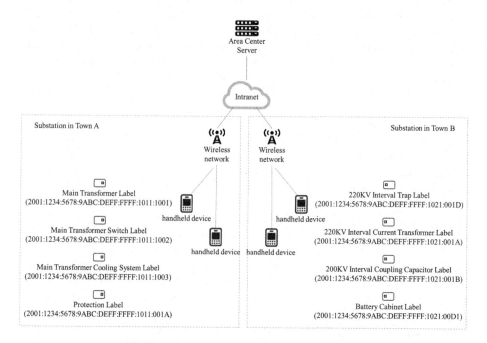

Fig. 2. Label management in inspection process.

Label management in Inspection process is shown in the Fig. 2. Through the above example, it is very intuitive to show the storage of IPv6 on the label. At the same time, the content of inspection equipment labels add some important information about equipment. For example, equipment manufacturers, equipment type, equipment name, service life of equipment, the temperature and humidity of equipment for the normal operation. Some information about the use of equipment, such as the usage time, GPS information, people who are responsible for the equipment, dangerous point of the equipment and notice. It also need to record the repair person and related equipment number, when equipment occur problems. Using high capacity RFID, it will record down comprehensive information of the entire equipment. Workers use handheld devices according to the different inspection process, operation and manage the equipment through the RFID reader. This information can be classified into MifareClassic type of label partition, each kind of information data can have one or more blocks. And some data in the label may need to change, workers can use RFID to access and modify the contents quickly. As mentioned above, the workers use the short distance radio frequency technology of RFID to get the inspection equipment list by the mobile terminal. Then we can use the GPS information in the label to locate the equipment on the map and display them in real time. Workers can use this to generate inspection route, when one equipment is inspected, system can hints the next place and equipment [13]. So it can improve the inspection process, and realize the efficient inspection process.

In short, manager can use inspection handheld devices as the intermediary to manage the inspection label. Instruction is sent and stored in the handheld devices through the network. When workers carry out the inspection tasks or management tasks, instructions will automatically be executed which is stored in the handheld devices, workers can use the handheld devices to communicate with RFID labels, inspection labels can be read and written, then workers finish inspection task. The task execution results will be send to the center server by the handheld devices, so that the system can judge and record the inspection task results.

6   Conclusions

The power industry is the premise and guarantee in people's daily life and national industrial production. With rapid economic development and the improvement of people's living standard, China has increased investment in the power system to enhance technical and managerial levels to ensure safe operation of the power system. This paper study on the device label for substation inspection process, mainly related to RFID and IPv6 technology, and propose the use of RFID in equipment label. RFID manages some of the basic information about equipment, and provides real-time monitoring functions for equipment. Because workers need to manage existing inspection labels, this paper also propose to use IPv6 technology as marked way for inspection labels. System binds the virtual IPv6 address with specific inspection label, so that the inspection label is incorporated into the network of inspection system, communicate in all the network, make the inspection label manage effectively, and enhance the accuracy and effectiveness of the inspection work.

Acknowledgments. The work was supported by the key technology research on IPv6 application in state grid china (TX71-13-045) as a technology project of State Grid Corporation of China (SGCC) and the National Natural Science Foundation of China (no. 61100066).

References

1. Smith, T.F., Waterman, M.S.: Identification of common molecular subsequences. J. Mol. Biol. **147**, 195–197 (1981)
2. Xie, X.: Research on navigation and positioning of robot for substation equipment inspection. SWUST, Mianyang (2008). (In Chinese)
3. Jiafang, W., Xiaoxia, J., Jing, F.: Substation inspection robot encoder inertial trackless navigation. Water Conserv. Electr. Power Mach. **35**(8), 11–14 (2013). (In Chinese)
4. Wu, G., Li, C., Ma, Y., Guo, K., et al.: High voltage grid inspection robot research and application review. In: The Collection of the National Power Transmission and Transformation Equipment State Maintenance Technology Exchange Conference (2009). (In Chinese)
5. Xu, Z., Shenli, W., Sunan, W.: Research on key technology of outdoor mobile robot autonomous navigation based on information fusion. In: The Sixth National Conference on Fluid Power Transmission and Control (2010). (In Chinese)
6. Wei, J., Wang, J., Zhou, F., et al.: Structure design and kinematics analysis of mew inspection robot. Coal Mine Mach. **6**, 45–46 (2005). (In Chinese)
7. Huq, R., Lacheray, H., Fulford, C., et al.: QBOT: an educational mobile robot controlled in MATLAB Simulink environment. In: Proceedings of Canadian Conference on Electrical and Computer Engineering, St. John's, NL (2009)
8. Deng, P., Zhang, J.W., Rong, X.H., Chen, F.: A model of large-scale device collaboration system based on PI calculus for green communication. Telecommun. Syst. **52**, 1313–1326 (2013)
9. Deng, P., Zhang, J.W., Rong, X.H., Chen, F.: Modeling the large-scale device control system based on PI-calculus. Adv. Sci. Lett. **4**, 2374–2379 (2011)
10. Zhang, J.W., Deng, P., Wan, J.F., Yan, B.Y., Rong, X.H., Chen, F.: A novel multimedia device ability matching technique for ubiquitous computing environments. EURASIP J. Wireless Commun. Netw. **2013**, 1–12 (2013)
11. Rong, X.H., Deng, P., Chen, F.: A large-scale device collaboration resource selection method with multi-QoS constraint supported. Adv. Mater. Res. **143**, 894–898 (2011)
12. Rong, X.H., Chen, F., Deng, P., Ma, S.L.: A large-scale device collaboration mechanism. J. Comput. Res. Dev. **9**, 1589–1596 (2011)
13. Chen, F., Rong, X.H., Deng, P., Ma, S.L.: A survey of device collaboration technology and system software. Acta Electronica Sin. **39**, 440–447 (2011)

The Application of Inspection Platform in Substation Inspection

Yang Wang$^{(\boxtimes)}$, Geng Zhang, Ziwei Hu, and Dongmei Liu

China Electric Power Research Institute, Beijing, China
yangw@epri.sgcc.com.cn

Abstract. Based on the field-operation requirements of electric power companies, the servers and mobile terminals must be combined. In this paper, a field-operation mobile platform has been developed. This platform can improve field-operation management of electric power companies, achieving a new level in aspects of informatization, real-timing performance and paperless. According to this platform, the safety and quality of field-operation system could be improved significantly, and more social and economic benefits could be created.

Keywords: Field-operation mobile platform · Electric power company · Real-timing · Informatization · Paperless

1 Introduction

Currently, patrol officers use the method of paper registration to inspect with their experience in the grid field operations. The operation is tedious and easy to make mistakes, so missing and wrong inspection may happen. The staff assessment cannot be put in place by the consciousness of patrol officers, and information management cannot be achieved. State Grid Corporation has asked to use a standardized management in the electrical equipment inspection, maintenance and test site. In order to achieve information and modern management of the grid field operations, urgent demand makes field-operation mobile platform emerged.

Field-operation mobile platform can improve the efficiency and quality of inspection, and achieve electronization, informatization, standardization and intelligentzein the substation equipment inspection. It also can minimize the missing, wrong inspection and ensure the planning, execution, completion confirmation forming a closed loop for patrol officers. Therefore it will ensure the safety of the facilities and stability of the power system, and achieve long-term, stable and efficient operation of substation equipment. Currently mobile terminals become more and more convenient to carry, high performance, easy and efficient to use, and real-time communication, so in the field-operation platform, the staff can complete specific tasks of substation inspection and overhaul by mobile terminals and its application. The field-operation mobile platform makes the staff get rid of the use of paper and make workflow standardized, so the user complete the job by following the prompts of the mobile terminal [1, 2]. Platform passes job information and provides browse, query and approval services for users by the communication with the mobile terminal.

© Institute for Computer Sciences, Social Informatics and Telecommunications Engineering 2015
V.C.M. Leung et al. (Eds.): CloudComp 2014, LNICST 142, pp. 240–244, 2015.
DOI: 10.1007/978-3-319-16050-4_25

2 System Architecture

The field-operation mobile platform is divided into two main parts, mobile job server and mobile terminals. Platform uses a mobile terminal as a tool to perform the job, and the mobile terminal communicates with the mobile job server and exchanges job information via the 3G network and Wi-Fi network. Substation inspection, substation maintenance, line inspection, maintenance and other operations can be completed by mobile terminal. Of course, users can also directly land the mobile job server and perform related operations by network [3]. The structure is as follow: (Fig. 1).

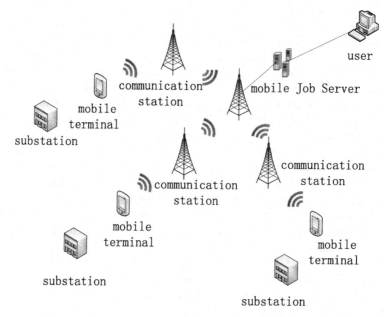

Fig. 1. system architecture of the field-operation mobile platform

The role of mobile terminal in the figure: it is mainly used for communication with the mobile job server, performs job-related processes and saves relevant results; finally it uploads the results to the mobile job server via 3G network or Wi-Fi network. The role of mobile job server: it provides job-related data to the mobile terminal and provides functionality which is needed by jobs for users. "Substation" is the object where you want to execute the job, "communication station" provides basic network, while "user" is the user of mobile job server.

3 System Functions

3.1 Functions of Mobile Job Server

The mobile job server is an important part of the platform, its function is to: (1) communicates with the mobile terminal and transfers job information; (2) the users apply and approval work orders, browse and query operations results through the mobile job server.

Based on the work plans and specifications of inspection and repair, the server generates annual inspection and maintenance programs. Certainly users can also add new work plans, that is to say plans generation, according to the current situation. Work plans include inspection plans and maintenance plans of substations and lines. Users of the relevant departments login mobile job server to audit generated work plan, after that is adopted, the server will automatically generate plan and execute the plan; if the plan is not passed, the reason why the approval is not pass need to be filled out and the result is passed to relevant user by the server, namely plan approval. For unplanned operations or tests such as special inspection of substations around thunderstorms, new jobs can be applied through the server and new work orders will be generated, namely work order application. Then users of relevant departments login the server to audit the work order that is applied and determine whether implement the work orders or not, namely approval for work orders. Mobile terminal needs to perform data transmission and information exchange with the server and the mode of transmission is HTTP, namely data synchronization transmission. Mobile terminal can be added, deleted and modified and its software can be upgraded in the server, namely management function of the mobile terminal. The information of substations, such as the increase, modification and deletion of the substation, can be configured in the server, what is more, the personnel, equipment, and location of the substation can also be configured, namely substation management functions. Users of the server and mobile terminals can be added, modified and deleted, namely user management functions. Workflow of the services can be added, modified and deleted, namely workflow management functions. Users can manger work condition of the mobile terminals through GIS function [4], which can show the locations of the mobile terminals and substations, That is to say GIS services of the server. The mobile terminal can take the way of problem ticket to communicate with experts on difficult problems by pictures or voice, namely expert diagnostic functions. Patrol officers need to take photos of equipments and positions which need to be checked. In the future inspection, patrol officers can check the picture and the current state of the equipment. If current state is in accord with the picture, the equipment can be considered to be normal; if not, the equipment needs further diagnosis. That is to say processing of inspection image function. Users can look over tested content and conducted operations of the substation through the server, namely display of job logs function. Users can inquiry the job records that users want to view, namely search of job function. Users determine whether the device of the substation needs an overhaul by the evaluation of the equipment status. Then the server generates initial evaluation report of the equipment, by which experts whether the equipment needs to be repaired or not, namely assessments of equipment condition function.

The main functions of the mobile job server are shown in the following figure: (Fig. 2).

3.2 Functions of Mobile Terminal

The mobile terminal is a equipment used by on-site staff when they perform specific operations. Through an application on the mobile terminal, the staff can accomplish

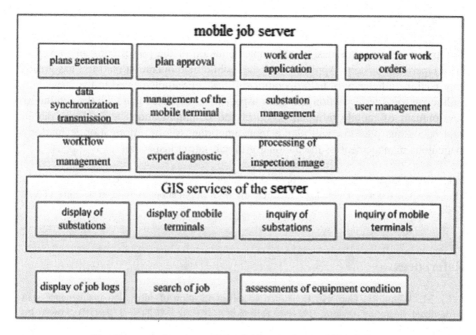

Fig. 2. server functions of the field-operation mobile platform

specific work of the inspection and overhaul of substations. It gets rid of using the original paper work orders and standardizes work processes. Following the prompts to the user's mobile terminal process, you can complete the job [5].

The user is able to log on to the platform, namely the user login function by entering the user's name and password assigned by the platform at the mobile terminal screen, after which the mobile terminal is connected to mobile field operations through a network server. The mobile terminal obtains substation inspection work orders from the mobile work platforms and displays, the user can operate the work orders, performing various tasks of substation inspection, which is the substation inspection function. When the mobile terminal performs operations or experiments, there will be some problems difficult to judge and solve. At this time, the mobile terminal can communicate with experts through pictures or voices by way of issue tickets. After the problems are photographed by mobile terminal camera and photos and related information uploaded to the platform, then experts diagnosis through photographs and related information, gives feedback and add advices to this homework and tests' results, namely the expert diagnostics.

The main function of the mobile terminal is shown in the following figure: (Fig. 3).

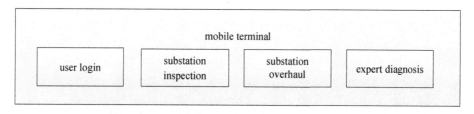

Fig. 3. mobile terminal functions of the field-operation mobile platform

4   Conclusion

This paper describes the design and implementation of the power company's Mobile Field Operating System. Application of the mobile field operation platform has greatly improved the efficiency of field operations. It has been implemented in the inspection, fault repair, on-site inspection and other aspects. It is expected that with the continuous development of mobile terminal products and communications technology, mobile field operations platform will play a more important role in information technology, meticulous management of the national grid substation inspection.

Acknowledgement. The work is supported by Technology Project of State Grid Corporation of China(SGCC), the key technology research on IPv6 application in state grid china (TX71-13-045).

References

1. Li, M., Wang, H., Gao, H.: Construction and application of substation maintenance standardized operating system (变电检修现场标准化作业系统的建设与应用). Power Inf. (09) (2011)
2. Chen, D., Long, H., Tan, H.: Research and implementation of on-site standardized job management system (现场标准化作业管理系统的研究与实现). Microcomput. Inf. **26** (12-3) (2011)
3. Shu, Q., Cheng, Z., Zhang, L.: Design and implementation of mobile marketing metering of electricity field operations systems (电力移动营销计量现场作业系统的设计与实现). Comput. Knowl. Technol. **35**(7) 09 (2011)
4. Liu, Z., Sun, J.: Mobile GIS-based Power Distribution Field Operating System (基于移动 GIS 的配电现场作业系统). Electric Time, 1 (2010)
5. Ma, K., Gu, Y., Wang, X.: Research and Exploration of the Integration Programs of the State Grid Corporation of PMS and Shanxi Grid Production Mobile Operating Termina (国家电网公司 PMS 与陕西电网生产移动作业终端融合方案的研究与探索). Shanxi Power, 03 (2011)

Author Index